Narrative Pleasures in Young Adult Novels, Films, and Video Games

Critical Approaches to Children's Literature

Series Editors: **Kerry Mallan** and **Clare Bradford**

Critical Approaches to Children's Literature is an innovative series concerned with the best contemporary scholarship and criticism on children's and young adult literature, film, and media texts. The series addresses new and developing areas of children's literature research as well as bringing contemporary perspectives to historical texts. The series has a distinctive take on scholarship, delivering quality works of criticism written in an accessible style for a range of readers, both academic and professional. The series is invaluable for undergraduate students in children's literature as well as advanced students and established scholars.

Published titles include:

Margaret Mackey
NARRATIVE PLEASURES IN YOUNG ADULT NOVELS, FILMS, AND VIDEO GAMES
Critical Approaches to Children's Literature

Michelle Smith
EMPIRE IN BRITISH GIRLS' LITERATURE AND CULTURE
Imperial Girls, 1880–1915

Forthcoming titles:

Clare Bradford, Kerry Mallan, John Stephens & Robyn McCallum
NEW WORLD ORDERS IN CONTEMPORARY CHILDREN'S LITERATURE

Elizabeth Bullen
CLASS IN CONTEMPORARY CHILDREN'S LITERATURE

Pamela Knights
READING BALLET AND PERFORMANCE NARRATIVES FOR CHILDREN

Kate McInally
DESIRING GIRLS IN YOUNG ADULT FICTION

Susan Napier
MIYAZAKI HAYO AND THE USES OF ENCHANTMENT

Andrew O'Malley
CHILDREN'S LITERATURE, POPULAR CULTURE AND *ROBINSON CRUSOE*

Critical Approaches to Children's Literature
Series Standing Order ISBN 978–0–230–22786–6 (hardback)
978–0–230–22787–3 (paperback)

(outside North America only)

You can receive future titles in this series as they are published by placing a standing order. Please contact your bookseller or, in case of difficulty, write to us at the address below with your name and address, the title of the series and the ISBN quoted above.

Customer Services Department, Macmillan Distribution Ltd, Houndmills, Basingstoke, Hampshire RG21 6XS, England

---

Narrative Pleasures in Young Adult Novels, Films, and Video Games

Margaret Mackey

palgrave
macmillan

First published 2011 by
PALGRAVE MACMILLAN

Palgrave Macmillan in the UK is an imprint of Macmillan Publishers Limited, registered in England, company number 785998, of Houndmills, Basingstoke, Hampshire RG21 6XS.

Palgrave Macmillan in the US is a division of St Martin's Press LLC, 175 Fifth Avenue, New York, NY 10010.

Palgrave Macmillan is the global academic imprint of the above companies and has companies and representatives throughout the world.

Palgrave® and Macmillan® are registered trademarks in the United States, the United Kingdom, Europe and other countries.

ISBN 978–0–230–29300–7   hardback

This book is printed on paper suitable for recycling and made from fully managed and sustained forest sources. Logging, pulping and manufacturing processes are expected to conform to the environmental regulations of the country of origin.

A catalogue record for this book is available from the British Library.

Library of Congress Cataloging-in-Publication Data
Mackey, Margaret.
Narrative pleasures in young adult novels, films, and video games / Margaret Mackey.
p. cm. — (Critical approaches to children's literature series)
Includes bibliographical references and index.
ISBN 978–0–230–29300–7 (alk. paper)
1. Young adult fiction—History and criticism. 2. Narration (Rhetoric) 3. Discourse analysis, Narrative. 4. Rhetoric and psychology. 5. Motion pictures—Psychological aspects. 6. Video games—Psychological aspects. 7. Media literacy. I. Title.
PN3443.M33 2011
700'.4—dc22   2011012066

10   9   8   7   6   5   4   3   2   1
20   19   18   17   16   15   14   13   12   11

Printed and bound in Great Britain by
CPI Antony Rowe, Chippenham and Eastbourne

'... a well modulated, coherent monograph which reveals the strengths of all the contributors. The care that has been taken in the editing phase to create the sense of a unified vantage point is worthy of praise in its own right.'

– Lydia Kokkola, International Research Society
for Children's Literature

Contents

List of Figures and Tables

Figures

Tables

Series Preface

The *Critical Approaches to Children's Literature* series was initiated in 2008 by Kerry Mallan and Clare Bradford. The aim of the series is to identify and publish the best contemporary scholarship and criticism on children's and young adult literature, film, and media texts. The series is open to theoretically informed scholarship covering a wide range of critical perspectives on historical and contemporary texts from diverse national and cultural settings. *Critical Approaches* aims to make a significant contribution to the expanding field of children's literature research by publishing quality books that promote informed discussion and debate about the production and reception of children's literature and its criticism.

Kerry Mallan and Clare Bradford

Acknowledgements

A project of this nature, of course, involves the help of many people, and the official acknowledgements only scratch the surface of my obligations. My first debt is to the 12 undergraduates who so willingly articulated the subtleties of their interpretive observations. I appreciate their good will and their eloquence, and only wish I could name them to thank them more effectively. It will be apparent to every reader that their contribution to this project was enormous and essential.

A number of research assistants worked ably and imaginatively on this project. Dale Storie, in particular, was my right-hand man for many, many months. He frequently manned a camera during the recording sessions, and also, more crucially, supplied the technical expertise that I comprehensively lack, organized the Transana loading and coding, and provided a sounding-board and an intelligent and sympathetic ear on many occasions. His intimate familiarity with the transcripts and his understanding of games (much deeper than my own) made his contributions to our discussions a crucial part of my thinking.

In the early stages of the project, James MacDonald was in charge of the technical demands, loading the huge video and audio files onto the website that was our link with the transcriber and finding ways to make the massive data set readily accessible to me even before the transcripts began to return. James also served as a camera operator, which meant he had a detailed grasp of the dynamics of different sessions. It is difficult for me to exaggerate the benefits of being able to talk through the implications of this work with these two men, who watched it develop from an idea to a reality.

Two research assistants attended every session, running the cameras and audio recorders, and taking field notes where appropriate. With four sessions running every week in the early stages, this called for a long roster, and I am grateful to all of the graduate students in the School of Library and Information Studies and the Department of Secondary Education at the University of Alberta who served as RAs, both for their effective management of the equipment and also for the informed and lively interest they took in the whole operation. Again, discussion with them after each session was one of the more illuminating pleasures of the whole project. I would like to thank Karyn Goodwillie, Tamara Guillaume, Jyoti Mangat, James Nahachewsky, Dai Newman, Sarah Polkinghorne, and

Jennifer Snowie, who, along with Dale and James, comprised the team. Thanks to their diligent and cheerful attention to all the technical details, I was able to relax and pay attention to the content of the sessions. Tanya Rogoschewsky did significant work in locating reviews of my three chosen texts, and Shelagh Genuis provided some background searching that also contributed to my initial understanding. At the very end of the operation, Jane Zaïane provided meticulous proof-reading and copy-editing and saved me from myself in a variety of large and small details.

The transcripts, for the most part, read smoothly and clearly, and give little sign of the audio crisis that dominated the first two weeks. To record three participant voices, plus my own, against the background of the game soundtrack and with enough clarity for the transcriber to have a chance of distinguishing all the contributing elements was a challenge. Before the project began, the research assistants and I piloted a recording arrangement that we thought would be effective, but by the end of the first week, it was evident that the quality of the audio recording was inadequate. The nature of the scheduling meant that we had between Friday of the first week and Wednesday of the second week to get an improved apparatus in place. The scrambling to locate and acquire a more elaborate sound system may be imagined. Sarah Eccleston and her husband Tom stepped into the breach after I located an efficient but intimidating mixer system; Tom very helpfully supplied instant sound system training for the RAs. Nobody, however, could fix it when, at the end of the first session with the new equipment, I accidentally pulled out the wrong plug before the system had saved and shut down. That session, full of intriguing discussion among the members of Group A, would have been lost entirely if not for the low-tech backup records of the two analogue tape recorders I never omit from the equipment list.

The hero who salvaged most of the conversation of that day out of the old-fashioned cassette tapes and who supplied all the remainder of the transcripts from the much more audible digital records was, as always for my projects, Deidré Johnston. No researcher could be better served. Deidré's dedication to clarifying every reference, however obscure, makes my job a lot easier. She completed this massive task (almost 2000 double-spaced pages of transcript) with her usual commitment and care, and took her regular intelligent interest in the participants. My debt to her is very great.

I am differently obliged to the Wisconsin Center for Education Research, University of Wisconsin-Madison, who have developed and maintained the Transana analytical software and made it readily available to researchers. Transana was originally created by Chris Fassnacht; David K. Woods is now responsible for it. Transana made it possible even to contemplate managing the enormous data set that I knew I would acquire. In the end, I made less use of its excellent coding capacities than I had anticipated, but in thinking through why it offered something different from what I needed, I came to a much clearer and more helpful understanding of my own priorities in this project.

As ever, my work was made easier by the contribution of colleagues at the School of Library and Information Studies at the University of Alberta, particularly Sophia Sherman in the office. I also owe a debt to the Department of Secondary Education at the University of Alberta, who made me very welcome for a year.

The first reader of all these chapters was my good friend and colleague, Anna Altmann, whose intelligent encouragement and criticism was always astute and thoughtful. As usual, I also benefited greatly from the insights of Gail de Vos, Ingrid Johnston, and Jill McClay (in alphabetical order!), and from the input of the young adult book group with whom I read *Monster* in the first place and with whom I discussed many stages of this project. I am further in Ingrid's debt for the very helpful suggestion that Palgrave Macmillan's new series might be a good home for this work. At Palgrave Macmillan, Kerry Mallan and Clare Bradford have facilitated this project in ways that every author dreams about. I am also substantially obliged to Palgrave Macmillan's anonymous reader who made stringent and productive suggestions about tightening up the later chapters of this manuscript; everyone who reads this book to the end will benefit from that reader's counsel!

I have been involved in some aspects of this project since 2003, and, during that time, almost every one of my students at the School of Library and Information Studies has had some impact on my thinking. I am grateful to all of them, both those currently in residence and those who have graduated but still think of me when they spot a notice of some new media technology development. Who would not become a better scholar with an army of working librarians acting as her eyes and ears – in the world, on the web, and among the databases? The pleasure of keeping in touch with these terrific people is even more significant than the intellectual value of the materials they forward to me. I am grateful to the School for giving me a teaching assignment that largely meshes with my research interests. Both my research and my teaching are the better for it.

The University of Alberta has treated me generously during this seven-year period. The Faculty of Education granted me a McCalla Research Fellowship in 2006–7, which gave me the most precious contribution of working time away from teaching. The final stages of readying the book for publication were completed while on sabbatical, which offered similar benefits.

This project was very generously funded by the Social Sciences and Humanities Research Council of Canada. Being able to work with a budget that allowed me to plan (and to improvise in a hurry when the first plan fell through!) made all the difference to this study.

Finally, as always, I would like to thank my family, which has increased in size since I started this project. In addition to Sarah and Beth, who have supported (and often improved) my work from the outset, I must now also thank Jamie Burns and Dave Waldbillig, who are very welcome additions to my life and my family. Terry, as ever, puts up with my enthusiasms, preoccupations, and obsessiveness in equal measure; there should surely be some sort of award for the thankless task of being an academic spouse, and if there were, he would be first in line to win it. I thank them all with all my heart.

An earlier version of Chapter 5 appeared in Loading... (Volume 2, Number 3, 2008), the journal of the Canadian Game Studies Association.

1
Asking the Questions: How We Understand Stories

Meaning [is] something that happens.
(Wolfgang Iser, 1978, p. 22)

A story is an event over time, no matter how it is told. Knowing only part of the story is an essential step in the ever-incomplete experience of coming to know it all. We draw data from a text, composing a story from the bits and pieces we are given, assembling the elements in ways that make increasing sense, retreating from too-hasty assessments and dropping our first tentative assumptions when necessary. We may enter the story world, becoming attached to characters and settings, and experiencing real emotion on their behalf. Alternatively, or additionally, we may attend to the surface of the text, admiring and critiquing the ways in which the components of the story are woven together or registering the audacity with which fragments are left floating.

However we approach it, to be engrossed in a deliberate form of partial understanding, driving for completion and maybe never entirely letting go, is a multifaceted experience. Iser, in the quotation that begins this chapter, is right about its temporal qualities, but it is not simply something that 'happens'. It is something we *perform*. How do we do this complex thing?

We are inclined to take it for granted that, once we have learned the basic code-cracking rules, we will be able to sit down with a story in a variety of formats – a novel, say, or a movie, or a digital game – and readily deal with whatever demands it makes of us. We may perhaps be uneasy about our ability to master the controls of an unfamiliar game console, but we assume we will be able to understand the story. But what skills and capacities enable us to make sense of a fiction via a range of different media? How much do we transfer understanding

1

developed in one medium when we initiate the processing of a story told in a different medium?

Such a question is particularly timely in an era of proliferating formats. New variants of electronic readers, 3-D versions of movies and television, radically sophisticated online games, and many virtual community sites of creation and commentary, all challenge the limits of contemporary storytelling. Now is a good time to gain a better understanding of the transferability of narrative awareness. What tools and strategies can we take for granted when we approach a new format? Those who are at ease with the implications of this question, even if they never articulate it in such terms, will be at an advantage in the years to come.

Carol Lee rightly observes that we do not know enough: 'In literary reasoning ... determining what concepts are *generative* has not been well specified' (2007, p. 113, emphasis added). In this book, I want to explore some story-processing skills and strategies that *generate* fictional understanding in three specific media: book, game, film. In these modes, the story's objective existence is confined to abstract black marks on the paper, or assembled pixels on a screen, or frames flickering by at a rate of 24 per second. What enables interpreters to take this unpromising, inert raw material and incarnate it as a vital, living story world inside their own minds? What processes allow this astonishing transformation to take place in ways sufficiently reliable that people can talk to each other in mutually comprehensible terms about the mental worlds they have created, even in times of rapid change in all our communication technologies? And what methods can we develop to observe these highly internal processes at work?

Much of our analysis of the activities and processes of interpretation involves a scholarly exploration of those static objects, the texts. And certainly there is much to be learned from and about the affordances of these texts, to understand what they make possible for interpreters to bring to life. In this book, however, I take a stronger interest in the activity itself, in what people *do* to enable them to draw from the given symbols and awaken the imaginary in their own minds. And to escape from the solipsistic fallacy very common in much theoretical hypothesizing about reading, viewing, playing – that what *people* do inside their heads is simply the same as what *I* do inside my own – I have invited other people to articulate their interpretive processes.

What happens inside our minds as we read, to a certain extent, occurs inside a kind of 'black box'. We cannot read and talk about our reading at the same time (though we can switch very swiftly between the two activities). Consequently, insofar as we truly comprehend what occurs in anyone's mind while reading, we really have access only to our own experience. It can be useful to think visually about this fact: here is the closed-off black box of my own mind while engrossed in reading:

This drawing would win prizes for the least informative diagram ever inserted in a book, but it gains resonance when we look at how we attempt to gain access to other minds. We cannot enter those minds (even fMRIs and PETs give only shadows of the experience), so we extrapolate from what other readers tell us. As we assemble accounts from these other readers, we may perhaps align them to afford maximum coherence, and our mental image may look like this:

The human eye finds it very difficult to look at such a diagram and not *see* a circle, even though there is no drawn circle in my image. The human temptation is to *insert*, metaphorically speaking, the circle of our own black box, to assume (in ways that easily convince *us*) that our own internal understanding of reading is the same as that which fuels the reading of others.

But there is no circle there! We must be very careful, as we listen to other interpreters, to resist the temptation to assert our own understanding as a default. If we can really hear what they have to tell us about interpretive pleasures and challenges, we will enrich our understanding beyond the limits of what our own brains can tell us.

Abstract and particular understanding

Questions about how we interpret are fascinating in large, general terms but they may actually best be explored in concrete and particular ways. Theoretical perspectives on the phenomenon of narrative understanding remain at the level of the abstract, but investigation of the nouns and verbs of interpretation entails concrete and particular specimens. My examples will involve 12 young people in late adolescence, aged between 18 and 22, meeting in groups of three to read a novel, watch a feature film, and play a digital game on PlayStation 2 – from beginning to end in each instance.

This book focuses on the behaviours of ordinary readers, viewers, and players, and on what we can learn from their ability to articulate the tacit and explicit skills and strategies they bring to bear on three particular and individual stories. The specific texts are the young adult novel *Monster* by Walter Dean Myers, the subtitled German movie *Run Lola Run*, and the PlayStation game *Shadow of the Colossus*, also subtitled; these adolescent narratives serve as the 'nouns' that scaffold interpretative behaviours. The audio and video records and transcripts of the young people's interactions with these texts, and their commentary on those interactions, supply the 'verbs' of what these interpreters *do*. Theories of narrative provide a supporting framework that, in the manner of all frames, directs our attention to particular phenomena of narrative interpretation as we observe how meaning 'happens' in these stories. My framework orients me to the ongoing activities of interpretation; to reflect that focus, the chapter titles all appear as present participles of verbs.

'What are the mental tools, processes, and activities that make possible our ability to construct and understand narrative?' ask Scholes, Phelan and Kellogg (2006, p. 290). Scholars in the field of cognitive narratology address this question, although often through the vehicle of exploring the nouns: the texts and what they make possible. I will explore this topic using both nouns and verbs, through an investigation of the actions of particular interpreters meeting particular texts.

Working exclusively with a text confines us to the limits of the medium through which it is presented. Working with interpreters allows us to take account of how they bring a panoply of experience in *many* media to the interpretive problem at hand. I believe that our understanding of the 'mental tools, processes, and activities' will become simultaneously broader and subtler as a result of exploring how these young people behave with different texts, and how they articulate their own awareness of narrative strategy in different media. Studying the particular will offer a constructive way to ground the general.

A tripartite approach to narrative understanding as manifested in three media allows for certain kinds of triangulation. If the same patterns of behaviour materialize across all three media, they may be taken to manifest a robust approach to the interpretation of fiction. There is a further advantage to this kind of study. It is a necessary inconvenience of investigating reading and viewing that the activity must stop for discussion to begin. We cannot simultaneously read and talk about reading, and the same is largely true for viewing (at least in any film with a soundtrack). Gaming, however, works on a very different basis. With my social set-up, which entails three gamers playing together and sharing one controller, the way is open for ongoing natural tactical and responsive conversation, which allows much more direct access to the kinds of thinking that fuel narrative interpretation. If we can establish that many of the same kinds of activity occur in each medium, the discussion around the gaming process offers us a relatively natural vehicle for exploring strategic, affective and narrative speculation and decision-making *as the interpretative efforts are actually taking place*. The consequence is a rich dataset of contemporaneous discussion that has an almost slow-motion effect. With appropriate precautions about taking the similarities too much for granted, the gaming experiences can be invoked to shed greater light on the reading and the viewing. Exploring interpretive processes in this interactive way also has the virtue of echoing the cross-media learning processes of contemporary media users.

Gaming, since it is not taught in school, also offers an interesting point of access to what Barton and Hamilton call 'vernacular strategies' (1998, p. 13). Narrative understanding manifested in gameplay originates in native intuition augmented by prior gaming experience, and/or in strategic understanding imported from other media – most likely both. *Ad hoc* bootstrapping by other players is often a significant factor as well. This unschooled element of narrative thinking adds another dimension to this project.

Finally, this project offers a broader way of thinking about young adult literature, one that more truly represents the literate experiences of today's adolescents. *Run Lola Run* and *Shadow of the Colossus* supply forms of young adult fiction that are every bit as important to today's teenagers as the novel. *Monster*, as the very first winner of the Printz Award for young adult literature, awarded by the American Library Association, represents the still-important form of print storytelling for adolescents; by exploring its connections to a film and a game, through the activities of interpreters who move from one format to another, I hope to expand ways of thinking about the field.

The actions of verbs take place over time, and I want to explore these actions in expansive ways. In order to foreground this kind of developmental understanding, I will often explore relatively lengthy extracts from the transcribed conversations.

'Reframing literacy'

Before beginning to describe this project in any detail, it will be useful to delineate its reach and its limits. Undoubtedly, the idea of what constitutes contemporary literacy is a highly contested question, and I am not going to investigate every corner of this disputed territory. Right from the beginning I would like to demarcate what I will and will not be exploring.

There are many labels for a contemporary culture that is convergent, mobile, interactive, and participatory. A helpful starting point for my purposes, one that allows me to define this project more clearly, comes from Mark Reid, the Head of Education at the British Film Institute. He has suggested a core definition of literacy that will 'reframe' twenty-first century elements in a coherent way. He addresses current disagreements as follows:

> Jonathan Douglas, Director of the National Literacy Trust, recently clarified the literacy debate quite helpfully when he said that on the one hand we have a 'strong' core definition of literacy; while on the other we have literacy as metaphor – visual, digital, media, cine-, emotional, and any number of other literacies. This bifurcation, between 'core' or 'basic' literacy, and other 'add-on' literacies has two impacts on teachers and policy makers: the core 'strong'

definition of literacy stays unchanged ('it's about words') while the literacy cognates, like distant cousins, clamour for a hearing, making a noisy din, scaring the 'word' people with their unreasonable demands.

(2009, p. 19)

Reid argues that we should consider the idea that literacy involves the interpretation of one or more language systems, rather than get bogged down in ever-changing media of communication; and he suggests a short but robust list of languages.

It seems clear to me in fact that there are a small number of language systems or modes that together constitute what it means to be literate in the 21st century – and that they were pretty much the same for the 20th century too. The modes are: speech, writing, pictures and moving pictures, music, and the dramatic modes of performance and gesture and the 'mise en scène' of theatre design.

(2009, p. 20)

Reid paraphrases a charter for media literacy issued in 2005 to suggest that, 'To be media literate means being able to choose and access, understand and analyse, create and express oneself from and in a range of media forms' (2009, p. 21). These six verbs, he suggests, 'operate independently of the media in which we access them' (2009, p. 21).

It is helpful to think in these terms, but this book sets out to deal with only part of this list, indicated by the emphasis in the entries:

- choosing
- accessing
- **understanding**
- *analysing*
- creating
- expressing oneself.

My project short-circuits the first two verbs on Reid's list in ways that I will clarify below. I chose the texts and I made them available to participants; they had no say in selection. Furthermore, this project was never designed to investigate issues of creating and expressing oneself, so the last two verbs are also not considered in detail in this study except as introduced by the interpreters themselves, a topic to which I will return at the end of the book. Instead, this study focuses chiefly on processes of *understanding*. To a lesser extent, some questions of *analysing* are necessarily involved, but the idea of analysis entails the explicit; my main interest lies rather in the mix of explicit and tacit that forms our developing understanding, and I have not explored the more analytical comments of the participants in the same detail.

To be able to locate this study in the larger set of verbs is a useful step forward in clarifying what this project does and does not attempt to investigate. It also provides a framework for investigating the degree to which it is actually possible to separate these elements of the interpretive process.

A complete literacy

Reid's six-part list of successful literacy includes four components not addressed in this project. Before moving on to consider understanding and analysis, I want to take a brief look at the four elements I have chosen not to investigate directly.

Choosing and accessing

The first two items on Reid's list, choosing and accessing, were ruled out right at the very beginning by my decision to pre-select and present particular texts to the participants. What are the conceptual implications of this decision?

In this book I recount the responses of 12 interpreters, working together to explore the story worlds of three narratives. Obviously, very many elements of these interpretive encounters were artificial. Readers, viewers and players are not normally asked to account for their responses in immediate detail as they progress through a story, nor are they often video-recorded as they do so.

In one very significant way, the artificiality of this project actually resembles the unnatural nature of classroom reading. Frank Hatt, writing from a library perspective, takes account of the importance of the reader's choice in the whole experience that we call reading, and he addresses Reid's categories of choosing and accessing as he does so.

> Even the more thorough of the models of the reading process take the coming together of the text and the reader as 'given', and locate the commencement of the reading act at the point where the reader starts to perceive the words on the page. This is hardly satisfactory. If we accept that a reader's mental 'set' is a key factor in reading performance, then it would seem that the approach route to the

text is crucial. If what the reader gets from the text depends on the questions he addresses to it, then these questions derive initially from expectations which are roused *before he encounters the text*. In effect, a reading act, extended to include the 'finding' of the text, can be seen as a series of questions which the reader puts to a store of messages.

(1976, p. 66, emphasis added)

The significance of being able to choose – having the right to make the selection of what will be interpreted, the skill needed to locate an appropriate and appealing text, and a sufficiently expansive text set from which to make a selection – applies *in absentia* to this project. Hatt develops this important idea further when he turns to the classroom.

One effect of extending the reading act to include the 'finding' of the text is to draw attention to the shortcomings of much of the reading done in educational situations, where students are obliged to read prescribed texts. The 'finding' in these cases is highly artificial. The students [*sic*] does not go through the process of selecting a preferred need, nor of matching a text to it on the basis of descriptions or clues. Having had the first part of the reading act done for him, he has to behave as if it were his own work and assume the right set for the rest of the reading act, and so reading becomes a kind of simulation game.

(1976, p. 67)

In exactly the same terms, the participants in this project took part in 'a kind of simulation game'. They had no say in the selection of the material and therefore stepped into the process of interpretation partway through, so to speak. The ability to muster an interpretive stance towards preselected and unknown texts is in many ways a schooled response, and these undergraduates certainly knew how to behave in the face of already-chosen material. Nevertheless, it is important to keep in mind that all my elaborated descriptions here outline only a partial form of the complete interpretive experience. The significance of Hatt's observations that the choosing is an essential part of the full process should be kept in mind throughout this project.

Simulations can indeed provide valuable information, and it is difficult to imagine a way of gaining access to the private experience of privately selected texts that does not involve some component of simulation, except perhaps when we explore our own personal experience.

But relying on our own singular interpretive strategies to provide a universal lens is an approach that also has the potential to mislead; our own behaviour, as I have pointed out, is not a template for everybody else's. In this project, accepting that all perspectives are partial, I opted for the simulation, with all its limitations, as the most productive route to explore the complexity of other people's interpretive experiences when faced with a particular and pre-selected novel, movie, and game. In this way, I could provide a common starting-point for all the interpretations I hoped to explore.

Creating and expressing oneself

A chorus of commentary addresses the fact that our communication media and modes of expression are merging. Henry Jenkins highlights the importance of media convergence, participatory culture, and collective intelligence, as markers of a new communication economy (2008, p. 2). Gunther Kress, discussing digital multimodality, explores the notion of interactivity both in terms of the user 'writing back' to the producer and also in terms of the user making links between different texts (2003, p. 5). Victoria Carrington and Jackie Marsh discuss new developments in literacy in terms of ubiquity, convergence, mobilization, and personalization (2009, Section 1). All of these approaches to contemporary literacies emphasize participatory forms of text use.

Such developments are not directly explored in this study. At the outset of this project, I deliberately opted to focus on the 'reception' components of interpretation (that is, understanding and analysing). As I commenced this work, my rationale for such a highly focused approach included the following reasons:

- Reception-only activities are still important in people's lives (they still watch the movie, play the game, read the novel; they move into the fictional zone often very intensely, brooking no interruption). Not every interpretive activity is socially oriented or geared towards simultaneous or subsequent production.
- Activities involving dedicated reception often precede many of the production-oriented interactions that form such an important feature of contemporary literacies. For example, how many bloggers, fan-fic creators, and critics of various persuasions and modalities paused in all their varied activities in order to read the final *Harry Potter* novel or the latest instalment of the *Twilight* series – from cover to cover and maybe more than once – before moving back into the world of commentary?

• We still do not comprehend the complexities of how we process narrative in any one medium, let alone how we draw on cross-media experience to fuel our understanding. There is a *generative* core of receptive activities and strategies that we would benefit from exploring in more subtle ways.

Reading, in its broadest meaning of interpreting, still fuels much of how we come to understand the world, and the aim of improving our understanding of that expansive sense of reading fuelled the design of my study. In the end I discovered, in ways clarified in the final chapter, that the social nature of my project elicited and highlighted a performative stance among the participants. It may be that in some crucial ways this project also offers only a simulation of *private* routes to understanding, which must be inferred from the public performances.

This project is thus contemporary in its attention to cross-media flow, based on acts of interpreting rather than on the texts. I deliberately chose singular, free-standing texts in each of my three media with a view to increasing the possibility of controlling sources of information; participants could not bring understanding gleaned externally from the film of the book or the game (though a movie of *Shadow of the Colossus* is now in the works); they could not consult a novelization of the film. Even without being able to call on such transmedia supports, however, the participants in this project clearly draw their narrative understanding and narrative processing skills from experience in a variety of narrative formats. This book attempts to illuminate that process.

Understanding and analysing

How we come to understand a fiction in each of three different media is the issue at the heart of this book. The word 'understand' incorporates a variety of meanings and connotations. We may be said to understand a story when we grasp the basic elements and can, for example, plot them on a diagram. We may desire a more organic and personal definition of understanding that requires us to find some way to animate these basic elements in our minds, whether through virtual images, virtual sounds, virtual emotions, or some compound of these and other components. We may hold out for a Platonic definition of complete, critically informed and/or true – and ultimately unobtainable – understanding. Or, we may think of many different points along the spectrum between these varying definitions: I may understand a story on an emotional level while being baffled about some of the surface details (a situation familiar to colonial interpreters).

I may grasp all the important details of the story but be blind to its appeal (many classroom readers know this feeling). I may appreciate the source of the appeal to other readers but be resistant to the story on the basis of some aspects of my own life (this kind of interpretive experience has been explored through feminist studies of women's reading of male-oriented materials). Given that meaning-making takes time, I may shift between stances even during a single interpretive episode.

A definition of reading that allows for the dynamism and fluidity of such contradictory processes comes from Chittenden and Salinger with Bussis in their groundbreaking longitudinal study of children's early reading. They describe reading as 'the act of *orchestrating* diverse knowledge in order to extract meaning from a text while maintaining reasonable fluency and reasonable accountability to the information contained in writing' (2001, p. 44, emphasis added). Only the last word of this definition is restrictive. If we substitute Reid's list of speech, writing, pictures and moving pictures, music, performance, gesture and *mise en scène*, we may maintain the complex notion of orchestrating while broadening the context; the definition thus retains its formative and summative utility.

To the extent that understanding precedes analysis, interpreters of stories may be vulnerable to the ideological biases of the story in wholly unquestioning ways. It is a truth often unacknowledged that many readers are perfectly happy to leave it at that – or to leave it at that, at least when it comes to some kinds of book or movie or game, while enjoying the pleasures of analysis in other corners of their fictional experience. To what extent is emotional comprehension of a story equivalent to an uncritical submission to the creator's intent? To what extent is such submission a poor shadow of the richer experience that comes with an analytical and critical approach? Alternatively, to what extent does analysis interfere with the rich sensory wash of immersed commitment to a fictional world?

All stories contain ideological freight. John Stephens talks about how such ideology is conveyed through the vehicle of a fiction.

> [I]deology is never separable from discourse. Its presence is only more or less apparent … [T]he discourse of a narrative fiction yields up both a *story* and a *significance*. Ideology may be inscribed within both. On the one hand, the significance deduced from a text – its theme, moral, insight into behaviour, and so on – is never without an ideological dimension or connotation. On the other hand, and less overtly, ideology is implicit in the way the story an audience derives from

a text exists as an isomorph of events in the actual world: even if the story's events are wholly or partly impossible in actuality, narrative sequences and character interrelationships will be shaped according to recognizable forms, and that shaping can in itself express ideology in so far as it implies assumptions about the forms of human existence.

(1992, p. 2)

Ideology is also present in *how* the story is told. Thomas Elsaesser, for example, suggests that what he calls contemporary 'mind-game films' (a category of puzzle films that includes *Run Lola Run*) play an important role in making us better suited to living under late capitalism:

[M]edia consumption has become part of the 'affective labor' required in modern ('control') societies, in order to properly participate in the self-regulating mechanisms of ideological reproduction, for which retraining and learning are now a lifelong obligation. Undergoing tests – including the 'tests' put up by mind-game films – thus constitutes a veritable 'ethics' of the (post-bourgeois) self: to remain flexible, adaptive, and interactive, and above all, to know the 'rules of the game'.

(2009, p. 34)

All three titles in this project raise questions about understanding the rules of the game entailed in each story's composition, and I think it is fair to say that all the participants understood and accepted that figuring out the rules for participation was part of the pleasure of the story. The degree to which such pleasure feeds 'ideological reproduction' is beyond the limits of this study, but the question is certainly important.

Ultimately, however, I am interested in how the participants in the project *make sense* and explore the potential pleasures of the three stories they are given, how they select the elements to orchestrate and how they weave these components together and bring them to life in their minds. In a few cases, they comment directly on the ideological assumptions of the story or of the way it is presented; in other cases their observations suggest an implicit awareness of ideology at work; in some cases they seem content to take the story at face value. But I did not push for analysis; if it presented itself it was as part of the initial impetus towards understanding and/or as an artefact of the social situation in which all these interpretive efforts took place.

All forms of interpretation, all ways of making personal and collective sense out of a story at whatever depth of penetration, remind us that the static page and disc represent an inherent potential for dynamic interaction. In important ways, it is only the static matrix that we hold in common; all dynamic interpretations begin to diverge from the very first moment. We see this divergence in the responses outlined in this book; at the same time, we see the power of the collective to contribute to the energy of each individual reaction.

The structure of the book

In the next chapter, I describe how this project was created and provide information about both the participants and the texts. In Chapter 3, I provide a more extensive theoretical framework. Chapters 4 through 9 explore the temporal process of interpretation, starting with the most preliminary forms of attention and the step 'into' the fictional world, and then looking at the details of how interpreters do the following: orient themselves in relation to the text; fill gaps and make inferences; move through the middle parts of the story after most of the preliminary interpretive deductions have become operational; sometimes meet with difficulties that stall their progress; and reach, first provisional and then more definite and wide-reaching conclusions. Chapter 10 presents explicitly comparative conversations with the participants about the specific pleasures of reading, viewing and gaming (and returns to the image of the circle and the spokes with which I began this chapter). Chapter 11 draws conclusions from the project as a whole, exploring possible contradictions between the integrative framework of interpretive actions that I describe and the fragmentary nature of the texts themselves and of the contemporary culture in which they are located. It also returns to the contemporary question of what forms and formats constitute a young adult literature.

Interpretation of research data is also an event that takes place over time. In the final chapter, I will return to the assumptions outlined in this introduction; some of them will benefit from reframing in light of what the transcripts have to offer.

2
Beginning: Designing the Project

To move from a set of relatively abstract questions about narrative comprehension to an operationally effective project is an elaborate process, and like the story itself, it involves time. For this project I invited 12 undergraduate volunteers at a western Canadian university, working in groups of three, to read a complete novel, watch a complete film and play a digital game to its conclusion. I will address the elements of this project in the order in which they arose.

The texts

I was aware from the outset that in eliminating the option of selection for these participants, the burden was on me to locate materials that would offer an interesting challenge to their interpretive capacities, preferably comparable in each format. I wanted to provide a set of titles that might reasonably represent a new kind of canon of young adult fiction. My strong preference was to locate one-off titles, rather than sequels or adaptations, simply to reduce the complexity of the project. I knew, whatever the virtues of specific examples for grounding broader theory, that these choices would have a major impact on every other aspect of this project, including the theory-building that might ensue. Selection was crucial.

As well as these questions of principle, I needed to address some practical issues. I have done a great deal of work with young adults and their media experiences, a history that served me well at this point. For the sake of comparability, my first preference was to capture a first encounter with each text, rather than a re-encounter, which supplies quite different kinds of data. Finding texts that participants had not seen before was one of my biggest challenges – and I knew well that the film would offer the major stumbling block. In previous sessions with young adults, showing them film extracts, I found it almost impossible to come up with a Hollywood movie that no one had seen. I owe thanks to Jyoti Mangat, my research assistant at the time, for suggesting *Run Lola Run* as a possible solution to this particular problem; the exceptional ingredient of the subtitles seemed a fair exchange in order to maximize the chances of obtaining comments on a first viewing. I solved the video game conundrum by choosing a brand new game; *Shadow of the Colossus* was released as I was making my final choices and some of the research assistants who worked on the project ran a quick pilot play of the early stages that established its potential to be satisfactory for my needs. Choosing a book was much simpler. It is not so much that these participants read less than they watch or play; it is rather that the supply of book titles is enormously larger, and I was happier to take my chances with a pre-selected book. *Monster* had the opposite virtue in being a few years old, and therefore not at the forefront of contemporary publicity or word-of-mouth.

My care in taking these considerations into account was well rewarded; none of the participants were familiar with any of the texts and so all the discussions recorded are of a first meeting with each story. And my three texts had a surprising amount in common.

In the interests of drawing participants' attention to the surface construction, as well as the created storyworld of each text, I looked for titles that included structures with cross-media implications. Each of these chosen stories contains an element of unreliable narration, achieved by different means. Each story also involves a quest of some kind, though in each case the quest component is open to interrogation, at least in part because of the way the story is told. Although each fiction is short, by the standards of its medium, they all offer challenges to interpreters.

Joseph Tabbi (2002) suggests that our experience of stories told and retold through multiple vehicles makes us more conscious of the medium we have chosen, and thus draws the surface of the text more sharply to our attention. Contemporary interpreters are therefore inclined to value stories that deal, explicitly or indirectly, with the phenomenon of their composition. All three of the narratives chosen for this project do play self-conscious games with the means of storytelling: *Monster* by providing two narrative formats, *Run Lola Run* by telling the same sequence of events three times over with small changes, and *Shadow of the Colossus* by withholding large amounts of essential plot so that the skeletal sequence of events that remains is permanently open to interrogation.

Another way of describing these three texts is that all of them offer elements of remediation, as described by Bolter and Grusin (1999). Remediation is the reworking of old media forms into new forms, and offers a balance of immediacy (or direct commitment to the world of the story being told) and hypermediacy (awareness of the form in which the story is being conveyed).

[N]ew digital media oscillate between immediacy and hypermediacy, between transparency and opacity. This oscillation is the key to understanding how a medium refashions its predecessors and other contemporary media. Although each medium promises to reform its predecessors by offering a more immediate or authentic experience, the promise of reform inevitably leads us to become aware of the new medium as a medium. Thus, immediacy leads to hypermediacy. The process of remediation makes us aware that all media are at one level a 'play of signs' ... At the same time, this process insists on the real, effective presence of media in our culture. ...

New digital media are not external agents that come to disrupt an unsuspecting culture. They emerge from within cultural contexts, and they refashion other media, which are embedded in the same or similar contexts.

(1999, p. 19)

Bolter and Grusin address new media in their seminal book, but knowledge of new media also opens contemporary interpreters to a kind of 'backwash' effect of more general media awareness, whereby oscillation between immediacy and hypermediacy are more likely to occur within old media forms as well.

The three texts used in this project provide many opportunities for such oscillation.

Monster, by Walter Dean Myers (1999), is a novel told in two configurations and two distinct typefaces: in part as a journal written by a young man held in custody and facing trial for murder, and in part as the screenplay for an imaginary movie of the court events, developed by this same young man as a means of psychological survival during his ordeal. Thus, *Monster* combines conventions from both novel and film. A few pages also feature images.

Run Lola Run (1998) is a film that has been said to resemble the structure of a digital game (although various commentators have also suggested other models such as a feature-length music video, a narrative database, the Internet, or even a simple video with a rewind button).

The same short incident is replayed three times with differing outcomes. When a character dies, the story restarts, and slight differences in the timing of the initial events lead to widely divergent conclusions each time.

Shadow of the Colossus (2005) has been described as a 'literary' video-game (Ciccoricco, 2007); players, on a quest to locate and kill each of 16 different colossi in order to restore a dead girl to life, are invited to empathize with both hunter and prey in a way more common to print fiction than to many 'quest' videogames. David DeRienzo goes further and declares, 'Where other games are novels, *Shadow of the Colossus* is a poem. Its ideas and expressions aren't spelled out for you. They're subtle' (n.d.).

These three hybrid stories all make use of conventions from other media to draw attention to the surface features of storytelling in ways that might be said to 'bounce' readers/viewers/players out of the engrossed moment into paying attention to how the story is being constructed. By choosing these particular titles, I made room for different stances towards the story that can be described in terms of immediacy and hypermediacy.

For several reasons, I chose texts that make a point of offering the potential for oscillating among different perspectives. One reason was simply to challenge the participants. Another was that I hoped that offering texts whose surface features borrowed from another medium would encourage participants to articulate comparisons between how different media invite interpretation. A third reason was slightly more complex. From earlier work with readers, I know that one risk of a very immersive text is that readers get 'lost in the book'. Crago, describing his efforts to annotate his reading responses to a single novel, notes that his ability to surface and make his annotations fades as he moves further into the story, and experiences 'the familiar process of gradually increasing immersion in the world created by the novel, an immersion which enables the reader less and less awareness of anything but that world' (1982, p. 173).

I was anxious not to intrude external promptings on my interpreters any more artificially than was necessary. Selecting texts that draw attention to the surface by the nature of their composition was one way in which I could make use of the logic of the materials in a relatively organic way to reduce (though not eliminate) the invasiveness of my requests for commentary. At the same time, such choices offered me a way to explore the degree to which immersion survives, or is even enhanced through multiple perspectives. Would my participants be absorbed by the story at least some of the time, even when the storytelling mechanisms themselves are potentially disruptive? Would they behave in ways that Murray ascribes to active meaning-makers, using their 'intelligence to reinforce rather than question the reality of the experience' (1997, p. 110) as they assembled a narrative from a variety of sign systems? Or would the surface features of the different texts intrude on their immersed experience and lead them to resist the stories on offer?

Another feature of this little text set is that it comes not just from three different countries (the US, Germany, and Japan) but also from three continents. I would be lying if I claimed such cultural variety as an explicit selection criterion, but I was happy to see it as a by-product of my attempt to find materials either new enough or far enough from the mainstream that my participants would not have encountered them before. It is very striking that they all took this heterogeneity completely in their stride. Two of the three titles (film and game) include subtitles, a topic to which I will return at a later stage.

All three of these stories have attracted critical commentary, and it may be useful before going any further to gain some sense of what each story offers, to look at the responses to these works or interpreters external to this study, and to consider what the creators themselves have to say. My argument for a new kind of canon is strengthened by the richness of critical discussion around each of these texts, represented here by sample quotes taken from a more extensive debate about each title. In addition, our exploration of the *verbs* of interpretation will be more subtle and complex if we have a sense of the specificity and complexity of the *nouns* of the texts themselves.

Monster

Myers' novel was lauded in the year of its publication, 1999: it won the American Library Association's first-ever Printz Award for the best young adult novel of the year, was listed as an honour book for the Coretta Scott King Award, and was a finalist for the National Book Award. Reviews applauded the book's dramatic shape and moral ambiguity.

The book tells the story of Steve Harmon, who is being tried for murder because of his alleged role as lookout in a drugstore robbery that went wrong. We first meet Steve through his diary as he describes his panic over being incarcerated and his terror of his upcoming trial. He decides that one way to preserve his psychological balance throughout this ordeal is to turn his experiences into a screenplay, as he learned to do in film class at school. From this point onwards, the story alternates unevenly between the journal (a total of 59 pages) and the screenplay (a total of 213 pages), and is further enhanced by 11 pictures: ten photos (some digitally obscured) and one court drawing. The journal sections are displayed in a script-like font and the size of words varies according to their emotional import. The screenplay is presented in conventional script format, in a Courier-style font, with indications of camera angles and brief descriptions of settings and characters included. Occasionally the surface of the text conveys further information. Page 24, for example, is over-written with six renditions of the word 'monster', three crossed out. A passage on the page explains what is happening:

> CUT TO: STEVE HARMON. Then CU [close-up] of the pad in front of him. He is writing the word *Monster* over and over again. A white hand (O'BRIEN's [Steve's lawyer]) takes the pencil from his hand and crosses out all the *Monsters*.
>
> (Myers, 1999, p. 24)

Since the words are only half crossed out in our version, we may have to assume that the page has been frozen in the middle of O'Brien's remedial action.

Similar complexity attends the double-page spread of 220–1. Stephanie Yearwood outlines some of the ambiguities that these pages highlight:

> Through varying accounts, we view and review the scene of the robbery/murder from a different point of view each time. Witness Lorelle Henry testifies that she did not see him in the drugstore, and he testifies that he never entered the drugstore that day. But in his notes he writes, 'I walked into a drugstore to look for some mints, and then I walked out' (p. 140). And on page 220, we find two photos of Steve which appear to have been taken by a security camera in a store, with the 'hand-written' marginalia 'What was I doing?' and 'What was I thinking.' [*sic*] Are these actual evidence in the trial or shots he envisions as part of his film? Steve Harmon re-fashions the past, again blurring the fact/fiction line.
>
> (2002, pp. 52–3)

John A. Staunton, in a 2002 review of the book, draws attention to elements both at the surface and within the content of the story that highlight ambiguity:

> The narrative conceit of the screenplay is a stylistic risk. On one level, the language of cinematography interrupts what is otherwise a rather

routine court transcript. But as *Steve's* narrative conceit, the language of film – fade in, long shot, close up, cut to – importantly reveals how he sees and wants us to see his experience at the trial. Together with his journal, these highly structured cinematic blockings are witness to Steve's own internal division about being scared or being tough, about being a good student and a good person or being a 'look-out' at a 'getover.' The interleaving of journal and script reinforces the sense of dislocation and confusion that arises amid competing representations and images of young urban lives. The effect becomes so disquieting for Steve that even at novel's end he confides that 'I want to look at myself a thousand times to look for one true image' (281).

Throughout the novel Steve is set on locating and identifying that single image or capturing that one moment that will explain him to himself. His lawyer, Miss O'Brien, cautions him 'not to write anything in my notebook that I did not want the prosecutor to see' (p. 137). It is a key moment in the text, one that puts into question the very confessional, truth-telling mode Steve has put in motion.

(Staunton, 2002, pp. 792–3, emphasis added)

The witnesses contradict each other in the courtroom, but more importantly we are never allowed to believe that Steve himself knows whether he is innocent or guilty. His lawyer turns away from him after his acquittal, and he is perturbed that she still perceives him as a monster. His relationships with his parents and younger brother are permanently altered. As we learn from the journal entries, he continues to describe himself as a good person but he remains exceptionally vague about his actions at the time of the crime.

The screenplay invites us into the courtroom but also provides flashbacks to points in Steve's life that may lead him to possible participation in crime. The ambiguity begins early, as witnessed by a flashback scene of Steve aged 12. He and his friend Tony are messing around, throwing some rocks at a post. Steve's throw misses the post and hits a young woman.

(The TOUGH GUY she is walking with turns and sees the two young boys.)
　　　　　　　　TOUGH GUY
Hey, man. Who threw that rock? **(He approaches.)**
　　　　　　　　STEVE
Tony! Run!
　　　　　　　　TONY (taking a tentative step)

What? (TOUGH GUY punches TONY. TONY falls – TOUGH GUY
stands over TONY as STEVE backs off. YOUNG WOMAN pulls
TOUGH GUY away and they leave.)
TONY and STEVE are left in the park with TONY sitting on the
ground.
>   TONY
> I didn't throw that rock. You threw it.
>   STEVE
> I didn't say you threw it. I just said 'Run.' You should've run.
>   TONY
> I'll get me an Uzi and blow his brains out.

(Myers, 1999, pp. 42–3)

Tabbi suggests that contemporary fiction explores the challenges of
what used to be taken for granted as objective realism and instead offers
the concept of cognitive realism.

> Cognitive realism ... comes precisely from the narrative interplay
> *between* first- and third-person accounts as the reading mind fluctu-
> ates between concrete and conceptual discourses. For what is rep-
> resented in these journal-like narratives is not thought as such but
> its systems of *notation*, material marks on a material page written by
> a particular thinker in the course of her thinking.

(2002, p. xxi, emphasis in original)

In this novel, Myers certainly does foreground questions arising from
systems of notation, questions that are all the more complex because
the more impersonal third-person rendition of the screenplay becomes
open to interrogation through our knowledge that Steve himself is creating it. The small scene above allows us to observe Steve's capacity to
evade blame through passivity, a characteristic that is crucial to our
understanding of his role as lookout in the drugstore robbery. Yet, even
as we register the importance of this scene, we should also be aware that
Steve is the person who has chosen to present it to us.

Myers himself speaks of the moral function of the dual format.
Talking about research interviews with incarcerated young black men,
he says,

> The picture that was emerging was that of a body of young men
> who were clearly separating their concept of self from their
> deeds. ...

They were all repeat offenders who could give a history of escalating offenses. It became evident that the separation of their self-images from their deeds was not just a face-saving gesture, but an avenue by which a crime could be committed without the burden of an uneasy conscience.

Even the way the prisoners related their tales was interesting. They would often talk in the active first person about themselves, and then switch to the passive voice when talking about the crime.

'The guy grabbed for the gun, you know, and there were some shots fired.'

Shots fired? I had read the trial transcript. He had pumped three shots into a drug dealer's back.

(Myers, 2001, p. 701, emphasis in original).

In a brief interview included in the reader's guide at the end of *Monster*, Myers very clearly makes the connection between these observations and the format of the book:

In interviewing inmates I noticed a tendency for the inmates to attempt to separate their self-portrayals from their crimes. In *Monster* I have Steve speak of himself in the first person in his diary, but when he gets to the trial and the crime he distances himself through the use of the screenplay.

(1999, *Reader's Guide*, pp. 8–9)

The deployment of surface resources to create an impact on the moral depth of the story comes across very clearly in these comments. Yet the surface play also functions *at the surface*, drawing attention to ways of composing a story, and to the particular deliberate decisions that were made both within the fiction by Steve and also by Myers as the external creator. The fiction thus incorporates consideration of how we compose fiction – and how we may use fiction to think about ourselves and/or evade thinking about ourselves.

Myers is very explicit about an ideology of responsibility for one's actions, and it may be argued that the book ends with Steve still unable to face what he actually did. We as readers cannot face what he actually did because, by the end of the story, we still do not know exactly what that deed was. The ambiguity of how much outsiders can ever understand the nature of an event, the tendency of some of these outsiders to revert to stereotypes as a way of making sense of a situation, the questioning of the American justice system – all these issues feed into the complexity of what seems at first glance to be a quick read and a simple story.

Run Lola Run

Like *Monster, Run Lola Run* was feted when it first appeared, both in Germany and elsewhere in the world. Wikipedia (2009) claims,

> In total, the film was nominated for 41 awards, 26 of which were won. These included the Audience Award at the Sundance Film Festival, Best Film at the Seattle International Film Festival, and seven separate wins at the German Film awards.

For more details, see also the Internet Movie Database (IMDB, 2009).

The highlights of the story, which is told in a total of 81 minutes, can be recounted briefly. Lola receives a phone call from her boyfriend Manni. He has bungled a test job for a criminal boss, Ronnie, and fears he will be killed if he cannot find 100,000 Deutschmarks in 20 minutes' time. Lola's response is to scream and throw the phone in the air and then to leap into action, running to find the money and deliver it to Manni at a specified square in Berlin by noon. She tries to get the money from her father, a banker, but he refuses. She is a bit late arriving at the square, and Manni has already moved on to Plan B: robbery of the grocery store on the corner. Lola joins forces with him and is shot by the police. As the camera focuses on her dying face, the scene merges into a red-filtered image of Lola and Manni in bed together. Their discussion leads to Lola rejecting death; the bag of money that has been flung in the air at the grocery store as Lola collapsed mutates into the telephone Lola tossed upwards at the beginning of the story, and the 20-minute plot starts again, with tiny differences in chronology that lead to substantially different outcomes. This time Lola's father rejects her plea and she robs his bank. This time Manni dies, the scene shifts back to the bed interlude and Lola rejects Manni's death rather than her own. Once again, we move back to the beginning of the story; Lola runs again, with further slight changes in speed and progress and a third set of results. Lola misses her father completely (he leaves the bank with a colleague, Herr Meyer) and wins the money at a casino instead. Manni meanwhile retrieves his own money from the vagrant who stole it. This final outcome sees Manni successfully paying the boss and Lola and Manni walking away together.

The film includes many more forms of complication than this simple tripartite reiteration of the plot. As Lola runs past certain people in the film, the camera freezes and a series of Polaroid-style still photographs flashes forward to represent possible futures for these individuals (different each time). At the beginning of each 'run-through' Lola is briefly represented in animated form dashing down the stairs from her apartment, and it is in the animated action that the crucial variation in chronology occurs. The first time she runs past a boy and a dog on the stairs, the second time the boy trips her and delays her, the third time she jumps over both boy and dog and arrives at the bottom slightly sooner. The impact on all subsequent events of this small shift in the timing of her arrival at street level is significant.

The story of Lola's father provides an example of the complex interweaving of the three plot puzzles. On Lola's first visit to the bank where he works, she distracts Herr Meyer who is pulling his car out of a driveway on his way to pick up Lola's father. Herr Meyer shunts his car into another vehicle, coincidentally containing Ronnie, the criminal boss who has so terrified Manni. Lola interrupts her father at his office just as his mistress has told him she is pregnant. On the second instantiation, Lola arrives a few seconds later. She distracts Herr Meyer a moment later than on the first occasion, and he hits the back half rather than the front of Ronnie's car. Meanwhile, inside the bank, the mistress has used that extra minute to inform Lola's father that the baby is not his. On the third time around, Lola is a bit earlier and she rolls over the hood of Herr Meyer's car, slowing him down as he exits from the side passage. There is no crash and Herr Meyer successfully picks up her father from the bank, so that when Lola arrives her father is not there. (Then the car is involved in a different crash that appears to leave both men dead.)

There are many such variations, intricately linked and equally intricately altered. Yet the forward drive of the story mysteriously survives. Author-director Tykwer considers it a story featuring a single strong theme:

> Despite the manic pacing and grab bag of visual techniques on display in *Run Lola Run*, Tykwer feels that from a narrative point of view, his film is still a conventional motion picture. 'It's a new kind of film, but only externally,' he concludes. 'It still functions according to the structural principles of classical drama. We have a clear and passionate love story, action principle and a mission that continues throughout. As far as theme and content are concerned, it is absolutely universal. This woman's passion brings down the rigid rules of the world surrounding her. Love can and does move mountains. Over and above all the action, the central driving force of *Run Lola Run* is romance'.
>
> (Rudolph, 1999, p. 26)

Tykwer used various forms of film 'language' to convey his romance. Scenes involving Lola and Manni are shot in 35 mm film; all other scenes are shot in video. 'In a sense', says Tykwer, 'the film images are true and the other images are untrue' (Rudolph, 1999, p. 22). Lighting was controlled by filters of coral and sepia, in the cause of maintaining audience engagement in the forward movement of the story.

> 'I felt that if we let the film go too bluish and cold, the audience would become more aware of it's [*sic*] construction, which I didn't want,' Tykwer notes. 'The most important thing for me was for the audience *not* to think about how we did things. I don't like films that show off so that you are distracted from the emotions, story developments and characters'.
>
> (Rudolph, 1999, p. 24)

While Tykwer emphasizes the importance of the audience being swept away by the story in conventional film fashion, critics are quick to make comparisons between this movie and other media forms. Robert Lauer notes a connection with the Internet with its 'back' button: 'a new technology, where everything is possible upon returning to a previous icon that enables one to access other potentially available albeit previously un-invoked routes' (2003). Stuart Klawans compares Lola to a 'punked-out Road Runner, pursued not by Wile E. Coyote but by an accident-prone Fate, whose assaults are as reversible as the workings of Acme products' (1999, p. 35). Jim Bizzocchi compares the movie to a feature-length rock video (2005, p. 1) and a video game (2005, p. 2), before moving on to categorize it as a narrative database.

> It is a highly structured set of parallel plot events. The film can easily be read as a narrative database with three records and a dozen fields. The 'records' of this database are the three iterations of Lola's run. The 'fields' are the events which are repeated (with variations) within the three iterated runs: the cartoon stairs, the Polaroid tales, the dream sequences, Lola hitting Mayer's [*sic*] car, etc.
>
> (2005, p. 4)

Viewers making comparisons across this database supply the interactivity that is associated with video games. 'If cinema does not afford explicit physical interaction, it can and does support implicit psychological interaction', says Bizzocchi (2005, p. 5).

Vadim Rudnev draws on three cultural patterns ('hermeneutic keys' [2003, p. 389]) at work in this movie: the computer game with its built-in re-start potential, the fairy tale with its recurring tripartite organi-zation, and 'the semantics of possible worlds' (2003, p. 390) with its perception of an infinity of possible futures.

Robert Lauer suggests that in the transitional scenes of Lola and Manni in bed, they are 'imagining ("developing") the scenarios the viewer has already seen' (2003). Others, such as Bizzocchi, see the bed scenes them-selves as the dream sequences. Similarly, it is possible to argue that, if the movie behaves like a computer game, either (a) the animated scenes of Lola running down the stairs and being variably delayed by the boy and the dog are the 'cut scenes' (that is, the non-interactive filmed interludes that punctuate games as either set-up or reward for players), while the three different runs constitute the game – or the opposite, (b) the variations in the animation are the game and the subsequent run is the cut scene, set in motion by Lola's different decisions during her descent down the stairs.

There are, in short, many accounts of the energy that fuels this branching story. All who mention it, however, are in agreement about the driving force of the music. Jim Bizzocchi suggests that one forebear of the movie is the rock video, and I will quote extensively from his development of this idea and the connections he draws to Bolter and Grusin's concept of remediation:

Lola is a rock video remediated through the magnification of scale. It merits this classification for two reasons. First, it borrows many of the specifics of the rock video form such as the reliance on music, the bold use of cinematic craft (quick cuts, dramatic angles, moving cam-era), and the rapid delineation of character and type. Second, it meets the two-fold requirements [of] rock videos... : combining immediate engagement with sustainability. In the process of achieving those goals, it actively explores the dynamic boundary between immediacy and hypermediation.

(2005, p. 2)

Bizzocchi lists the elements that invite immediacy:

The solid continuity within the dramatic scenes makes it easy to fol-low the flow and the emotional arc of the story. The design of the narrative also affords an early engagement. At a high level the story is a standard quest/love story. As such it presents us with romantic love, challenge, danger, and suspense – all leavened with a sense of wit and humour. The characters are human enough to relate to, and idiosyncratic enough to maintain our interest. Stylistically, the use of insistent and engaging techniques (such as the exquisitely tracked running shots, or the driving techno beat) quickly draws the audience into the work, and makes it easy for them to stay in the film world.

The hypermediation, on the other hand, helps to sustain repeated viewings. The mix of embedded media components gives the film a heterogeneous texture: live-action cinema, live-action video, animation, Polaroid stills. Multiple viewings enable the viewer to savor that texture, to anticipate the radical media shifts (such as the polaroids) and to appreciate the subtler ones (such as the use of video footage for the scenes with Lola's father and his lover).

It is, however, the richness of the plot that most profoundly supports multiple viewings ... This multi-variant and multi-level plot structure extends traditional concepts of cinematic continuity, causality, and narrative.

(2005, p. 2)

It is interesting how Tykwer's declared ideological infusion – that, despite the random nature of tiny and uncontrollable variations in an arbitrary universe, love really does conquer all – is manifest in some components of the story. I would suggest that the pulsing forward drive of the music, for example, supports the more coherent version of life that he proclaims in his interview – whereas the hit and miss nature of the futures forecast in the Polaroid photographs contradicts this singular framing of the story.

The complexities of these competing analyses provide us with an intriguing snapshot of the many narrative variations that contemporary interpreters may recognize. Despite or because of its complex and multi-textual composition, *Run Lola Run* remains a highly watchable and engaging movie. It was striking throughout the sessions that none of the participants in this study was unduly puzzled or put off by its convolutions, and most were intrigued by its branching format.

The question of translation deserves attention. Even the title of the film is not exactly the same in English and German. *Lola Rennt* (Lola Runs or Lola is Running) offers a different kind of invitation from that given by the English title, *Run Lola Run*. The second person imperative of the translated title, for example, makes a link to the second person address of a video game that is completely missing in the original German title.

I will return to the significance of viewing with subtitles in the final chapter. There is no doubt their presence led to a specialized form of viewing, one for which nobody in the project expressed great enthusiasm. There was little evidence, however, that viewing through the frame of the subtitles interfered enormously with making narrative sense of the movie. From inside my own black box as a viewer, I find that although I have to distract attention to reading the words, my attentiveness to the nuances of the actors' voices still supplies a great deal of information even when I know nothing of the language, as in this case. Personally I would always rather watch a subtitled movie than a dubbed one; I find it interferes less with my reading of the entire screen.

But I have no way of knowing if the participants feel the same way. I did not ask about the subtitles, and there was remarkably little conversation about them among the participants. Here is the most extended conversation in its entirety; Group D is discussing the identity of the man in the ambulance:

Adam: I don't know, again, it wasn't developed well. Maybe it was because we were watching the subtitles.

Margaret: Does it matter?

Adam: I think so.

Sandra: No, I think that the director – he or she – they're just using the characters to get across like, bigger points like, a bigger story and I don't really think the characters themselves really mean a whole lot, but I think the main *message* is what –

Lewis: They're all kind of pawns in the big game.

Sandra: Yeah exactly.

Of the 12 participants, Adam is the only one to blame the subtitles for specifically interfering with his comprehension, and Sandra is quick to disagree. It would be foolish to conclude from this observation that the subtitles did not affect response, but it would seem arguable that, overall, they were not at the forefront of the viewers' attention.

Shadow of the Colossus

Shadow of the Colossus provides only the barest bones of a story. Superfluous detail has been removed and some essential information is also missing right up to and even after the ending. The story begins with a long cut scene showing the arrival of a solitary young man on horseback at an isolated and enormous temple. When he dismounts, we see he is carrying the body of a young woman, which he places on the altar. Mysterious shadowy creatures emerge from the floor of the temple but he dissipates them by pointing his sword at them. Communicating with a voice that speaks from above, he asks for restoration of the young woman's soul. The voice, identifying itself as Dormin, says that only a human being in possession of that particular, ancient and powerful sword has even a slight chance of such restoration but that, even for such a sword-bearer, the price will be very high. As with *Run Lola Run*, the language itself is not English, and subtitles convey the gist of the dialogue.

Sixteen stone idols line the temple walls. Dormin tells the young man that he must seek out one colossus for each idol and destroy it, an act that will bring the statue tumbling down. To locate each colossus, the hero is advised to hold his sword to the sun and follow in the direction where the light beams focus. At this stage, the cut scene ends and the player takes over, helping the hero to re-mount his horse, Agro, and to gallop off out of the temple into a vast and empty land.

Sixteen times the hero must first locate, then arouse, then slay the colossus. Each time a colossus dies, black shadows emerge from its body, wrap themselves round the hero, and transport him back to the temple where the body of his beloved still lies. Dormin gives him a cryptic clue about the location and identity of the next colossus before he sets off again. As the game progresses, the hero looks more and more haggard.

Each massive colossus is different and lives undisturbed, sometimes asleep, in a different corner of the empty and beautiful wilderness. The hero's journey to find each colossus is lengthy and carries him across bridges, down valleys, through forests, over mountains, alongside meadows. There is no musical accompaniment for these explorations, and the silence of the landscape is interrupted only by the occasional birdsong and the clop of Agro's hooves.

Once the colossus is located, it comes to life in a brief cut scene, and then battle ensues. The colossi are indeed enormous and they fight for their lives with epic intensity. Many times the hero must literally climb their gigantic furry limbs and torsos to reach and stab the weak spot, known as a sigil, which alone makes them vulnerable to slaughter. Sometimes he must decoy them down from the sky or out of the water in order to launch his assault. Each colossus is differently shaped, armed, and skilled, but all are determined to survive and keen to kill the hero instead. The music that accompanies each heroic struggle is driving and dramatic. The hero never possesses more in the way of weaponry than his sword and a bow and arrow, which he must use in different ways to obliterate his foe. Figuring out how to find and then how to kill each different colossus is the main challenge of the game.

The colossi are themselves magnificent, usually in quite intimidating ways, and often apparently harmless until aggravated. Their end, as the sword is thrust into the glowing sigil, involves gushes of black blood and a complete collapse, portrayed in a cutscene. Tendrils of black shadow surround the hero's limp body as it is conveyed back to the temple. The shift from active and very tense game-play to the sudden relaxation of the cutscene means that the player's physical and emotional response mirrors the hero's post-victory collapse.

Equivalence of player experience and story experience is not limited to the moment of the colossus' defeat. Ben Sherman has explored parallels between story mechanics and game mechanics in this game, and highlights another example:

> After each successive colossus, you are transported back to the main temple near the center of the world map. Your immediate goal is to use the light from the sword to find the colossus. What you then have is between 5 and 20 minutes of galloping around a very desolate and isolating landscape. The game designers could well have made it a far shorter distance. Why make the player gallop, sometimes in an unbroken straight line, for an extended period of time? The answer: it makes the player feel the isolation that the story tells the player they should feel.
>
> Rather than the player galloping a bit, hitting a spot on the map and fading to a cut scene where he or she is told that the protagonist 'Traveled for many a day before he came upon the great Colossus,' the player must experience it. And the travel is not a simple extension of time. Each step is carefully considered. Each colossus is an unknown piece of the map. The player experiences the travel through unknown territory without a companion.
>
> (Sherman, 2006)

Sherman refers to the guilt that many gamers feel about killing the colossi, and claims that it is exacerbated by the encounter with the fifth colossus, one shaped like a giant bird.

> This colossus does not immediately attack you. You must get its attention by shooting it and only then does it fly down to get rid of you ... In the story line, this is where the player learns that not all colossi will attack. Sometimes the player must instigate the battle ... In *Shadow of*

the Colossus, it unfolds as a story would, but the hand of the protagonist is synonymous with the hand of the player, so the protagonist's guilt becomes the player's guilt.

(2006)

David Ciccoricco suggests that guilt is also associated with the long travels in between battles:

> As adventure games go, *Shadow of the Colossus* is unique in that it makes time and space for a reflective response ... that is, it makes you think about what you've done after you've done it while, experientially, it may seem as though you're not *doing* anything in terms of a material outcome in the gameworld. ...
>
> What does one do when riding alone all that time? You think. You think about the fact that you are about to bring down another one of these awe-inspiring creatures even though you know that they have not wronged you in any way, and they are definitely not expecting you and your sword. All you know – all you remember – is that you must kill them in order to complete your quest.
>
> The sense of moral ambiguity evoked by the storyworld is one of the main reasons why *Shadow of the Colossus* is an aesthetically compelling video game. ... [T]he lengthy cut scenes and long stretches of riding in isolation are both design qualities that allow the player to respond reflectively to the storyworld, a response that calls on the player's own form of narrative memory. In effect, the player not only inherits the task of the wanderer and the tools with which to accomplish that task, but also (potentially and ideally) the psychological baggage that his ordeal entails.
>
> (2007)

This game confounds Ryan's assertion about games that, 'if players had to debate the morality of their actions, the pace of the game, not to mention its strategic appeal, would seriously suffer' (2006, p. 196). Pace is certainly implicated; the long hunt for each colossus can be almost leisurely – but the visceral battle scenes that ensue when the colossus is found and awakened, lack nothing for fast pace and complex strategic appeal. 'Literature seeks the gray area of the ambiguous', Ryan asserts (2006, p. 196), and, to the extent that this game moves in exactly that gray area, it can perhaps be described as literary.

For all its mix of ambiguous reflection and regret with high-intensity battle scenes, *Shadow of the Colossus* shares with the other two texts in this project a forward-moving impulse. Creator Fumito Ueda was intent on developing a game that flows, and on evoking emotion (which will vary from player to player). 'Emotions tend to usually work the same way, over and over again', he says. 'There aren't many levels to them. They're profound, they're big; you just need to make something that, visually, matches up with that' (Rogers, 2005).

Prior to *Shadow of the Colossus*, Ueda was responsible for the cult classic game *Ico*, which he describes as a game 'designed by subtraction' (Rogers, 2005). Subtraction plays a major part in the story of *Shadow of the Colossus* as well. Rogers suggests that 'What *Shadow of the Colossus* does is pin down the way narrative should be in videogames. That is, it should be spare' (2005). *Shadow of the Colossus* is certainly spare in narrative terms, though lush in its geography and challenging in its conflict scenes. We do not know what killed the young woman who lies on the altar; we have no idea where the hero obtained his miraculous sword. Dormin exists as a disembodied voice, and his only context is the temple, which is otherwise utterly empty. The vast landscape is similarly devoid of people. After the twelfth colossus is slain, a brief cut scene shows us a group of masked men riding towards the temple, but we are ignorant of their purpose. The lengthy hunt for each colossus and the vivid moment-by-moment detail of its slaying is acutely portrayed for us, but the narrative compulsion that fuels the hero's movements is decipherable mainly through the actions it engenders. The horse Agro's apparently fatal fall down a deep crevice during the hunt for the last colossus is almost the only singular plot detail in the highly repetitive iterations of hunt and battle. As a story, it is both partial and austere in its limitations, yet that austerity is part of its appeal.

The lengthy cut scene of the ending provides a lot of story in a short time but solves only some of the mystery of the game. The concluding cut scene lasts for the better part of half an hour. Briefly put, the masked men arrive in the temple just as the sixteenth idol collapses. The body of the hero is returned once more to the shrine. The hero's face and demeanour have coarsened through the trials of the game and by now he is less than human; horns are sprouting from his head. Lord Emon, leader of the masked men, reveals that the hero has stolen the ancient sword and violated the taboo of entering the cursed land, using a forbidden spell to call up Dormin. But the hero is only being used, he says, and he orders his execution. A man runs the hero through with a sword – but like the colossi he emits a black stream of blood, absorbs all the shadows and grows into a monstrous colossus himself – a new Dormin. It seems that Dormin's evil had been contained by being distributed through the

16 colossi; now reunited in the body of the hero, it poses new threats to the world.

Retreating from the temple in order to seal it off, Lord Emon throws the ancient sword into the pool, creating a flash of light and a vortex that inexorably drags the hero under, shrinking as he tumbles towards the water. The men gallop off over the bridge, which collapses behind them, thus isolating the temple. The dead heroine comes back to life; the missing Agro limps back into the temple, badly injured. When the girl goes to the pool she finds it drained, and in it lies a horned baby. These three – girl, baby, horse – face a closed-off world, but as the game ends a deer comes to visit and the birds sing. There is at least the possibility of a new, though compromised, beginning as the credits conclude.

Like Tykwer, Uedo claims that emotions are big. Uedo's story also asserts that emotions are dangerous, that they can open up a person to manipulation by evil forces. 'Love loses all' might be a short theme statement for this game. The inherent peril of focusing only on your own heart's desire, oblivious to any other cost, is implied in the story. There is some vestigial sense of social cost, conveyed only through the dialogue of Lord Emon, but the moral cost is conveyed throughout the game-play, and the ending suggests more direct dangers to the hero as a result of his desperation and hubris.

Shadow of the Colossus is relatively short by the standards of many contemporary narrative games. All the players testified to the intensity of its battle scenes, and every one of them at one point or another commented on its moral ambiguity.

The Participants

So much for the materials. Locating participants for this project was a little simpler. With my text selections made, I advertised for participants in the student newspaper in the fall of 2005, inviting undergraduates aged between 18 and 21 with at least some minimal competence in digital gaming to join the project. A total of 12 volunteers could be slotted into timetables so that they could work in groups of three. I said I was interested in working with friendship groups or with individuals. One group of three and one pair of friends applied; the rest were strangers to each other.

I acquired very little information about these participants except date of birth and undergraduate major. The disciplinary range was broad (see Table 2.1). Nine men and three women took part in the study, reflecting the natural gender bias of the pool. Not everyone was white but I asked no questions about ethnic or racial background.

Table 2.1 Participants

Group A		
Dan	general science	age 20
Keith	chemical engineering	age 20
Neil	microbiology	age 21
Group B		
Martin	English	age not known
Sumana	political science	age 22
Tess	English	age not known
Group C		
Jacob	general arts/business	age 20
Jarret	education (English/history)	age 20
Seth	engineering	age 20
Group D		
Adam	English/drama	age not known
Lewis	genetics	age 21
Sandra	psychology	age 19
Group AB		
Dan	general science	age 20
Martin	English	age not known
Neil	microbiology	age 21

The gender bias perturbed me slightly, but I did not think it worth re-advertising to attempt to level it out. I have encountered imbalances in prior studies: when I advertise for participants with at least minimal gaming experience, the pool skews male; when I look for enthusiastic readers, the majority is female. In this case, my first priority was to gain insight into narrative thinking that included the element of game experience. These volunteers were certainly qualified to offer perspectives different from my own.

Here are the groups with disciplinary background and age included (four participants did not provide a date of birth, but all appeared to be aged 20–1). Groups A and C were all-male, and Group B was the only group with a majority of women. Sumana was probably the least experienced gamer of the whole group and certainly the most diffident about taking the controls. Some experienced gamers such as Dan and Neil never became really comfortable with the controls of the PlayStation 2, so their general comments were more assured than their actual play.

Group AB developed after the Christmas break, as timetables shifted and it became necessary to re-schedule. All the work with the novel and the film was completed by the four groups; Group AB as a unit dealt only with the game.

The project

Each group watched the movie, read the book, and played the game in its entirety – with the single exception of Group AB who, for the sake of completing the project before the end of the winter term, skipped the slaughter of two late colossi. I worked hard to make each group's experiences, interruptions, and questions as comparable as possible, and in this section I outline some of the details of the sessions.

Louise Rosenblatt famously distinguishes between an 'efferent' reading (reading to take information away) and an 'aesthetic' reading (reading for the sake of living through the experience, indwelling in the text) (2005, p. 85). In this project, I was anxious not to skew the responses towards the efferent by asking questions about content, and I drew on Rosenblatt's advice:

> Questions can be sufficiently open to enable the young readers to select concrete details or parts of the text that had struck them most forcibly. The point is to foster expressions of response that keep the experiential, qualitative elements in mind. Did anything especially interest? annoy? puzzle? frighten? please? seem familiar? seem weird?
>
> (2005, p. 85)

'Tell me what struck you' and 'In what ways did that matter to you?' were my guiding themes throughout the sessions.

Participant responses to these materials were both video- and audio-recorded. The records were transcribed and both transcript and video record were mounted for analysis on Transana software (http://www. transana.org/), though my account makes rather less use of the Transana coding than I anticipated.

Working in four – and then three – groups of three, the participants articulated their responses in ways appropriate to each format.

With the movie, the group watched it together, with six breaks for conversation about their interpretation of the story so far (all at roughly the same points in the film, as I clicked the pause button), and an extended discussion at the end.

With the novel, they read the first 58 pages in five specified instalments, silently reading a few pages at a time (always the same for all groups) before speaking together about what struck them as noteworthy in that segment. I asked them to put a sticky note down beside any resonant phrase, to serve as a prompt for later discussion. They took a copy of the novel and a set of sticky notes home to read the remainder of the novel in private, after which we conducted an extensive follow-up discussion about the book as a whole. They made some use of their sticky notes as *aides-mémoires* in the subsequent conversations. After the session, I retained the labelled copies of the novel complete with readers' placed markers.

In the case of both film and novel, the conversations involved a kind of simulated, naturalized 'think-after' account of their processing activities (Pressley and Afflerbach, 1995; Branch, 2000; Afflerbach, 2002).

With the PlayStation game, the three participants took turns with a single controller. They were invited to advise freely when not manning the controls, and did not hesitate to do so. The nature of the game is that it allows conversation during play; the story need not be stopped for discussion as was required by both film and book. The result is a naturalized version of a 'think-aloud' (rather than 'think-after') protocol; the game-playing observations were contemporary with their play, rather than retrospective. We also discussed the game as a whole after they reached the end of the story, for varying lengths of time.

Further details of the sessions can be found in Appendix 1.

The methodology

As the participants viewed, read, and played their stories, a team of graduate assistants recorded them, with one camera trained on the group and a second on the screen (we turned off the second camera as they read *Monster* and made no attempt to record any individual page). I sat with them and invited them to talk about their experiences. We loaded the video records and the transcripts onto the analytical computer program Transana, and synched the video and the written record. Transana permits coding of the data, and research assistant Dale Storie took the first pass at marking links and associations. I used his coded version to search the transcripts and found it very helpful in coming to terms with the scale of the dataset. There is little overt record of that coding in this volume, however. In the end I decided that prising particular quotes away from their social setting was counter-productive as a route to demonstrating how the participants gradually sorted out meanings that were satisfying to them. Instead, for the most part, I present embedded quotes in their organic settings of a developing conversation. On the other hand, for the sake of readability in these extended excerpts, I made the executive decision to eliminate silently the 'thinking noises' such as 'um' and 'like', and I have occasionally smoothed out repetition without giving notice.

The challenge

With my texts selected, my groups assembled, my assistants recruited, I embarked on the complex process of pursuing insight into other people's interpretive capacities. While I tried to be as open to discovery as possible, there is no doubt that what I perceived – both during the live sessions and later in reviewing the various records – was shaped in part by my own understanding. As I explored and analysed the records, I also turned to theories of narrative to help me to see further. In the next chapter I outline some theoretical approaches that applied in significant ways to what I was discovering.

3
Thinking It Through: Theoretical Frameworks

Contemporary definitions of literacy would fill a large conceptual map, featuring many battlegrounds where conflicting ideas about what counts as literate behaviour are negotiated. This book occupies a territory that amounts to a small corner of this map. Overarching general theories about changing communications are important, but so are smaller-scale projects that attempt to improve our awareness of particular forms of understanding. In this study, I am specifically looking at ways in which we come to comprehend narrative fiction in three distinctive media, one very old, one middle-aged, and one young and new. To use a distinction that Andrew Elfenbein borrows from psychologists, I will investigate many online and some offline interpretive processes.

> Online processes such as inferring, elaborating, summarizing, paraphrasing, and integrating information, take place during the act of reading and lead to, or fail to lead to, a coherent memory representation. This representation is modified by offline processes (which occur after reading): for example, accessibility decreases over time, and new sources of background information may be integrated.
>
> (2006, p. 486)

One question of interest will be whether the social construction of understanding occurs online or offline or in some mixture of both. In this chapter, however, I will pay particular attention to the theoretical framing of activities described as online in this account (pausing, in passing, to take note of the power of cross-media metaphors in academic thinking; we will see more of them in Chapter 10).

Does narrative itself change when new formats provide new channels for story? Marie-Laure Ryan, exploring this question, recommends a relative answer: 'I suggest regarding the set of all narratives as fuzzy, and narrativity (or ("storiness") as a scalar property rather than as a rigidly binary feature that divides mental representations into stories and nonstories' (2006, p. 7). Ryan provides a list of eight criteria of relative 'storiness', divided under four headings: the spatial, the temporal, the mental, and the formal and pragmatic dimension (2006, p. 8). Under these headings, all three of the texts chosen for this study qualify to be considered as narrative. Interestingly, despite those who argue that a game cannot be a real narrative, it is *Run Lola Run*, in my view, that plays fastest and loosest with at least two of the conditions (#6, 'The sequence of events must form a unified causal chain and lead to closure,' and #7, 'The occurrence of at least some of the events must be asserted as fact for the story world'), rather than *Shadow of the Colossus*, which seems to me to meet all the tests satisfactorily.

Ryan outlines relatively conventional narrative attributes. In addition to colonizing various platforms and formats, however, contemporary narrative also experiments with the 'rules of the game'. Eliza Dresang (1999) talks about 'radical change' affecting books for young people as a result of cultural and technological shifts in how we develop narrative understanding. Games of course, are digital and open to interaction. Much current popular film also plays complex and daring games with interpreters. Thomas Elsaesser speaks of 'mind-game films' that disrupt the implied narrative contract with the viewer. *Run Lola Run* does not establish its temporal parameters in any clearcut way, disrupting the 'spectator-address' (Elsaesser, 2009, p. 16). As the story events themselves are altered, reworked, brought into question,

> the spectator's own meaning-making activity involves constant retroactive revision, new reality-checks, displacements, and reorganization not only of temporal sequence, but of mental space, and the presumption of a possible switch in cause and effect.
>
> (2009, p. 21)

How the interpreters in this study deal with the need for 'constant retroactive revision' is one of the interesting questions. Do they apply normative narrative interpretations until it becomes clear they will work no longer, or do they begin with an assumption that all bets are off? Does disruption of expectation lead to a sense of distraction, chaos, and interpretive failure, or are their schemas elastic enough to continue to provide support? How flexible is the 'mental space' they bring to the complex narrative presentation of *Run Lola Run*, for example? We will explore these questions as they arise 'online' during the temporal act of viewing.

Nouns, verbs, and temporality

Lisa Schade Eckert draws our attention to the significance (both scholarly and pedagogical) of looking at verbs rather than nouns.

> Literary scholars have long used the term *reading* as a noun; a student is required to construct a *reading* of a text, somehow understanding that this really means a critical *interpretation* of the text. Used as a verb, however, *reading* is relegated to a lower, less scholarly, cognitive activity in which the reader has little agency in constructing meaning from text.
>
> (2008, p. 112, emphasis in original)

In this project, I will investigate the verbs, the processes of reading, viewing and playing, both those that occur so automatically that they may pass for unconscious and involuntary, and those that involve more explicit agency and decision-making. Although the participants in the project often did develop critical opinions about the texts under consideration, I did not ask them to 'construct a *reading*' in the deliberate, critical form described by Eckert.

The main emphasis of this project is on the component of understanding, which is never complete. Novels, films and games are all temporal media. An interpreter never has total grasp of the whole text at any one time, and the most complete understanding arises only as the act or interpreting comes to an end, or maybe even much later. We may gain a deeper awareness of interpretive processes if we look for theoretical approaches that acknowledge this temporality, that explore the partial nature of understanding as it develops over time. Exploring this temporal process as it plays out in different media may expand our understanding of its complexities and limitations.

Literacies and textual artefacts

In this study, I explore the relationship of interpreters to *finite* texts *created in advance* and relatively *impervious to alteration* within the limits of the artefact provided. In such ways all these texts are 'locatable' (Bazelgette, 2008, p. 14); you could go out this afternoon and acquire your own copy of the materials I brought to this study, and they would effectively be the same artefact. Each of these texts begins as something we can hold in our hand.

Asserting the finite nature of these texts is not the same thing as saying that they always lead to the same interpretation. Nor is it true that the texts remain sacred and that nobody messes with them after the fact. There are many playful (and/or school-related) encroachments on the stories I chose for this project. See for example, *Run Leia Run*, an animation that crosses *Star Wars* with *Run Lola Run* (Force, 2009); or the spoof preview of the promised movie version of *Shadow of the Colossus* (YouTube, 2009). It may be telling that when I searched the Internet for *Monster*, I turned up lesson plans rather than parodies, but some of these also invite tampering with the given text.

Nevertheless, as artefacts, these texts – my locatable copies and the identical copies you buy this afternoon – are straightforwardly designed for reception. They contrast with multiplayer online games, for example, where players develop plot and character; with YouTube mash-ups that merge story elements in new ways; with the Penguin Wiki novel and other experimental forms of collective fiction writing that mutate as they develop.

In open texts, such as an online role-playing game, it is possible that the time of telling and the time of the event are simultaneous. In closed texts, there is always a discrepancy, one that leads to the distinction between *story* and *discourse*: 'what happens and the presentation of what happens' (Hogan, 2003, p. 115).

Even for the closed forms of text that I selected for this project, though in certain ways they are reiterable, reception is never instantaneous and never occurs twice in exactly the same way. Interpreters must find ways of processing the story as it is told to them and the story as they infer it to have occurred in its untold, un-related state. Such a process involves a building-up of comprehension, involving eye, brain, and also hand.

It is too simplistic to say that if we can *lay our hands* on a text we have more control over its pacing, but the issue is worth pursuing, at least briefly. Our page-turning hands help us to pace our reading; holding the remote control enables us to pause or rewind the video. Certainly hands play an important role in the speed with which the digital game progresses. Not every medium, however, is susceptible to manipulation in this way; pressing the pause button brings the audio recording to a complete halt, rather than enabling us to listen timelessly to the frozen chord. The role of the 'intelligent hand' in interpretation (Sennett, 2008, p. 149) is significant, however, and should not be overlooked;

we will return to this topic later, and delve more deeply into manual components of comprehension.

In the meantime, we will explore some of the implications of how the locatable and finite 'page' turns into a temporal event. Theorists of the act of reading who focus on the temporality of the event provide a useful starting point for a preliminary framework; other theoretical approaches will be fleshed out in later chapters.

Making meaning

Meaning, says Wolfgang Iser, is 'something that happens' (1978, p. 22), a perspective that enforces temporality in all forms of interpretation. Iser's description of the reading process involves movement from the familiar to the new, but he begins with the great miracle of reading itself. Over time, as we read, says Iser,

> *we think the thoughts of another person.* Whatever these thoughts may be, they must to a greater or lesser degree represent an unfamiliar experience, containing elements which at any one moment must be partially inaccessible to us. For this reason our selections tend first to be guided by those parts of the experience that still seem to be familiar. They will influence the gestalt we form, and so we will tend to leave out of account a number of other possibilities which our selective decisions have helped to formulate but have left on the fringes. But these possibilities do not disappear; in principle they always remain present to cast their shadow over the gestalt that relegated them.
>
> (1978, p. 126, emphasis added)

Our tentative assessment of what is familiar to us, helps to shape our even more provisional appraisal of what is new, and so, out of the matrix of the words presented on the page, we carve a reading experience that is not entirely alien and are thus able to absorb it into our own sense of ourselves and our world view. It is a performance of the text that makes it our own; it is also the process that turns the locatable page into a temporal event.

In similar ways, we bring the familiarity of our own experience to bear on the newness of the images we encounter in films and games. Over time, we amalgamate what we initially brought to the experience with what we did not previously understand. The familiar, as Iser suggests, may well overpower the new, but the new remains in our minds, if only in the form of questions that may haunt and/or corrode our best efforts to feel authoritative and clear. In very real ways, we must learn to recognize what we have never seen before.

Reading is not the same as viewing or playing in one very important cognitive way. If, in reading, we often 'think the thoughts of another person', it may be more precise to say that in viewing or gaming we think thoughts that are not our own. Neither of the latter activities offers the same insight into the internal perspectives of others; we must infer character attributes from external observation. Slightly different forms of social intelligence are involved.

Rules of reading

Nevertheless, cross-referencing among theoretical approaches to reading, viewing, and playing can take us a long way towards understanding the complexity of our capacity to explore narrative in its many forms. For example, Peter Rabinowitz's rules of reading provide a more detailed breakdown of the *gestalt* formation that occurs during the act of reading; they also supply an interesting elision between the 'nouns' and the 'verbs' of reading. Rules are definitely nouns, but in his rules of notice, rules of signification, rules of configuration, and rules of coherence, Rabinowitz provides a useful key to what it is that interpreters *do*, and how they behave differently at different points in the fiction. In effect he discusses textual artefacts in terms of the 'online' behaviours they invite. He draws his analysis from the reading of standard nineteenth- and twentieth-century print fiction, but it is worth noticing that I have found these rules equally useful in exploring how people interpret films and games (Mackey, 2007). Viewers and players, just like readers, explicitly notice, make decisions about how to think about what they've noticed, put the pieces of the story together in terms of their understanding of the conventions, and reflect on the story in ways that help them to understand it as a coherent whole. Whether they work with page or some kind of moving image, they develop and refine their sense of the text over a period of time.

Briefly expressed, Rabinowitz's four sets of conventional tools involve the following:

- *rules of notice*, which help us distinguish what to attend to in the initial presentation of a mass of details (1987, p. 53). We will explore the rules of notice in Chapter 4.
- *rules of signification*, which enable us to decide *how* to attend to what we have decided to notice: is a narrator reliable, do the normal

conventions of contemporary society apply to the world of the story, and so forth (1987, p. 76). Who speaks? Who sees (Stephens, 1992, p. 22)? To what extent can we trust these eyes and voices? We will return to the rules of signification in Chapter 6.

- *rules of configuration*, which allow us to assemble the components of the story into a plausible unit. Our expectations are important, whether authors decide to meet them or to confound them. Rules of configuration will figure substantially in Chapters 7 and 8.
- *rules of coherence*, which are often applied 'offline' (Elfenbein, 2006, p. 486), after the story is finished. Rules of coherence are brought to bear in order to make the best story possible out of the assembled elements, and we often work on the assumption that 'apparent flaws in its construction are intentional and meaning bearing'.

(Rabinowitz, 1987, p. 147)

My experience to date is that Rabinowitz's observations apply readily to the interpretation of film and game as well as print story. His sample, however, derives from nineteenth- and twentieth-century print literature, and twenty-first-century interpreters may well be more experienced in dealing with ambivalence beyond what would have been tolerated earlier. The impact of such a cultural shift would appear more strongly in the application of rules of configuration and coherence, and we may see some examples of this factor at work in the selected texts.

'Rules of configuration', says Rabinowitz, 'are prescriptive only in the following way: they map out the expectations that are likely to be activated by a text, and they suggest that if too many of these activated expectations are ignored, readers may find the results dull or chaotic' (1987, p. 113). These rules of configuration certainly work well in the nineteenth- and twentieth-century fiction that Rabinowitz uses as his test bed. His analysis, however, does not apply in straightforward ways to all versions of twenty-first-century popular fiction: for example, massively multi-player online role-playing games do not necessarily follow these rules, nor do some of the improvisations on core stories that are beginning to move onto the web. The Penguin Wiki Novel (Penguin, 2009) offers one example of an open-endedness that makes configuration much more challenging. Whether such a text offers the potential for a successful reading experience is a different question; some readers may well find the Wiki novel 'dull or chaotic', and it may take years of experimentation before we can decide whether the concept of forms of narrative open to participant contribution has succeeded or failed in terms of words, moving images, and games.

In this study, however, the focus remains on one-off, stand-alone, closed-ended fictions of the conventional kind described by Rabinowitz here, and so his rules of configuration retain much of their utility for this exercise.

The importance of prior experience in developing a sense of what makes for satisfying coherence cannot be over-emphasized. Rabinowitz, drawing on relatively conventional print examples, describes relatively 'neat' examples of coherence. Perhaps the most interesting example I know, of readers applying expectations of 'neatness' to their stories, comes from James Squire's 1964 study of high-school readers interpreting short stories; in many cases he described them as imposing tidy conclusions on relatively open endings:

> Many adolescent readers in this study seem to be incorrigible romantics. Regardless of the logic of events and circumstances, they continually assume, infer, and hope for the best. They are 'happiness bound' both in their demand for fairy tale solutions and in their frequent unwillingness to face the realities of unpleasant interpretation. Consequently, their sentimental overemphasis on the good frequently leads them to distort and misinterpret both characters and their actions.
>
> (1964, pp. 41–2)

Squire's participants forced 'happy' endings onto the stories he asked them to interpret, over-riding textual information where necessary.

The participants in this project were only a few years older than these high-school students from the 1960s, but were radically more sophisticated in terms of accepting ambiguities, insufficiencies, and tampering with the 'rules' of telling a story. There are many possible explanations. My participants had a slight age advantage, which may be enough to explain the difference. The cultural changes of the 45 years or so between the two studies may account for increased sophistication. It may broadly be that Canadian culture is somewhat less sentimental than American. In any case, the undergraduates who took part in this project have a lifetime of experience in aspects of contemporary culture that open up plurality: multiple platforms, transmedia reworkings, extended opportunities to revisit texts in many formats, support structures such as websites and extra DVD tracks, and so forth. That experience informs their understanding of *what to expect*, an awareness that fuels much of what they then perceive.

Rabinowitz's insights figure in many subsequent chapters, but it is worth noting that they do not address the questions raised in Chapter 5 about how we step 'into' the story, how we engage with the subjunctive. His rules of reading deal more with the rational than with the imaginative elements of interpretation, more with design and shape than with the intangibility of creating and accepting forms of mental life from words activated in the mind.

Envisionments

Rabinowitz's rules have a prescriptive, almost puzzle-solving edge to them. Judith Langer, discussing much the same conceptual territory, takes a more descriptive stance, and makes more room for the mysteries of make-believe. She highlights the temporal nature of the reading experience, pointing to

> the complexity of the text-worlds in people's minds when they engage in the literary experience. How do these text-worlds develop? In the most direct explanation, they grow from people's active quest for sense as they read.
>
> (1995, p. 9)

Such a quest is driven by 'the passion for meaning' (1995, p. 9). Langer uses the term 'envisionment' to describe a condition of great tentativeness and provisionality, and

> to refer to the world of understanding a person has at any point in time. Envisionments are text-worlds in the mind, and they differ from individual to individual. They are a function of one's personal and cultural experiences, one's relationship to the current experience, what one knows, how one feels, and what one is after. Envisionments are dynamic sets of related ideas, images, questions, disagreements, anticipations, arguments, and hunches that fill the mind during every reading, writing, speaking, or other experience when one gains, expresses, and shares thoughts and understandings. Each envisionment includes what the individual does and does not understand, as well as any momentary suppositions about how the whole will unfold, and any reactions to it.
>
> (1995, p. 9)

Importantly, Langer points out that an envisionment 'is always either in a state of change or available for and open to change' (1995, p. 9).

Concentrating on the fact that reading occurs over time, Langer describes four shifting stances:

Stance 1: Being Out and Stepping into an Envisionment
Stance 2: Being In and Moving Through an Envisionment
Stance 3: Stepping Out and Rethinking What One Knows
Stance 4: Stepping Out and Objectifying the Experience

(1995, pp. 16–18)

In this project I will apply the concept of these four stances to all three media – book, film, and game – developing Langer's categories in the context of the interpretive stages of the story. But, of course, the idea of 'envisioning' alters when images are supplied by the text, as in movies and games. What is not seen in the film, what viewers must supply in their expanded 'envisionment' of the story, is the internal awareness of the characters, which must be inferred from their actions, words, and expressions. Gamers also are not supplied with any extensive sense of characters' internal lives, and are often not motivated to supply much depth in that regard since the game story often does not entail much psychological subtlety. Instead, their first priority in terms of envisionment may be to activate a sense of the mind or minds that set the terms within which they play. The logic of the environment (which may or may not be affected by the actions of other players but inevitably at a minimum reflects the intentions of the designer) must be inferred in a vital, 'alive' way if the game is to proceed.

In all cases, the 'envisionment' serves to bring the story under consideration to some kind of more vivid life. The energy of the reader, the viewer, the player, is *invested* into the world of the story in a personal way that begins with the stepping in, *animates* the awareness of story events, and *mutates* again with the stepping out (though animated consideration of the story may linger in the mind, and the stepping out may be very partial indeed in psychological terms). It is an extended form of attention and awareness that yields understanding that is, for the most part, provisional and partial – and kept alive in the mind of the interpreter by means of its very limitations and the questions thus raised. This intriguing process occurs across many stages, and takes place in encounters with all three media forms.

In short, there are many common components to the ways in which books, games, and films invite the investment of interpretive energies. Books and films operate on the basis of a spectator role for the interpreter, while games involve interactivity and a different kind of participation. D. W. Harding reminds us, however, that the spectator role in the interpretation of fiction is more complex than simple onlooking:

> The imaginary spectatorship of fantasy and make-believe play has the special feature of allowing us to look on at ourselves, ourselves as participants in the imagined events ... In spite, however, of seeing himself as a participant in the story, the daydreamer or the child engaged in make-believe remains an onlooker, too; in all his waking fantasy he normally fills the dual role of participant and spectator, and as spectator he can when need be turn away from the fantasy events and attend again to the demands of real life.
>
> (1962, pp. 136–7)

With book and film, the mental involvement can be very intense; we do not lightly use the phrase 'lost in a book' and it is easy to consider an absorbing movie in the same immersive terms. Nevertheless, the book and film have been created and closed before we, as interpreters, come along to spectate. With the game, however, our role is more 'hands-on', more interactive.

The game question

Novels and films do not have to assert their story-bearing capacities, perhaps because the place for the spectator has been so well established. The issue of computer games as narratives is not as clearly settled. For example, Mark Reid, outlining the general overview of contemporary literacies we saw in Chapter 1, is not completely convinced about where games belong. In a footnote, he is fairly dismissive about including computer games under his general umbrella. 'I'm not certain how useful it is to call computer games a text, for example: isn't its "game" status the point – you play it, rather than watch or read it' (2009, p. 23). But computer games match his six categories of literate activity very exactly. Like films and books, they are also chosen and accessed, understood and analysed, and used as a basis for creating and expressing oneself, although this final category is still relatively limited (but see McClay et al., 2007, for a study of how swiftly contemporary teenagers learn to create stories with game engines adapted for popular authoring use).

Even if we conceded (which I do not) that playing the game is a separate and different activity, interpreters would need to interpret the mediated information they are given in order to get started on that play.

Shadow of the Colossus, for example, entails understanding all of Reid's language systems:

- speech (Dormin does not speak English but his portentous tone of voice must still be interpreted)
- writing (the subtitles of Dormin's enigmatic cues)
- pictures and moving pictures (the basic unit of information)
- music (absent for the exploring sequences, dramatic and driving in the battle scenes)
- the dramatic modes of performance, gesture and *mise en scène* (these dramatic modes represent the key point of interface with the screen. Interpreting the information contained in the *mise en scène* is crucial to the successful development of the narrative. How the hero performs the approach to the colossus and how he gestures with his weapons [expressed physically as different, smaller gestures through the buttons on the controller] makes the difference between success and failure with each colossus).

The game maps completely onto this list as a story, but its hybrid nature – a game as well as a narrative – manifests itself in the final entry: the elements of performance and gesture are *in part* created by the player; in this particular example, all the other elements are givens of the game story, exactly as they are in the narratives of novel and film. I will return later to some of the ways that performance and gesture are shared between creator and player at the moment of interpretation, distinguishing between activity and agency as a route to assessing the balance of responsibility for creation between game designer and player.

There are other complexities about the issue of whether games qualify as narrative fictions. A dispute between narratologists (games tell stories) and ludologists (games are for playing) (see Aarseth, 1997; Frasca, 1999, 2003; Juul, 2001 for more details) has more or less abated and the possibility of compromise or hybrid options has gained respectability. Greg Costikyan offers a version of the new compromise:

To get a good story out of a game, you have to constrain gameplay in a way that ensures that a story is told through play. There are direct conflicts between the demands of story and the demands of gameplay, because constraints that benefit the story aspect of the game may sometimes make the game aspect less interesting; yet any game *is* a system of constraints. Players have free action only within those

constraints; there are always limitations on behavior, and indeed, gameplay often emerges *precisely* because of those limitations. ...
In other words, since a game is a system of constraints, and since if we want a story to emerge from a game we must constrain it in such a way that it does, it is not a priori impossible to imagine constructing a set of constraints that both produces a story and also fosters interesting gameplay. Solving the problem is not easy, but it is conceptually possible.

(2007, pp. 6–7, emphasis in original)

Andrew Burn, who has long explored the overlaps and discontinuities between interpretive strategies for books, films and games, investigates how games exist between the constraints of the story and the constraints of the gameplay.

The game system means the rule-based system of the game, which in computer games is produced by the procedural work of the game engine, while the representational system refers to how the game represents the world, and includes the visible and audible game world, the narrative and the characters overlaid on the system ... [T]he avatar-protagonist operates in both systems and understanding the avatar enables us to see how the two systems work together to produce the player's experience of the game.

(2006, pp. 73–4)

Moving within the game system allows the player, operating as a character but also as a manipulator of the game engine, to share control of the dramatic modes of performance and gesture with the game's authors. In a game more open than *Shadow of the Colossus*, it might well be that player-characters could share in speech and/or writing as well.

It remains to be seen whether novels and films may eventually make the equivalent of the game engine more open to interpreters. It is arguable that the fictions created in the interactive verbal worlds of MUDs and MOOs resemble a kind of novel told by means of a shared 'engine'. The Penguin Wiki novel may represent another experiment with the story's 'engine', and it would not be surprising to see further tests and trials of story-making engines in the coming years.

In a game, the character is brought to life by the player in ways that are more active and tangible than the animating imagination of the reader processing words or the viewer absorbing images. In the game, nevertheless, activity is not enough; the imagination must be engaged as well as the hands on the controller. At the level of 'representation', in Burn's terms, the mind is as active as in reading or viewing, and in many of the same ways.

The role of the player is described as interactive, but Janet Murray points out that it is useful to distinguish between degrees of control in the interactive environment. She contrasts agency and action.

> But activity alone is not agency. For instance, in a tabletop game of chance, players may be kept very busy spinning dials, moving game pieces, and exchanging money but they may not have any true agency. The players' actions have effect, but the actions are not chosen and the effects are not related to the players' intentions. ...
> Agency, then, goes beyond both participation and activity.
>
> (1997, p. 128)

In the closed environment of *Shadow of the Colossus*, players have a finite amount of agency. They may certainly travel where they please, they may make a large range of decisions about how to battle the colossi, but, ultimately, the game play must meet certain criteria for the end of the story to be accomplished. Each colossus must be stabbed in the various weak points outlined by the glowing sigils for the game to move onwards to the next stage; there is no flexibility in this part of the story.

If we invoke Ryan's rubric of narrativity (2006, p. 8), *Shadow of the Colossus* has clearly met the challenge of creating a story in game terms. Italics indicate Ryan's requirements for narrative, which include:

1. *a world populated by individuated existents* (the hero, Dormin, the dead girl, and 16 individualized colossi)
2. *a world situated in time and undergoing transformations* (the colossi die and the temple permanently alters to correspond as the statues collapse)
3. *transformations caused by nonhabitual physical events* (definitely! – the battles are all distinctive)
4. *some intelligent agents with mental life and emotional reactions* (this role is shared between the hero and the game's players, as the conversations documented in this book make very clear; players also, from time to time, impute motivations and emotions to the colossi)
5. *events as purposeful actions by these agents, motivated by identifiable goals and plans* (the slaughter of the colossi fits well here)

6. *a sequence of events forming a unified causal chain and leading to closure* (the deaths of the 16 colossi lead to irrevocable changes in the temple and in the hero)
7. *the occurrence of at least some events asserted as fact for the story world* (the story begins *in medias res* in a firmly established world)
8. *the communication of something meaningful to recipients* (the motif of slaughterer's remorse recurred in every iteration of this game)

The goodness of fit between these requirements and the narrative of the game is very striking.

Bringing the story to life: The eye and the hand

Torben Grodal, in a very interesting chapter about the embodied experience of computer games, points out the significance of being able to move within and in response to the given images and sounds. He describes video games as

> the medium that is closest to the basic embodied story experience ... In earlier media, story progression is controlled by the author/director. To follow protagonists through space only demands rather vague mental models (for instance, to imagine that a character somehow gets from his apartment in Berkeley to Golden Gate Bridge), not detailed cognitive maps and hand-eye coordination. Watching John Wayne shooting an opponent only demands crude models for actions, not precise motor programs for grasping the gun and aiming precisely. But in video games such activities often demand rather detailed cognitive maps and motor skills, and playing therefore often requires extensive training of necessary skills.
>
> (2003, p. 139)

Players need to take actions that are specific and detailed in order to make progress through the story.

> The perceptions have to be fast and precise, the motor control coordinated with the perceptions, and thus the computer story demands the acquisition of a series of procedural schemas. From another point of view, therefore, video games are not imploded stories, but on the contrary the full basic story that the retelling has to omit, including its perceptual and muscular realization.
>
> (2003, p. 147)

This muscular performance relies on information from both hands and eyes. Barry Atkins makes a distinction between the game gaze and the gaze of the film. The game, he suggests, relies on future thinking, although the screen shows the past of what has been accomplished to this point.

> The screen does not represent the present, let alone the future, on which the player is focused. Rather, the screen represents the past of play. It presents us with a report that conveys information about the game state that is essential to successful play, but the player's gaze actually lingers elsewhere ... To the outsider the screen may appear more or less visually interesting, more or less aesthetically pleasing. To the player, it is full of rich possibilities of future action, pointing always off to the moment at which it will be replaced by another image and then another. Its purpose, if it fulfills its function, is to insist on its own erasure, as it prompts the player to move on and look elsewhere.
>
> (Atkins, 2006, p. 135)

Atkins describes the gaze at the game screen as one of calculation:

> The focus, always, is not on what is before us or the 'what happens next' of traditionally unfolding narrative but on the 'what happens next *if I*' that places the player at the center of experience as its principle [*sic*] creator, necessarily engaged in an imaginative act, and always oriented towards the future. In effect, the game gaze might appear to rest on the image on the screen, but the player sees through and beyond the screen and into the future.
>
> (Atkins, 2006, p. 137, emphasis added)

The issue of whether the 'helpers' who do not hold the controller also apply a game gaze to the screen is an interesting one, and I am indebted to my students in the multimedia literacies class at the University of Alberta for assisting me to think it through. Helpers have a more vested interest in the future than a mere spectator, but they do not have the immediate ability to test future-oriented hypotheses via physical movement. In Atkins' terms, they are not quite at the centre of the experience but neither are they on the outside simply looking on.

Atkins refers only to the eyes and the mind in this account of gaming, but the hands are part of the equation too, and may contribute very substantially to the ability of the player to think in terms of 'what happens next *if I – ?'* Richard Sennett, in a very absorbing book about the achievements of the craftsman, discusses *prehension*, the common yet startling ability of the hand to anticipate the size and shape of what it is about to grasp:

> In the familiar physical gesture of grasping a glass, the hand will assume a rounded shape, suitable for cupping the glass, before it actually touches the surface. The body is ready to hold before it knows whether what it will hold is freezing cold or boiling hot. The technical name for movements in which the body anticipates and acts in advance of sense data is *prehension*.
>
> (2008, pp. 153–4, emphasis in original)

This familiar capacity of the hand involves a future orientation that maps well onto Atkins' future-directed gaze, as Sennett makes clear:

> Prehension gives a particular cast to mental understanding as well as physical action: you don't wait to think until all information is in hand, you anticipate the meaning. Prehension signals *alertness*, *engagement*, and *risk-taking* all in the act of looking ahead.
>
> (2008, p. 154, emphasis added)

That sense of directing the body, even in advance of complete information, may make a strong contribution to the player's sense of agency in the game, even when what is achieved is mere activity rather than agency. Yet the manual engagement *per se* is not what makes games distinctive as forms of narrative. Hands are also meaningfully involved in the act of reading, as Elaine Scarry elaborates:

> The imaginer, although almost wholly immobilized in the process of reading, is still performing sustained actions with her eyes (moving across all the words) and hands (turning the pages) ... first, the fingers must discriminate the delicate edge of the page from the full array stacked in the book, and then they must lift or flip it away from the others. Often the fingers are engaged in this act during the whole time that the left and right pages are being read: while the left-hand page is read, the right-hand fingers find the upper right-hand edge of the page that must eventually turn; then, as the right-hand page is read, the fingers move down along the page edge to the bottom corner, where, once the reading of the two pages is complete, the turning motion will be carried out; the right-hand page will be folded over

and smoothed into place where it now becomes a left-hand page, and the hand moves back across the two-page surface and up to the upper right-hand edge to prepare for the next turn. Meanwhile, new worlds keep swimming into view.

Reaching, stretching, and folding are the actual motions the hand carries out – like a spell of hand motions performed over the book – as one reads.

(1999, p. 147)

Such activity – the small, repetitive, profoundly automatized movements – involves a modest form of anticipation as the fingers prepare the page turn, but, while alertness and engagement are entailed, there is no component of risk. The role of the hands in reading is almost invisible. In gaming, however, even in its most predictable and reiterative forms, the hands are on display as obviously important participants in the process.

A large amount of the muscular realization of the game occurs in the actions of the hands, yet the hand's motions are as abstract as any letter of the alphabet. Holding R1 as you press the square is not an intuitive activity and definitely resembles 'a spell of hand motions'. If it allows you to stab the colossus' weak point, it is an abstract manual action that becomes imbued with significant specific meaning.

The muscular contribution to the perceptual realization occurs explicitly with the motions of the hands that create what the eyes then see, via the game engine. It is with the hands on the controls that players share the creation of performance and gesture with the game's creators; it is with the hands that players move from engine level to representation level. The abstract movements of the hands dancing over the buttons convert into a participatory element in the story, and create an interface between player and game that appears on the screen and can be observed from the outside. In many ways, this visibly realized interface behaves in the same way as the less tangible conversion of the black marks of print into mental imagery. Reader must cooperate with writer just as player must cooperate with game designer. The movement from tool to representation takes place meaningfully inside the mind of player and reader alike.

(The Wii, of course, alters the relationship between abstract controller and specific movement on the screen – an example of the 2-D world bursting at its edges. Here I will do no more than acknowledge its stylized verisimilitude of action as a feature of game narrative worth watching.)

We know too little about whether or how we may watch a film differently with our hands on the remote control. In this particular study, I controlled the remote and decided when to stop for conversation, both for administrative convenience in the moment and also to keep the study within manageable limits. So no reflection on the introduction of a manual relationship with the images on the screen can be deduced from this project, but I do think the question is a significant one.

The 'full basic story' of the game, worked out in all its 'perceptual and muscular realization', offers an unanticipated research bonus. Writers and film-makers can 'cut' to the chase and short-circuit the time it takes to move the plot forward; in the game world where players must make the action happen in muscular detail, they have plenty of leisure to discuss their sense of the story's development. With a shared controller, they are motivated to make their hypotheses explicit, in order to advise the one actually playing about the details of what his muscles should be accomplishing. There is no need to stop the story processing in order to talk about it (as is the case with novel and film). The complex process of realizing 'full basic story' is explicated in full basic conversation about some of the essential tools of sense-making – tools that are muscular but also cognitive. There is potential, therefore, for the more detailed and expansive game-playing conversations to shed light on more generic questions of understanding a story, that may help us also understand what happens in the more opaque world of reading a book or watching a movie.

The theoretical elements of text processing are complex and absorbing and could fill a book of their own. It is time, however, to turn to the actual behaviours of the interpreters as they moved into a relationship with *Run Lola Run, Monster,* and *Shadow of the Colossus.*

4
Paying Attention: Provisional Observations and Inferences

When the participants sat down in the meeting room, they had no idea what kinds of text they were going to encounter. It is an axiom of interpretation that nobody can pay heed to everything all the time and they had to decide swiftly how to allocate their attention. In Judith Langer's term, they had to establish 'orientations *toward* meaning' (1995, p. 24, emphasis added). Wolfgang Iser talks about meaning as 'something that happens' (1978, p. 22). The text on offer (*Run Lola Run* on the first day) would supply some of the energy that would make it happen, but some of the constructive effort also had to come from the viewers. They had to prepare to create a fiction out of both what was present and what was absent on the screen in front of them, as Iser describes: 'Communication in literature, then, is a process set in motion and regulated not by a given code but by a mutually restrictive and magnifying interaction between the explicit and the implicit, between revelation and conceal-ment' (1978, pp. 168–9).

Interpreters of a fictional text participate in a two-way relationship in which one side is relatively static (fixed in advance by author, by film director, and even, to a considerable extent, by game designer), and in which there is no external world of reference points. Iser makes the distinction between interacting with a text (even a relatively 'interactive' game would fit into this category), and interacting with another person.

An obvious and major difference between reading and all forms of social interaction is the fact that with reading there is no *face-to-face situation*. A text cannot adapt itself to each reader with whom it comes in contact [even a game is not infinitely adaptable]. The partners in dyadic interaction can ask each other questions in order to ascertain how far their views have controlled contingency, or their images have bridged the gap of inexperienceability of one another's experiences. The reader, however, can never learn from the text how accurate or inaccurate are his views of it. Furthermore, dyadic interaction serves specific purposes, so that the interaction always has a regulative context, which often serves as a *tertium comparationis*. There is no such frame of reference governing the text-reader relationship; on the contrary, the codes which might regulate this interaction are fragmented in the text and must first be reassembled or, in most cases, restructured before any frame of reference *can* be established.

(1978, p. 166)

Online role-playing games do combine some of the qualities of text-reader relationship with some of the qualities of personal exchange as interpreters do share more of a real-time frame of reference. This quality, however, simply highlights how *Shadow of the Colossus*, by contrast, shares many of its fixed qualities with the other two texts in this study.

How do interpreters begin to notice what is present and to judge the significance of what is not present in a textual construct that they are approaching for the first time? Judith Langer says the initial task is to establish what we hope to gain from the experience. Are we looking for information or for experience?

[P]eople approach meaning in essentially different ways when their reasons for reading, writing, or discussing are primarily to experience (to live through the situation in a subjective manner) as opposed to when their primary goal is discursive (to gain or share ideas or information).

(1995, p. 25)

Louise Rosenblatt famously makes a similar distinction in terms of the aesthetic stance and the efferent stance. Here is how she explains each approach:

The reader may be seeking information, as in a textbook; he may want directions for action, as in a driver's manual; he may be seeking some logical conclusions, as in a political article. In all such reading he will narrow his attention to building up the meanings, the ideas, the directions to be retained; attention focuses on accumulating what is to be carried away at the end of the reading. Hence I term this stance *efferent*, from the Latin word meaning 'to carry away.'

If, on the other hand, the reader seeks a story, a poem, a play, his attention will shift inward, will center on what is being created *during* the actual reading. A much broader range of elements will be allowed to rise into consciousness, not simply the abstract concepts that the words point to, but also what those objects or referents stir up of personal feelings, ideas, and attitudes. The very sound and rhythm of the words will be attended to. Out of these ideas and feelings, a new experience, the story or poem, is shaped and lived through. I call this kind of reading *aesthetic*, from the Greek word meaning 'to sense' or 'to perceive'.

(2005, p. 73)

The participants initially were not even sure which of these stances was being asked of them, and, in actuality, they were probably most conscious of a third stance, that of being a research participant, invited to simulate normal interpretive behaviours. Importantly, they also lacked any questions of their own that had led them to this choice of text. As they began to look at each offered text, they had to establish even the basic category of whether they were being asked to deal with fiction or non-fiction, and to make a decision at some level about how personal and invested an aesthetic response they were prepared to make in this circumstance of simulation.

In the first meeting they all looked at *Run Lola Run*. None of them had seen it before and most of them had never heard of it. The title and the image of a girl running on the cover of the DVD hint that this film is a narrative, but it could possibly be a documentary rather than a fiction. Only the title serves to delimit the movie in any way; apart from the kinds of constraints that such a title might inscribe on a movie, the film could have been about anything in the world. They watched it from a starting point that was very close indeed to completely blank.

But not for long. Even a glimpse of the image on the jewel box would irresistibly fire up schemas about the woman's artificially red hair and athletic appearance. As Barratt points out, '[O]ur first impression of a person or situation "primes" us to label that person or situation using a certain type of schema which biases the way in which we interpret, and attend to, subsequent information' (2009, p. 67). Even before the first frame of the movie rolls, therefore, the interpreters are already developing fleeting hypotheses, activating possible schemas, predisposing their attention to focus in some ways and not others.

When they picked up the novel *Monster* they acquired a little bit more preliminary information from the paratext: the title (again), the cover image, the three medallions on the cover indicating a range of prizes, and, in the case of those who turned over to the back, a little bit of blurb. Again, it was barely possible that the book might be non-fiction. Nobody was familiar with it, and they knew of it only that I was asking them to read it. Yet again, their preliminary response would be swift (too swift to be captured by my recording methods) but directional. The face of a black boy, possibly a mug shot, raises certain ideas that are perhaps never entirely erased – certainly not in the reading of *Monster* where many of these initial implications are proved to be reliably predictive.

Shadow of the Colossus was a similar enigma; it was brand new at the time I introduced it and none of the participants knew much about it. Some participants took a quick look at the little guide to the game contained in the jewel box. The cover image alone (a huge club-bearing colossus) was a strong indicator of fictional content. I made the official game guide available (Off, 2005) and different groups made varied use of this tool, but at the outset their chief source of information about the story lay in the lengthy cut scene that introduces it.

So how do we slant our awareness at the beginning stages of a text? What is it that we are trying to do? Peter Rabinowitz suggests that readers should 'try to duplicate the angle of the author's attention' (1987, p. 51). Louise Rosenblatt describes in some detail the very tentative initial stance towards a story told in words:

> The words in their particular pattern stir up elements of memory, activate areas of consciousness. The reader, bringing past experience of language and of the world to the task, sets up tentative notions of a subject, of some framework into which to fit the ideas as the words unfurl. If the subsequent words do not fit into the framework, it may have to be revised, thus opening up new and further possibilities for the text that follows. This implies a constant series of selections from the multiple possibilities offered by the text and their synthesis into an organized meaning.
>
> (2005, p. 73)

Torben Grodal, writing about film viewing, reminds us that as well as paying attention to the initial fragments of information that we may glean from a new text, we must move into a stance that discerns and provisionally accepts limits on our relationship to the text:

> When we agree to watch visual fiction, we accept a set of rules of experience and establish a viewer-persona, a mental model of the

viewer as spectator of fiction, and this viewer-model, this persona, feels suspense, happiness, fear, and sadness as if witnessing similar phenomena in the non-fictive world. In simple narrative forms, the subject-actant and the viewer-persona are merged, whereas more complicated narrative forms have every possible variety of distance between viewer-persona and actants. All fictional forms of identification and empathy are hypothetical simulations of non-fictional types of experience.

(1999, p. 103)

Early response to a story thus involves the development of a working hypothesis about the spectrum of connection – ranging from complete merging of identities to strong forms of detachment – between the characters of the story and the interpreter of the text. Such hypotheses can be readjusted during the course of the story; participants learned that they could not invest completely in any one version of Lola's effort to rescue Manni, for example, but the need to step back a bit did not become entirely clear until they were a third of the way into the story.

In short, tentativeness, combined with the involuntary initiation of schematic associations, probably did prevail as participants responded to all three texts – and, of course, for *Run Lola Run* and *Shadow of the Colossus*, they reacted to images and sounds as well as words, selecting, assessing and synthesizing a range of semiotic channels.

Langer's label of Being Out and Stepping into an Envisionment applies to this early stage of coming to terms with what a text may be offering. She defines this stage as follows:

> In this stance, readers attempted to make initial contacts with the genre, content, structure, and language of the text by using prior knowledge, experiences, and surface features of the text to identify essential elements in order to begin to construct an envisionment.
>
> (1989, p. 9)

Langer is also very clear about the extreme state of tentativeness with which an interpreter approaches an unfamiliar text:

> When we begin to read, we are out and stepping into an envisionment. We try to gather enough ideas to gain a sense of what the work will be about (as in real life, when we try to pull together as many ideas as possible about a new acquaintance). Although fragile, it is a place to begin a conversation with ourselves – in the real world

or in text-worlds. Because there is little to build on (because we are 'outside' an envisionment), we pick up any little clues that are available and try to make sense of them in terms of the little we already know. We search for as many clues as possible, but the meanings we seek (and derive) are usually superficial; the search is for breadth rather than depth.

(1995, p. 16)

From birth, we are hardwired to pay special attention to people. Martin Meisel, writing about how we read plays, has some interesting observation about this human-centric bias and its implications for our initial attention in a textual fiction. '[T]he main work of creating the world of the play depends almost invariably on the presence of the characters on the scene', he suggests (2007, p. 17), and certainly the arrival of the first characters can rivet attention in any medium. Meisel points out that we attend not only to these humans or human-like beings themselves, but also to the ways in which they are presented to us as characters.

The opening of the play addresses a set of implicit questions and sets the defaults. How do people speak in this world? In measure and rhyme? In ordinary prose? In dialect? To music? Are they allowed to express their deepest thoughts and most powerful feelings in commensurate language? Or is speech channelled into witty 'persiflage', a highly stylized polite exchange; or limited to the banalities and commonplaces of everyday; or to an impoverished monosyllabic street lexicon?

(2007, p. 17)

Meisel is talking about reading a stage play, moving in a paradoxical world that exists on the borders between abstraction and performance. In the performed play, as in the movie and the game, words are voiced; the cadence and sweep of the sentences are ready-provided. In reading, readers must add that voice; I have heard Margaret Meek say that they must 'tune the voices on the page,' a phrase that is both evocative and (as we say) 'telling'.

Rabinowitz supplies a detailed account of how we notice and ascribe importance to one detail over another. He is talking about reading but his approach works well with other media formats as well (see Mackey, 2007). Describing 'rules of notice,' he discusses 'two interrelated aspects of noticeability: concentration and scaffolding' (1987, p. 53). We apply rules of notice to decide where to concentrate our attention, and we use the details thus stressed to enable us to create 'a basic structure on which to build an interpretation' (1987, p. 53).

Here are some of the rules of notice, derived from print examples. Creators can tell us outright that something is important. They can emphasize significance through repetition. Language can be organized to highlight a particular detail semantically. More generally, Rabinowitz outlines three major categories of notice: rules of position, of intratextual disruption, and of extratextual deviation (1987, p. 58).

We tend to privilege particular forms of placement: titles, beginnings and endings, epigraphs, and so forth:

> Placement in such a position does more than ensure that certain details will remain more firmly in our memory. Furthermore, such placement affects both concentration and scaffolding: our attention during an act of reading will, in part, be concentrated on what we have found in these positions, and our sense of the text's meaning will be influenced by our assumption that the author expected us to end up with an interpretation that could account more fully for these details than for details elsewhere.
>
> (1987, p. 59)

Titles are particularly helpful; they 'not only guide our reading processes by telling us where to concentrate; they also provide a core around which to organize an interpretation' (Rabinowitz, 1987, p. 61); a title 'primes and colours expectation' (Meisel, 2007, p. 15).

Openings and closings – of paragraphs, of chapters, of whole books – are imbued with extra significance, according to Rabinowitz. Disruptions in the anticipated order also gain attention. The skimming eye pauses when it hits the unexpected. Deviations from the expected norm – either the norm of other similar stories or the norm of our own experience – provide another way for the creator to slow us down and make us think harder.

In addition to exploring our initial responses to characters and their language, Meisel raises further interpretive questions that need to be answered very early on. These could be described as issues of notice that connect to questions of coherence overall.

> Are gestures large, movements sweeping, and attitudes eloquent, as befits heroic and ideal figures? Or are they constrained and suggestive only, appropriate to cramped lives, cold climates, and domestic interiors? Is this a world keyed to laughter, where the consequences

of misbehaviour are unlikely to be serious? Or to romance? Or to suffering? Is it an observable social world, where the drama lies in complex interaction? Or is it the projection of an inner world of feelings and desires? Or a parabolic world of embodied ideas and arguments? As these questions are answered, they establish the law and logic – perhaps the grammar and syntax would be a better analogy – of the stage world. And as they are answered, they launch whole sets of expectations about what is to come, and about what would be 'in keeping' – a phrase from the practice of painting – and what would not. Some of these expectations are clustered in what are thought of as 'genres', like Comedy, Tragedy, Melodrama. But some are better thought of as belonging to a 'mode' or a 'key'. Expectations, however, are precisely the stuff that the playwright has to work with: promoting them, teasing them, deceiving them. What is called plot is usually a matter of anticipation and deferral, resistance and resolution, within a framework of managed expectations.

(2007, pp. 17–18)

Experienced interpreters are primed for pattern recognition, and part of the 'defaults' they set up in early stages of paying attention involve noting anything that could become part of a pattern later on. Attention and expectation work together; interpreters expect their anticipations to be 'managed' by the producers of the text. When they make inferences about the initial information they glean, they attend to their early glimpses of the story world but also to their understanding of how stories are actually put together.

Inferences, say Kendeou, Bohn-Gettler, White and van den Broek, 'are information generated by the reader to fill in information [*sic*] that is left implicit in the text' (2008, p. 260).

A central component of successful reading comprehension is the identification of meaningful relations between the various parts of the text, and between those parts and the reader's background knowledge. These relations are identified through an inferential process, in which the reader monitors his/her comprehension, allocates attention to past parts of the text and to his/her background knowledge and determines which semantic relations are supported by the text and are important to comprehension. ... If all goes well, the reader arrives at a coherent memory representation for the text in which the text elements are connected in meaningful ways.

(Kendeou, Bohn-Gettler, White and van den Broek, 2008, p. 259)

The capacity to generate inferences, Kendeou and colleagues assert, is separate from the decoding elements of comprehension and is generalized across media forms. We will discuss this idea in more depth in Chapter 6.

As interpreters gear up to move into a narrative, therefore, they establish a provisional stance, they attend to the elements of the story that need to be decoded, they make tentative inferences about the story world and also about the story-telling apparatus – and they begin to generate some potential understanding of what might be going on in the text before their eyes, ears, and fingers.

Starting up

The creators of each story set up the invitation into the fiction in particular ways that drastically affect response so, before I describe the ways in which participants explore and start to answer these invitations, I will begin each section with a description of the text's opening scenes. All three of the texts used in this study open in highly stylized ways. Interestingly, each of them could be said to have more than one beginning. And, interestingly, these complex openings seemed to be taken for granted by the participants in this project.

The Initial Scenes: *Run Lola Run*

The first screen of *Run Lola Run* contains two quotations about time. One quote is from T. S. Eliot's *Little Gidding*:

> We shall not cease from exploration
> And the end of all our exploring
> Will be to arrive where we started
> And know the place for the first time

> (1942)

The second is from S. Herberger, footballer: 'After the game is before the game.'

A giant gold pendulum swings across the screen and wipes out the quotes, to the accompaniment of a rapid ticking sound. The camera zooms up the shaft of the pendulum to a clock face with its hands spinning around. A gargoyle on top of the clock opens its mouth and the camera zooms through into blackness, as fast music begins. We see a number of blurry people moving inconsequentially past each other in quick-time; occasionally the speed of the film retards into slow motion and a single person is highlighted briefly: a woman in a dress, a man in a red shirt, a man in a suit, a woman with a child, a man in uniform. A male voice-over, speaking in German, asks a number of existential questions translated in subtitles as in the following sample:

Man – probably the most mysterious species on our planet
A mystery of unanswered questions
Who are we?
Where do we come from?
Where are we going? ...
But, in the end, isn't it always the same question?
And always the same answer?

(Run Lola Run, 1998)

By this stage in the commentary, the camera has focused on the man in uniform, and he is the first character to speak. Looking directly at the camera, he holds up a soccer ball and says (according to the subtitles), 'The ball is round. The game lasts 90 minutes. That's a fact. Everything else is pure theory. Here we go.' He drop-kicks the football into the air and the camera follows its upward motion. Below, the walking crowd turns itself into two words: 'Lola Rennt' (the German title of the movie).

At this point, the music revs up in intensity and we shift to a cartoon of a red-headed girl running through a sequence of abstract shapes that mutate and break. The credits begin to appear. The third change involves the display of a set of mug shots of different faces, accompanied by yet more forceful music. Two names (in two different fonts) appear with each photo: a character name and an actor name. This information supplies the first potential marker of the film as fiction; it is more likely that these actors are portraying fictional characters than any other explanation.

Finally we see an overhead photo of a city landscape. This time the camera zooms down and in on an apartment where a phone is ringing and the action of the story is finally set in motion. Manni is calling Lola, desperate for her to bring him some money. Lola starts to run – first in cinematic, then in animated, then in cinematic form again – and begins her encounters with a variety of obstacles.

There is certainly no shortage of disruption and deviation in this introductory sequence, and we have seen Lola in mug-shot and animated forms before the initial moving image of the human, acted Lola. There are many pointers to help us pay special attention to this moment when

Lola finally takes over the screen. Actress Franka Potente is first among the credits and we are able to recognize her as related to the animated runner because of the shock of bright red hair and because of the cue provided by Lola's name in the title. The zoom in from the aerial shot to the portent of the ringing telephone suggests that the show is about to begin at last, and when Lola picks up the phone we finally have a real character on 'stage'. Prior to this moment, as we waited for the story to begin, we have been treated to a range of philosophical language, supported by images of vague and blurry crowds with an individual singled out from time to time – a filmic discourse that matches the profound queries of the text concerning man and his place in the universe, and the significance of time.

Starting *Run Lola Run*

At last, after many explications of the framing project and its theoretical underpinnings, we hear the first voices of the interpreters. They do not use the vocabulary of this introduction but their specific comments illuminate these abstract formulations in interesting ways.

Run Lola Run opens with a flurry of different formats, and participants drew on their film repertoires to connect with the fast-moving set-up. Martin is quick to explore his assessment of the producers' intentions:

> The credits were interesting. It seemed like they were supposed to be disorienting – or, I'm not sure if it was supposed to be disengaging or engaging. It seems like the characters are set up sort of on the fringe of society, like they're operating outside of it, and so *that* makes the story exceptional.

Sumana also responds to the credits and the very first scenes of the story, but finds them immersive more than disorienting:

> So many changes and the medium ... They go from the love line with Manni to black and white flashbacks, and they've got the cartoons, and she's running really fast, and a lot of cutting back and forth. So you really get excited about what's going to happen next. It gets you right into the movie I find.

Dan is also positive:

> The beginning seems a little cartoon movie and I think they're kind of giving the impression of time moving by faster to add to the

suspense of the movie. The story's pretty [*inaudible*] messed up or whatever, he lost his money, they're just trying to convey a real sense of emergency behind the story line. It's interesting.

Tess is intrigued but puzzled by some components:

It's neat that we're seeing the clock again from the first credits. I'm pretty sure that's the clock anyway, it doesn't look quite the same. I have to say the soccer game threw me for a loop. What in heaven's name, where was that coming from? It reminded me a bit of *The Matrix*, the way the crowds were sort of not really corporeal at all, but then it focused on a couple of people. So far, so good – I like the music, really fast paced and again it keeps you really watching the film. I don't think it's giving away too many answers. I'm pretty sure he's not going to stay in that phone booth for too long.

Sebastian also wonders about the soccer game image: 'I'm curious what soccer has to do with it – maybe it will be a bet.' Given the random, aleatory nature of the introduction, this prediction makes thematic sense.

The highly crafted introduction draws references to the creators at this early stage of the film. Neil says, 'I think they are trying to hypnotize us', and, a few minutes later, 'It's definitely an interesting style, kind of a schizophrenic style.'

Sandra and Adam are not so sure about the stylized introduction, and their comments also make explicit reference to the creators:

Sandra: I think it's kind of over dramatic. The script's okay, there's nothing wrong with it. They're trying to jack it up more by all the filming techniques and everything.

Adam: Yeah, you can totally see where the director is using little things to try and catch your eye. He's definitely going for the 'art'.

These participants are largely discussing the surface of the film, though several of them mention pacing as raising anticipation about the movie's content. Their sense of a connection between the story's creators and the audience is perhaps enhanced by the artificiality of the early images. Perhaps the early absence of a focal character increases their inclination to make a connection with the 'they' or the 'he' behind the story. It is also interesting to note Tess's early reference to *The Matrix*; if, in Iser's terms, 'our selections tend first to be guided by those parts of the experience that still seem to be familiar. These will influence the gestalt we form' (1978, p. 126), Tess provides a useful reminder that the familiar may be intertextual rather than based on life experience. Iser suggests that a 'shadow' of *The Matrix* may linger to inform Tess's later interpretations. The half-life of early impressions is very difficult to disentangle from other, more specifically based forms of interpretation in a temporal process.

The initial scenes: *Monster*

The first page of *Monster* is printed in a font that varies in size and rather resembles hand printing. The opening sentence says, 'The best time to cry is at night, when the lights are out and someone is being beaten up and screaming for help' (Myers, 1999, p. 1). In terms of physical size, the word 'screaming' is the largest in the sentence. This personal writing continues for five pages, introducing a speaker with the very first words; because of the large font, it is very quick to read. On the third page, the narrative voice says, 'Sometimes I feel like I have walked into the middle of a movie. It is a strange movie with no plot and no beginning. The movie is in black and white and grainy' (p. 3). The cues to a dark story are in place from the beginning. The language describes suffering but is not really 'commensurate' in terms of eloquence.

By the next page the narrator is creating possibilities for himself: 'I think to get used to this I will have to give up what I think is real and take up something else. I wish I could make sense of it. Maybe I could make my own movie. I could write it out and play it in my head. I could block out the scenes like we did in school. The film will be the story of my life. No, not my life, but of this experience' (p. 4). On the next page, this voice says, 'I'll call it what the lady who is the prosecutor called me. MONSTER' (p. 5). The final word is printed in very large letters followed by a half page of white space.

Page 6 is blank, and page 7 establishes a completely different register, both a disruption and a deviation from the expected – and a new opening. With one exception (the date at the top right-hand corner – 'Monday July 6th' – written in the same script as the 'notebook' entries on the previous pages), it is typeset in a Courier-style font (with some family resemblance to a typewritten manuscript) and laid out on the page in the form of a screenplay. The title 'Monster!' is followed by these instructions:

FADE IN: INTERIOR: Early morning in CELL BLOCK D, MANHATTAN DETENTION CENTER. Camera goes slowly down grim, gray corridor.

There are sounds of inmates yelling from cell to cell; much of it is obscene. Most of the voices are clearly Black or Hispanic. Camera stops and slowly turns toward a cell.
INTERIOR: CELL. Sixteen-year-old STEVE HARMON is sitting on the edge of a metal cot, head in hands. He is thin, brown skinned. On the cot next to him are the suit and tie he is to wear to court for the start of his trial.

(Myers, 1999, p. 7)

The credits then appear over the page, in the *Star Wars* format of retreating words. Here we see the printed page being used to imitate the movement of floating credits on the screen; readers' knowledge of the famous introduction to *Star Wars* is invoked to help them mentally animate the fixed print and to set a movie frame of reference. Steve Harmon appears in these credits as author, actor, producer and so forth; reading the credits as we know how to do from the cinema, we learn that this movie is entirely a figment of his imagination.

On page 11 the story begins to move forward, still in screenplay form. For the rest of the book, it alternates between Steve's introspective reflections in free font, and the screenplay laid out according to the strict conventions of the genre. Occasionally an image is added to the page.

Starting *Monster*

The opening pages of *Monster* contain many surface features to catch the eye, and readers appeared to enjoy sorting through the implications of these design features. Here, for example, is Tess reflecting on the opening pages:

Even the first page of the novel, where the very first thing you see is *Monday July 6th* so that makes it look like a diary, sort of a confessional and then all of a sudden there's *Monster*. Big font, center of the page, and then you're sort of into the screenplay form. So it's a novel within a novel, because then you have the narrative at the very beginning so then you wonder how many layers, how deep this is going to go. Like one of those Russian dolls where you have them all stacked inside each other.

It is worth noticing here how Tess initially dismisses the first few pages of the journal entry in its script font (even though I watched her read them!) and refers to the first page of typeface (page 7, where the date appears) as the first page of the novel. Only after she establishes this point as the start of the novel does she refer back to 'the narrative at the very beginning' – the journal. At this point, she does not know that the journal entries will recur through the book (a pattern that becomes observable only later), so it is relatively easy for her to dismiss this section as some kind of lesser-status preamble. Nevertheless, we see her respond to the disruption and the deviation represented by the shift to the screenplay format. Her acknowledgement of the date helps her to place this narrative in a specific world, a potential, though far from definitive, marker of a fiction.

Lewis is explicit about his pleasure, right from his assessment of these opening few pages:

> I like the setup of how it is a movie. It's different. I've never seen a book like, done like that before, so at first I want to see what's going on with this trial, and how he's done this as a movie. And how that's going to affect how the book works, I guess, is my first thought.

Sebastian also enjoys the surface features, this time of the diary section:

> I like the first bit. It's kind of written by hand, how some things are bigger and some are smaller, and I like the directions.

Keith, on the other hand, is put off by the surface:

> Keith: It's a little gimmicky.
> Margaret: Uh-huh. In what way?
> Keith :   Well the strange fonts and the fact that he used to be [*inaudible*] sort of a screenplay type thing. All the weird thoughts is kind of distracting a little bit.

In this conversation with Tess, Sumana takes note of the introductory features as part of an assessment of genre potential, and also as part of establishing an emotional connection with the story:

> Sumana: Personally I found it was interesting that he decides to write a screenplay in the first place, because normally when you read – I don't know, just the fact that he's referring to *Star Wars* just makes him such a contemporary character who seems so real and so current.

Tess: Yeah

Sumana: Normally when you're reading a novel they don't usually refer to –

Tess: Pop culture or – ?

Sumana: Exactly, yeah. So in that way, I think that's something that's more common in books for young people and that's an interesting thing I thought.

There is plenty of surface information for the readers to assess, and they are variably intrigued or repelled by it. They also draw on their experiences of other texts to help them frame their initial impressions. Jarret discerns a 'Tennessee Williams-like feel' to the starting pages. Tess comments on its similarity to *Ulysses* (which she has just been reading in extract form in one of her classes) – an unlikely comparison on the face of it, but she explains the connection clearly and uses it to assess the main character: '[It's] just how the different methods of writing were all mixed together to make a somewhat coherent whole.'

Meisel's assessment that the play (or any other text) really begins when the character appears on the stage is borne out by the immediate focus of many of these readers on the character of Steve, even as they take note of the different ways in which the story is told. Nobody says explicitly, 'Here is a fictional character so this must be a fiction', but such an assessment is implicit in much of their analysis of Steve, right from their very early encounter with him.

The initial scenes: *Shadow of the Colossus*

The game opens with an elaborate and lengthy cut scene. An androgynous figure on a horse crosses an empty landscape and then a huge bridge to carry a body to an altar in a deserted temple and to ask for the return of life. He is told by a voice from above that the only way to achieve this end is to destroy the 16 idols whose statues adorn the temple walls. 'Hold your sword to the light and follow the path where the beams focus to find and kill the 16 colossi who represent these idols,' says the voice (according to the subtitles). The colossi are dormant in the landscape and the hero must locate, summon, and slaughter them all.

At this point, the story shifts out of the cut scene and the player must take charge of the action. Calling and mounting the horse, finding a sunny spot to raise the sword for direction, and riding down the stone steps into the barren landscape are all actions governed by the player, and they mark the beginning of the active game component of the story. Quickly the hero, led by the lightbeams, finds a cliff and learns how to shimmy up and around its grassy crags, and how to lean backwards and leap across a small chasm. Skill development becomes part of the texture of the story.

Starting *Shadow of the Colossus*

In the quotes about the film and the book above, we can see the participants gathering surface clues and beginning the most preliminary attempt to assemble these hints into the set-up of a story. The responses to the opening cut scenes of *Shadow of the Colossus* are similar. For example, here are sample comments from Tess, Sumana and Martin as they watch the opening scenes; it is easy to see them applying more than one schema to the interpretation of the material presented to them. Their remarks begin at the start of the cut scene. Martin is holding the controls, but at this stage of the game he is not using them The three have had a quick look at the instructions that come inserted in the jewel box, but otherwise know almost nothing about the story.

One immediate difference between this conversation and all preceding examples is that the participants are able to speak as they watch the scene. With the book and the movie, they have to stop attending to the story in order to speak about it, and their discussions have a summative quality. Here their observations are more formative as they converse while watching and playing; the passage below conveys their initial reactions as the hero crosses the deserted countryside:

Martin: Holiness.
Sumana: It's a beautiful game.
Martin: Purity.
Tess: There's our hero.
Martin: The first person that we see.
Tess: Mm hmm. The music reminds me of *Zelda* games actually. At the temples. I grew up playing those.
Martin: It reminds me of *Indiana Jones*.
Tess: Oh, maybe a little. Where is he?
Sumana: A generic forest.
Tess: (Chuckles) fair enough. It's a very dead forest, there's nothing else in it. No sounds … no birds, no squirrels –

The three players comment immediately on the atmosphere, and draw on their awareness of other games to help them decide what is salient. Is the forest simply generic, something that appears in numerous other games? Or is it a *dead* forest with quite different connotations?

Martin replies to Tess's observation with a technical comment: 'It's just a visual of him right now, though; none of the sounds from his tracks are being played.'

Commenting on the beautiful temple leads the trio back to more technical comments, which in turn give way to generic parsing of the introductory emptiness:

Martin: The graphics are really good for a video. Not great for a computer, but –

Tess: They're pretty amazing for a video game.

Martin: And nothing is happening. Usually in the intro there will be some sort of –

Tess: A fight sequence –

Sumana: Like action.

Martin: There'll be a fight scene.

Tess: There'll be numerous characters, but he's just walking and I think it gives you a sense of how *huge* this world is like, yet how empty.

Sumana: Yeah, it's totally empty. That's true.

Tess: Who built this? Where are they? Is this like – ?

Martin: Nice place.

Tess: It's beautiful.

Sumana: Yeah it's evoking like, a mystery you have to figure out.

Tess: It's too cold for me.

This discussion operates in the same spectator mode as those conversations interpreting the book and the movie. There are numerous comments on the atmosphere of the beautiful, deserted landscape and temple, and some preliminary moves into the subjunctive mode of prediction. The players seem to be enjoying the opportunity to comment in leisurely ways on the developing story. But immediately after this stage, participants find themselves having to master the controls to get the story moving in both literal and metaphorical senses of that term. At this stage they begin to merge their general, strategic noticing with a concerted step 'into' the world of the story. We will return to this trio of gamers later in the next chapter, after an exploration of that important move 'into'.

5
Entering the Fiction: The Subjunctive and the Deictic Centre

At some point, successful interpreters step *inside* the make-believe world of the text before them, whether in film, novel or game format. No matter how we configure the question of narrative, the gamer, or the viewer or the reader 'engages in an act of imagination' (Ryan, 2007, p. 13), and my study explores similarities and differences in how this act of imagination is *performed* with different media. I suggest that exploring overlaps and contradictions in the invoking of make-believe in fictions presented in different media can enhance our understanding of all these media, and of the act of make-believe itself.

The subjunctive

Monster opens with an offer to readers to step into a story:

> The best time to cry is at night, when the lights are out and someone is being beaten up and screaming for help. That way even if you sniffle a little they won't hear you. If anybody knows that you are crying, they'll start talking about it and soon it'll be your turn to get beat up when the lights go out.
>
> There is a mirror over the steel sink in my cell. It's six inches high, and scratched with the names of some guys who were here before me. When I look into the small rectangle, I see a face looking back at me but I don't recognize it. It doesn't look like me. I couldn't have changed that much in a few months. I wonder if I will look like myself when the trial is over.
>
> (Myers, 1999, pp. 1–2)

We are immediately invited into a world where the future is unknown, and persuaded to look into that future by taking on the fears and hopes of a character/narrator who sets up the opening scene. We may skip to the ending if we choose, because it *is* a narrative fiction and the ending has already been written, but even if we do so, when we return to page one we return to the situation of Steve's terror about the unknown future. This essential component of make-believe, this step into not-knowing, is helpfully explored through the idea of the subjunctive.

It is easy to take for granted how we have learned to shift stance between the world we inhabit and a created world. Even as we sort out the limits of the make-believe, we start adjusting to its parameters. We begin to locate what we are experiencing within the framework of the *as-if*.

Grammatically, make-believe is the realm of the subjunctive mood or mode. The *Oxford English Dictionary* defines the subjunctive as follows:

> Designating a mood ... the forms of which are employed to denote an action or a state as conceived (and not as a fact) and therefore used to express a wish, command, exhortation, or a contingent, hypothetical, or prospective event.
>
> (Oxford, 2009)

The *American Heritage® Book of English Usage* describes the subjunctive as 'used chiefly to express the speaker's attitude about the likelihood or factuality of a given situation' (Bartleby, 2009).

The hypotheticals created by the subjunctive can be expressed formally with verbal markers ('If I *were* you', 'If winter *come*, can spring be far behind?'), but contemporary English makes less use of these formal indicators. The subjunctive territory survives, however, no matter how much colloquial English flattens the verbal distinctions.

Questions about factuality, fictionality, contingency and make-believe entail somebody with an opinion: 'I hope that', 'I expect that', 'I believe that', 'I wish that', 'I fear that', 'I doubt that' (or, in the case of Steve, the narrator above, 'I wonder if'). A non-factual possibility or potentiality has no real-life existence, by definition, so there must be a person acting as the subject of the sentence to set the subjunctive verb in motion. In the successful development of fictional understanding between a creator and an interpreter, each has the potential to participate as the subject of the subjunctive; the relationship between the implied creator and the implied interpreter may sometimes entail a slide between a subject 'I' and a subject 'you' as each envisages the stance and intentions of the other. It is an intriguing territory that does not seem to be particularly medium-specific. It is not difficult to imagine an interpreter layering the subjunctive elements at the moment of processing: '*You* – the creator – *expect* that *I* – the interpreter – will *believe* that'. There are two different subjects and two different verbs invoking the subjunctive – and yet this complex exchange is a completely ordinary and taken-for-granted form of the discourse of make-believe. We will return to this territory in more detail below when we consider the nature of the deictic shift.

Jerome Bruner (1986) and Susanne Langer (1953) both describe the narrative experience in terms of the subjunctive mode, although only Bruner uses that explicit term. 'Narrative deals with the vicissitudes of human intention', says Bruner (1986, p. 16). He expands this idea with his clarification of what he means by the subjunctive: 'To be in the subjunctive mode is to be trafficking in human possibilities rather than in settled certainties' (p. 26). Langer is clearly referring to the same region of make-believe in her account of impressions:

> The poetically created world is not limited to the impressions of one individual, but it is limited to impressions. All its connections are *lived* connections, i.e., motivations, all causes and effects operate only as the motives for expectation, fulfillment, frustration, surprise.
>
> (1953, p. 265, emphasis in original)

In other words, inside the world of the *as-if*, the narrative is *lived*, is *felt* as hopes, fears, assumptions, surprises; it is experienced prismatically through the lenses of human emotions coming to terms with an unknown future. As Gerrig points out, even when we do actually know the end of the story, once we step into its purview we experience it as if we do not know what will happen. 'Anomalous suspense', says Gerrig, allows a reader to 'experience suspense with respect to an outcome about which he should not have any uncertainty' (1993, p. 158). He describes this experience as 'a compelling aspect of the real-life experience of narratives' (p. 161); although it sounds esoteric, it is a relatively commonplace element of our encounters with fiction, and most people will recognize its power.

According to I. A. Richards, that step into the subjunctive mode of wondering, expecting, hoping, fearing, is essential to making the story work: 'The persistencies of effects – no matter how well we make them overlap – will not systematize themselves into experience (knowledge that returns as power) unless they are heated by an immediate sustaining interest' (1942, p. 54). The events of the story are 'heated' for me by my hoping, expecting, and so forth.

In her description of aesthetic reading, Rosenblatt provides a clear account of how we activate our own experiences to breathe the tentativeness and uncertainty of the subjunctive into the words we read, 'heating' our interest in the story:

> In order to shape the work, we draw on our reservoir of past experience with people and the world, our past inner linkage of words and things, our past encounters with spoken or written texts. We listen to the sound of the words in the inner ear; we lend our sensations, our emotions, our sense of being alive, to the new experience which, we feel, corresponds to the text. We participate in the story, we identify with the characters, we share their conflicts and their feelings.
>
> (2005, p. 75)

So far, I am describing interpreters moving towards the state of being very completely absorbed in a story. Douglas and Hargadon refer to this condition as 'immersion' (2001, p. 156), the capacity of submerging oneself entirely within the schemas established by the fiction. The condition of being totally caught up in something that is known to be not true is certainly complex enough to challenge philosophers and psychologists for a very long time to come. But human interpreters can also take pleasure in moving in and out of this state of absorption. They can simultaneously commit themselves emotionally to the subjunctive unknowns of the story and also enjoy the way the story is constructed. Douglas and Hargadon call this second form of imaginative investment 'engagement' (p. 156), and refer to this condition as being able to manage a number of schemas at the same time. These schemas include those of the story world, those entailed in how it was made, and those needed for the interpreter to approach the story: 'Contradictory schemas or elements that defy conventional schemas tend to disrupt readers' immersion in the text, obliging them to assume an extra-textual perspective on the text itself' (p. 156). What Rabinowitz calls 'deviations' serve the same purpose, catching intepreters' attention in order to 'bounce' them into paying heed in different ways.

Andrew Stibbs describes the condition of engagement, of contending with multiple schematic frameworks, by means of an elaborate metaphor, offering advice about enhancing the pleasures of an *immersed* reading through a more *engaged* stance:

> Whereas good advice to immersed non-swimmers is to relax, competent swimmers can have more fun by thrashing about. They can pop

out of the water, sometimes, to remind themselves that the water is not – as fish believe – the only world. Competent readers are amphibious: they can enjoy both the air and the water; they know the difference; from the atmosphere they can enjoy the view of the textual pond, and when they're in the pond they can recognize its surface as neither a mirror nor a window but an interface to be played with.

(1993, p. 58)

Before any of this amphibious thrashing about can be truly enjoyable, the moment of first casting oneself onto the water and relaxing into a float is necessary for skilled as well as beginning interpreters. In exploring the responses of the participants as they started each fiction, I was very interested to establish whether the initial juxtaposition of floating and thrashing (to maintain Stibbs' aquatic terms) occurred in book, film and game in similar ways, or whether the game was, so to speak, more like a waterfall or a rapids: a situation where attention must necessarily be focused simply on *not drowning*, as players learn to manage the controls that make the story happen and thus remain so conscious of their own role in making the game happen that they can never be totally absorbed into the story.

Katharine Hayles suggests that there may indeed be an overlap between different media because of the effects of remediation:

When literature leaps from one medium to another – from orality to writing, from manuscript codex to printed book, from mechanically generated print to electronic textuality – it does not leave behind the accumulated knowledge embedded in genres, poetic conventions, narrative structures, figurative tropes, and so forth.

(2008, p. 58)

In other words, the initial step 'into' the story draws on an understanding of make-believe that is in crucial ways platform-neutral.

Hayles uses different terms in her discussion of electronic literature but it is not hard to discern the elements of the subjunctive in her phrasing: 'For two thousand years or more, literature has explored the nature of consciousness, perception, and emergent complexity' (2008, p. 59). The idea of the emergent is crucial to the experience of fiction. If we are aligning ourselves with the characters and thinking in the subjunctive mode ('I hope that', 'I wish that', 'I expect that', and so forth), we are looking at the future as it will *emerge* within the terms of the story.

Without using the explicit concept, Marie-Laure Ryan suggests that the subjunctive works in a game as much as in another form of fiction. She addresses the idea that games are located in the present (the action doesn't begin until the player activates the control) while narrative necessarily entails a past tense (the teller recounting what has already happened), but she suggests that the experiences of different media narrative have more in common than might be expected:

Even when stories are ostentatiously told by looking backward, they are experienced by readers, spectators, and arguably players by looking forward, from the point of view of the characters. There are consequently only superficial differences, in terms of the lived experience of time, between games, movies and novels.

(2006, p. 187)

'Looking forward, from the point of view of the characters' is exactly what the subjunctive is designed to facilitate.

Mark Stephen Meadows confirms that games entail this subjunctive step but suggests that the creation of the subjunctive is more collaborative than in other media formats:

The key difference between narration and this software-related writing is the opinion implied in the story – the individual perspective. The human element of interpretation needs to be present for writing to become narration.

A piece of writing requires an opinion – call it perspective or call it point of view – before it becomes a narrative. ...

Narrative requires opinion. But we're not suggesting that the opinion has to be of the narrator or the reader. This is a big swerve from the course of traditional narrative because, traditionally, the narrative opinion is the opinion of the author. Sometimes, with narrative that contains interactivity, the interpretation is made collaboratively (or simultaneously) by both the author and the reader. ...

It's the human element of the perspective that's significant in stories, not the quantities or its charts.

(2003, p. 29)

A human perspective may be interactively developed and shared between the game's author and its player, but it still entails a 'step into' that perspective on the part of the player.

Taking the first steps into a story world entails risks, as Crago warns. He suggests that complete immersion cannot be instantly achieved, because emotional threats distract us:

> For me, beginning a new novel, watching the curtain go up on a play or a movie, means a threat to the extent that I'm forced, temporarily, to submit myself to somebody else's world; some aspects of that world are bound to be alien to me, and may generate feelings of disquiet, even of anger. That I know I'm *choosing* to undergo this because I also expect to derive pleasure from it doesn't help. I have to pass through this stage every time, until the tale takes hold and absorption becomes more pleasurable than threatening.
>
> (1982, p. 180, emphasis in original)

Immediate immersion is difficult for a number of reasons: for one thing, we need to sort out what schemas are organizing the world of the story, which often entails reference to the outside world. At the same time, we are deciding on the degree to which we want to trust the creator of the story. In Stibbs' terms, there is likely to be much thrashing and splashing at the beginning of a connection with a fiction, as we get deep enough into the story to cast ourselves upon its surface and float away into the conditions of a different world. Experienced consumers of stories explore the surface for clues about the depth. Murray describes this active process:

> The pleasurable surrender of the mind to an imaginative world is often described, in Coleridge's phrase, as 'the willing suspension of disbelief.' But this is too passive a formulation even for traditional media. When we enter a fictional world, we do not merely 'suspend' disbelief so much as we actively *create belief*. Because of our desire to experience immersion, we focus our attention on the enveloping world and we use our intelligence to reinforce rather than to question the reality of the experience.
>
> (1997, p. 110)

In the examples that follow later in this chapter, we can see such activities being conducted in all three media. Before we get to these examples, however, I want to consider a different way of describing the move 'into' the narrative world.

The deictic centre

Another way of entering a story draws on our tacit skill in understanding and exploiting the grammatical category of deictics or deixis: that small group of words, sometimes called shifters, that take specific meaning only in the context of use; examples include *I, you, here, there, now, then, this, that, yesterday, today, tomorrow*. Tense markers may also function deictically, relating to the time of utterance in specific, situated ways. In a sentence such as, 'I will see you here tomorrow', every single word takes on a specific meaning only when the context of speaker and place and time of utterance is specifically known. Yet the sentence follows grammatical rules and makes a kind of context-free sense because of that fact. We understand it at the level of abstraction as well as grasping what the speaker communicates concretely.

Human beings are very skilled at shifting their sense of how these 'empty' words can be filled in specific circumstances. The circumstances do not need to be concrete or real. I had an experience while sitting in an airport listening to my iPod that demonstrated to me that my attention could actually toggle very swiftly between multiple focal centres, some fictional and some situated in the real world. I sat waiting for a plane with my mind idling, listening to Kathleen Ferrier sing an unaccompanied rendition of 'Blow the Wind Southerly,' a recording I remembered from childhood. My eyes moved around the waiting hall and took in a soundless television sitcom at the other end of the room. As I listened and looked, I realized my mind was moving between five centres of attention: the acoustic space of the recording (remarkable for its era and very arresting); my vivid memories of the record player in the living room of my childhood home; the fictional world of desolation and fear portrayed in the song's narrative of a woman waiting for her lover to return from a stormy sea; the comings and goings of my fellow passengers in the hall; and the fictional exchanges and antics of the characters on the television screen across the room. At any one time, I could focus on one of these possibilities, and I could shift between them very readily, moving from one 'here' to another, being the 'I' who sat in the hall, or the long-ago 'I' who first heard the song, or the 'I' who waited for a lost lover, and so forth.

The simplest focus for deictic attention is very often the character. Bower and Morrow, investigating the idea of the reader's mental model of the story, point out that, '[r]eaders focus attention on the protagonist whose actions usually determine the "here-and-now" point in the progress of the narrative' (1990, p. 45).

Deictic shifters have a role in placing a reader inside a story world in concrete ways that involve both conventional and social components. They supply the pivot point that makes the text able to move between potential and actual, between the abstraction of the words on the page and the instantiation of my own mental image during which I, as reader, *inhabit* the shifters, and become a different 'I' as character or narratee.

In the example from the opening of *Monster*, the first paragraph intro-duces the word 'you' and the second paragraph adds the word 'I'. We as readers know that the meanings inbuilt into these words are established in a world other than the one we occupy as the 'I' of our own universe, and that they remain only potential meanings until we move in as readers and occupy them. As David Herman expresses it, we move into 'the here and now that constitute the deictic center of the world being told about' (2002, p. 14). Erwin Segal describes the phenomenon in related ways:

> [I]n fictional narrative, readers and authors shift their deictic center from the real-world situation to an image of themselves at a location within the story world. This location is represented as a cognitive structure often containing the elements of a particular time and place within the fictional world, or even within the subjective space of a fictional character.
>
> (1995, p. 15)

Segal's point that readers and authors alike have to shift their deictic centre confirms that one point of connection between creator and interpreter lies in their relationship with the paradox of the shifter in its conventionally empty, but specifically 'fillable' role. I as writer, you as reader (or the other way around) insert myself /yourself in the deictic centre created on the page, and thus make a connection to the other.

Children struggle to master the complexities of the empty role of the shifter, and can often be heard in conversation at a very young age, trying to establish when it will ever 'be' tomorrow, or querying who truly is the 'I' of a picture book story. Yet before we even start school, most of us are able to normalize our magnificent capacity to shift deictic centre into an entirely invented universe. That pivot between the abstract emptiness of the formal vocabulary and the concrete vividness of the individual instan-tiation is a microcosm of how we understand fiction more generally.

The deictic shifter is a linguistic formulation, and most easily recog-nized in print literature. The concept of the deictic centre, however, applies more broadly to fictional worlds in many media, and it is inter-esting to see it functioning in film and game as well. Indeed, some of the conversations that took place during the game-playing are exemplars of shifter-talk (my favourite is a question from Jarret to his two game part-ners on the subject of the androgynous appearance of the hero of *Shadow of the Colossus*: 'We are a guy, right?')

In the previous chapter, we saw the participants assessing what seemed important to notice in each story. Here we observe them as they take the initial imaginative leap 'into' that world, and occupy an internal rather than an external observer's position.

Entering *Run Lola Run*

As Lola begins to run, viewers begin to move into the story world. For example, Dan, Keith and Neil rapidly assess plot possibilities:

Dan: I'm guessing that he's going to attempt the robbery and that she'll reach him just before he pulls the gun out or something to that effect. That's my guess.

Keith: I wouldn't know, but I assume he's going to rob this place.

Neil: Yeah I think he's going to rob this place and she's going to you know, just stand there and watch.

Similarly, Martin set up a prediction:

Martin: They started out the movie with this emotional – swearing and despair and – I imagine it's up to heroics and there's sure to be a twist.

Tess: Or a few twists.

Martin: Yeah, several.

Sumana: Yeah it seems that you're asking what we think is going to happen? And – it seems as though he's probably going to go try to hit up that bank or whatever it was. And just by the way he behaves I think they're kind of foreshadowing that it's not going to go very well and that he could end up dying or being injured or being arrested or something like that and then Lola will probably save him or something.

Martin: They set up the element of Ronnie as being this overriding authority that's going to come into play.

Tess regularly mentions that she is aware of the soundtrack ('I like the music, really fast paced and again it keeps you really watching the film'). Her comments offer an insight into a signifier that is available to the movie and the game but not to the novel: music. While these viewers are moving cautiously into the world of the film, with plenty of reference to its existence as a construction rather than as a felt story, the music of the soundtrack is providing an imperative forward momentum.

Marshall McLuhan expresses the contradiction between control and submission in these terms:

> Any medium has the power of imposing its own assumption on the unwary. Prediction and control consist in avoiding this subliminal state of Narcissus trance. But the greatest aid to this end is simply in knowing that the spell can occur immediately upon contact, as in the first bars of a melody.
>
> (McLuhan, 1994, p. 15)

The music of *Run Lola Run* does indeed hold the potential to cast a spell. Rhythmic, driving, catchy, it moves listeners into a world where breath and pulse may coordinate with the tempo of the song. It is interesting to see McLuhan highlight the importance of *resisting* the spell of the music. He dismisses the fully immersed interpretation as a 'Narcissus trance'. The participants are rather less averse than McLuhan to being swept away into a fully absorbed state, though it is clear they also enjoy inspecting the surface of the text. Critical attention seems to be part of the pleasure of engaging with this complex fiction.

Sumana makes an implicit statement about the subjunctive mode: 'It gets you right into the movie, I find.' 'You' are there as the subject of the subjunctive, expecting, hoping, fearing and all the rest. 'You' are also deictically re-located 'into the movie.' This common phrase says more than we customarily glean from its surface meaning.

Entering *Monster*

Monster signals early on that form is at least as important as content, and it is easy to see these experienced readers assessing the implications of that information.

Sumana is positive about the combined appeal of content and design as creating an invitation to move in:

> It's very well written, it's very evocative and you can see those images and it's really fast paced. So it's not slow and plodding like a lot of novels you might get. It borrows the things that attract people to films – like the fast pace and you can see the images even when it's just written ... I also love the way there are different fonts and sizes used. It makes it a lot more engaging to read and it's something really unusual for a novel that makes it stand out and makes you think that this novel might be different from other ones.

Lewis and Adam are quick to see the advantages of combining the journal with the screenplay, allowing for a more internal perspective on Steve the hero than might be possible in a conventional movie alone. At the first pause for discussion, after they have read just 12 pages of the book, they pick up the potential of the double format. Adam says 'I think the inner stuff is really good because it sort of forces you to almost interact with the character because he's right there.' A moment later, Lewis adds his initial assessment: 'You can relate to the character more if we see that thought actually, by doing it as a movie. We'll see their thought process and stuff like that and what he's thinking, because he's doing it himself so that might help us to maybe sympathize or something later on.'

In these comments, we can see readers assess the potential of the material before them, both in terms of the surface – fonts, layout, and so forth – and also the depths: anticipated complexity, and psychological insight. We can also see, especially in Lewis's comment, an articulation of the potential for deictic re-centring.

Even in the early stages, as the readers were still sorting out the representational forms, they were beginning to speculate about the story from the perspective of the interior schemas of the fictional world:

Neil: Normally you would pick somebody a little more credible to open up the story, but this witness has obviously got problems. [*chuckles*] The fact is that we have no idea whether he's telling the truth and there's no way to judge that he might be, just because of his past and his own admissions.

Keith: It kind of leaves the image that he might actually get off because of the lack of credibility of the witness.

Tess simultaneously moves between different components of the story and the telling, and reflects on the character's use of exactly the same strategy:

And so going from the introduction where it's a first person narrative to, I guess, a screenplay more or less – it's a bit of an interesting transition and I guess one of the things I was struck with was, I think, this kid really strikes me as being quite intelligent, like he's fairly eloquent, he's reverting to things he learned in school, which is interesting in a time of desperation it's not a survival, it's a 'I'm going to use my brain to try to record this, to write this down.'

Even in these very preliminary stages, we can also perceive the conversation pushing participants' thinking. Martin hears Tess's theory of Steve choosing to rise above his desperation and immediately disputes it:

Martin: I think that it *is* survival, though. Essentially I agree that he's recording, but I think the reason that he's recording is so that he's not experiencing it.
Tess: So is it an escape or – ?
Martin: It's easier to turn it into a discourse than to actually experience it, which is what he's trying to do with the movie. Hopefully by making it a discourse he's able to separate himself a little bit from it.

In short, while these readers reflect on the way the story is being told to them, they simultaneously make efforts to 'move into' the story world, using their intelligence to reinforce the created world in exactly the way that Murray describes, not simply passively waiting to be swept away. They become invested in imagining the world of the story from the very early stages of observing, predicting, and evaluating.

Entering *Shadow of the Colossus*

In the last chapter, we left Group B, Tess, Sumana and Martin, entranced by the opening cut scene of the game. It is striking how the relatively contemplative language of this trio shifts immediately as they move to take charge of the action. As we pick up their conversation at the very next line of the transcript from where we left off in the last chapter, Martin is trying to climb on the back of Agro the horse so he can leave the temple, and Tess is assessing where best to hold the sword up to the light in order to find the right way:

Martin: Pushing this down – all right, horse.
Tess: Where is the sunlight?
Martin: Okay, this is hard – extremely difficult! Agro is not hip. [*Chuckles*]
Sumana: How easy is it to point it in certain directions?
Tess: This horse is very stubborn – ooh.
(Hero struggles with the horse and eventually re-enters the temple)
          Do you remember how to do the sword-raising thing? You might want to do that then. He's running.
Martin: Here comes [*inaudible*]

Tess: It feels almost like a church altar. Like an African god.
(Martin pulls down map)
Sumana: What did you press?
Martin: Functions. *Zoom in; zoom out, turn back, map, move, left analog stick.* All right, so they don't have –
Tess: I still say you go to the sun and do the sword thing. It seems like that was the last instruction he really gave, short of kill those gigantic idols on the wall.
Martin: So you – left analog stick is movement. You press 'X' to make him go and make him stop or actually, not to make him stop. You press 'X' and you can go faster and then hard back on the left analog stick.

The sequence continues in this vein. Martin, who is activating the story, is highly focused on the need to sort out the controls for the horse. Tess and, to a lesser extent, Sumana, concentrate on the strategic need to locate a light source for guidance on the direction to follow; Tess also continues to admire the setting. Of the first 37 remarks after the cut scene ends and the action begins, 17 refer to the controls and 14 to wayfinding. A few of these contributions also discuss the wayward character of the horse. The horse's personality at this stage is largely a response to Martin's ham-fisted early efforts with the controls, so these remarks toggle between surface and depth in interesting ways; a technical problem soon turns into a subjunctive assessment of the horse's potential as an ally – and back to the technical again.

Martin: As soon as we get these controls underway it will go a lot smoother. And this horse is ridiculous!
Sumana: He's got a mind of his own.
Tess: Pretty much! ... Yeah. I'm still convinced that the middle of that room – you need to do something with it. Maybe the horse refuses to go back up? Maybe you're stuck.
(Hero and Agro seem to be stuck in a corner and are not moving)
Martin: The controls are really sensitive.

In this group's comments reported in the last chapter, in the passage of the transcript immediately prior to this section, these players were watching the cut scene and asking spectator questions: 'What is happening? What might happen?' In this passage, we see a very pronounced shift to the player's question: 'What do we have to *do*?' It is a model of Atkins' distinction between the 'What happens next?' question of the spectator stance and the related gamer question: 'What happens next *if I –* ?' (2006, p. 137). In this passage we see the players moving back and forth between these two questions, at least to a limited extent. Such oscillation increases as their manual control becomes more fluent. Tess also raises an issue she has previously mentioned in *Run Lola Run*: 'Left is movement – oh, I like the music!' This comment includes an involuntary component that often marks the beginning of 'floating,' though in this case she is struck by the aesthetics of the music rather than absorbed into the plot.

A more clear-cut example of 'flotation' into the fiction – of the button-pressers suddenly switching into story mode – can be observed in this conversation featuring Dan, Neil and Keith of Group A (Neil is in charge of the controls):

Dan: Hold the control in the direction on the other wall behind you and let go of triangle. Hold triangle, pull back and hold triangle.

(Makes it!)

Keith: Nice work!

Neil: That's nice. It's going to be like this learning curve for *Splinter Cell*.

Dan: *Splinter Cell* is a lot worse than this. With *Splinter Cell*, I couldn't figure how to get a weapon out for like 20 minutes.

Neil: Slow walk there.

(Finds the colossus)

Dan: Oh it's a colossus!

Neil: Holy crap, that thing is big! They weren't kidding. Do you think he's got some sort of poison?

Neil's last question is clearly expressed in the subjunctive mode of expectation and prediction. In this short exchange we can see the beginnings of the oscillation between Atkins' two questions: the spectator's 'What happens next?' and the player's 'What happens next *if I –* ?' (2006, p. 137). Both questions are important to the experience of the subjunctive world of the game story. But it is also worth noting that Neil's final question comes as the game shifts into the cut scene of the colossus' awakening. In the early stages, the cut scene offers relief from the learning curve of the buttons and allows a small space for reflection and anticipation.

The deixis of the game is strongly affected by the potential for action. 'This' and 'that' have precise meanings when the speaker is in charge of the cursor and his interlocutor can see the reference zone of the screen. In this situation, the empty signifiers are specifically filled in the same way that a pointing finger will establish a concrete meaning in real life.

Articulating the subjunctive role

Benton and Fox quote Claire, a 14-year-old reader, on how she perceives herself *within* the fiction of her print story:

> It's as if I'm a sort of dark watcher, who is there at the scene, but none of the characters pays any attention to me. I'm like a power, as if everything is happening because I'm there.
>
> (Benton and Fox, 1985, p. 9)

Claire's stance can be read as the power that activates the subjunctive. Everything happens because there is a reader *to hope that –, to expect that –, to fear that –*. But the 'dark watcher', though described by a reader, is a strikingly non-media-specific concept. My undergraduate participants, with the DVD of *Run Lola Run* projected on the screen of a darkened room, personified the dark watcher in very literal terms, but they also activated the story in their own minds through their concern over the different outcomes for Lola and Manni, as if they were inside the story looking on. In their readings of *Monster*, they were invisible observers of the actions in court and in the jailhouse and they drew the links between the two formats of storytelling through their own involvement in the possible guilt or innocence of Steve. In *Shadow of the Colossus*, the player's place behind the shoulder of the protagonist is manifest through the camera placement. The player's 'dark' invisibility is plain as the character moves through the landscape without ever attending to the one who makes him go. And the power of caring about what happens to the avatar and to the colossi is expressed in the investment of subjunctive wondering and suspecting and wishing on the part of the player.

In this chapter, I am exploring the implicit understandings of the participants as manifested in their approach to each fiction; in Chapter 10, we will return to this topic in terms of what participants explicitly articulate of their own sense of the spectator role.

It can be argued that I have loaded the decks, choosing texts from three media with a virtual space for the dark watcher so that my selected texts may have more in common with each other than with other examples from the same medium. In each case, for example, I chose a 'one-off' rather than an entry in a series, so that readers had to create the subjunctive space from the ground up rather than importing prior knowledge. In each case, I chose a narrative with a conclusion, however indeterminate, rather than a soap opera, a cliff-hanger, or the ongoing universe of an online multiplayer game. In the case of *Shadow of the Colossus*, I selected a game that supplies a metaphorical location for the consciousness of the player, a corner of the scene lacking only a labelled arrow saying 'dark watcher stand here', behind the hero. Many games alternatively place the player as the agent of the action, whether as the first-person who does the shooting or as a creator of the plot in a multi-player online role-playing game, but I chose a finite, third-person game with only camera control as a factor in point of view.

So any conclusions drawn from this study would not stand as gener-alizations about the entire universe of print, moving image or interactive fiction. Nevertheless, it seems important to point out commonalities in orientation efforts and in the mental shift that launches the fictional stance cross media boundaries in these three examples. Participants in this project could not import specific knowledge from previous texts in the same series; what they clearly did import were manifestations of fictional understanding that could be derived from several different media.

Subjunctive resources

Children learn tacit lessons about the subjunctive as soon as they start to listen to stories and to pretend. The bedtime story introduces the sig-nificance of 'What happens next?' Their make-believe games offer them ways of exploring possible answers to the question 'What happens next *if I* – ?' The undergraduates who encountered these three sophisticated texts brought a well-honed repertoire for the interpretation of fiction in various media.

In all the examples above, we see participants raising preliminary questions of interpretation: What do I need to know? How can I know it? What cues do I perceive and what significance should I allot to each cue? What understanding of previously encountered stories can I import to help me start up the fictional engines? What life knowledge can I use and what should I abandon in order to meet the terms of the fiction as I perceive them in this preliminary state? What happens next? What happens next *if I* pay a particular kind of attention/take a particular action? What can I expect, hope, wish, or fear?

The role of the subjunctive mode is apparent in the processing of all three formats. While the details of engagement differ, the need to step into the fiction is an important component of commitment. Although in this chapter I am reporting largely on the early stages of encounter, it is already possible to see interest 'heating up' (Richards, 1942, p. 54) under the pressure of looking ahead through the subjunctive lens. Even in the early moments, we see the beginnings of '*lived* connections' (Langer, 1953, p. 265, emphasis in original) in all three media. Participants' use of deictic markers to refer to the story world rather than the university meeting-room where the discussion was actually taking place reinforces this shift.

The subjunctive is not a mode confined to language, although we understand it through words. In its multimodal incarnations, it offers a relatively precise tool for understanding what makes fictions come alive for their interpreters in multi-sensory ways. In all formats, the subjunctive mode is sufficiently robust to survive oscillation between depth and surface, between immersion and engagement. In all formats, the subjunctive is the engine fuelling the creation of a suspension of disbelief that enables a dozen young men and women sitting in a university meeting-room, surrounded by cameras and research assistants, to describe a state of anticipating, reacting to, and caring about three sets of people and events that have never actually existed. The subjunctive enables them to sustain *lived* connections, even as they simultaneously explore how the stories that embody such connections have been constructed to draw them in. It is clear that they all understand the subjunctive, not only as they experience it themselves but also as they hear it expressed with differing nuances by their interpretive partners in this exercise.

'Trafficking in human possibilities' (Bruner, 1986, p. 26) is one of the major pleasures of fiction. This little study indicates that such pleasures are not medium-specific. It is also clear from these particular examples that the both immersion and engagement feed into the subjunctive mode; that, as Murray suggests (1997, p. 110), we vivify a fiction through our intelligent *creation* of belief, using the tools of whatever format is in front of us to a common end. Strikingly, we not only do this for ourselves, but also understand the process as experienced and articulated by others with different emphases.

Such a finding is not a definitive answer to the questions raised by ongoing culture wars that claim particular value for writing or for films or for interactive games, but it does suggest that one common component of all three forms is actually a very powerful activator of fictional experience. Clarifying our understanding of this common feature offers a route to clearer understanding of the many story-telling options now at our disposal. This study of the *performed* subjunctive does not provide a complete answer to Ryan's question: 'How can the concept of narrative be fruitfully invoked in game studies' (2006, p. 181)? What it does offer is another tool for exploring how the concept of narrative is activated in games as well as in fictions of other media.

To return to the metaphor of swimming, there are many examples in the transcripts of the participants pushing themselves away from the edge of the pool, away from the handholds of exploring the surface controls of the text (in whatever medium). The subjunctive draws them in – to wonder, fear, and yearn *with* and also *on behalf of* Steve, Manni or the game hero (that is, they infill the space created for the emotions of these heroes with their own feelings). They shift so that the deictic centre of their attention takes on a character's point of view. Their feelings are loaned to these fictional persons as a way of understanding them and of breathing life into the different kinds of flat surface on which each story is presented. It is an impressive cognitive achievement in each medium, and it is one that we do not truly understand. The concept of the subjunctive and the floating grammar of the deictic shifter offer us dynamic tools for approaching this black box of imaginative engagement and comprehension.

In the next two chapters, we explore ideas of orienting and making inferences, assessing these elements of the interpretive process in light of how they augment or disrupt the invested making-believe of the subjunctive stance. What matters is not that the subjunctive absorption be unalloyed and uninterrupted; we will see examples of interpreters looking up and out from the story world. What matters is that the subjunctive stance should continue to be available as an option for understanding the story; the alternative is a detachment that may be intellectually interesting but that will ultimately be an emotionally thin experience. The ability to be 'inside' that world is part of what makes our narrative experiences memorable.

6
Orienting: Finding the Way Forward

In an ideal world, this chapter and the next would be printed and read side-by-side. To divide the topic of how we make headway in a text, I have arbitrarily taken the idea of orienting as a kind of macro-level, top-down approach, while filling gaps and making inferences is taken as occurring at the more local level of sentences and paragraphs. In reality, interpreters almost certainly oscillate between the two.

As discussed in Chapters 4 and 5, interpreters gather cues and clues in an initial cast of their attention and muster enough information to springboard their leap into the subjunctive world of the story. Then what? Judith Langer talks about the second step of literary engagement, 'being in and moving through an envisionment' (1995, p. 17). What does 'through' mean in this context? What decisions and strategies allow you to 'move though'? Are they similar in the three formats or completely distinctive? Alternatively, do individual interpreters invoke what Sipe calls a 'signature response' (1998, p. 87), a distinctive personal reaction that manifests itself across media boundaries but varies from one respondent to another – that is, does 'through' look different for different interpreters? Can a group develop a collective signature response in its collaborative deliberations?

Iser combines some of these questions in his consideration of the importance of 'consistency-building' (1978, p. 18). 'As a structure of comprehension [consistency-building] depends on the reader and not on the work, and as such it is inextricably bound up with subjective factors and, above all, the habitual orientations of the reader' (1978, p. 18).

Implicit in the idea of 'moving through an envisionment' is the necessity of orientation, both in terms of the interpreter's habitual stances and behaviours and also in terms of the signposts suggested in the text. In the early stages of a story, one question is very important in both its literal and its metaphorical overtones: 'Where might we be going?' How does a text provide 'directional' markers for readers to orient themselves to the possibilities of the story? And how do interpreters learn to align themselves with the text in order to make sense of the story's development? Need they establish a vision of what the author expects them to do, or can they simply march into the story on their own terms? To what extent do their initial expectations shape their final understanding?

Rabinowitz suggests that we actually use consistency as a rule-of-thumb until it is made clear that we should not take it for granted. Discussing the rules of signification – those indicators that suggest how we should pay attention to what we have decided to notice – he talks about readerly short cuts:

> In addition to metaphorical rules of appearance, which make it appropriate to assume that physical or verbal characteristics stand for moral qualities, we have metonymical rules of enchainment, which make it appropriate to assume that the presence of one moral quality is linked to the presence of another that lies more or less contiguous to it. ...
>
> In another kind of chaining, many narratives also ask us, in the absence of evidence to the contrary, to assume a kind of innocence by association: we trust the friends of our friends, and the enemies of our enemies.
>
> (1987, pp. 89–90)

The word 'assume' appears three times in these two sentences. We have to start by assuming something as part of orienting ourselves to the text so we can begin to make more refined assessments. Rabinowitz's categories supply some of the rough-and-ready tools we bring to that initial process.

There is also a more macro level of assumption that needs teasing out more fully. Participants in this study assumed very early on that these texts were narrative fictions, and they applied default narrative schemas to shape their interpretation. As they moved through the stories, they not only checked out local content information, they also vetted whether their narrative schema was still functioning appropriately. In Tabbi's terms, these stories all draw attention to their mode of telling, their 'systems of *notation*' (2002, p. xxi, emphasis in original). These undergraduates were clearly at home with the idea that the practice of orientation includes the making of initial assumptions about the mode of telling. Their default start-up position may be relatively simplistic but they are not closed off to developing narrative complexity as well as thickening action *inside* the story.

We will return in the final chapter to that instant and irresistible flicker of identification of narrative potential, from which so many processing decisions descend. It is too swift to be visible even in microanalysis of the transcripts, yet the ripple effect of that moment of hypothesis reverberates through the actions of the interpreters. The assumptions described here follow from that initial, very swift assessment.

Moving through the story

To discuss how interpreters decide where to begin and what direction to consider, two spatial concepts are helpful. Firstly, it is useful to consider the idea of *texts* as legible environments, a term taken from Lynch's (1960) study of what makes cities comprehensible to inhabitants and tourists. Secondly, the behaviours of *interpreters* can be usefully encapsulated in the idea of reading paths. Before we move into any analysis of specific responses, I will consider these terms in more detail.

The question 'Where might we be going?' is more than literal; a story 'goes places' by more than the specific means of crossing an imagined geography. As we use the English language, a story 'goes' in 'directions' dictated by plot events, psychological development, emotional nuance, and so forth. The fact that our reading metaphors are so spatial is in itself telling. Beyond this metaphorical level, however (or perhaps beneath it, shoring it up), the actual spatial element is one concrete component of the story world, and its specificity may make it particularly useful in the early stages of the interpretation.

David Herman suggests that spatial reference 'plays a crucial, not an optional or derivative, role in stories' (2002, p. 264), and uses the term

> *narrative domains* to emphasize that narratives should be viewed not just as temporally structured communicative acts but also as systems of verbal or visual prompts anchored in mental models having a particular spatial structure. More exactly, narratives represent the world being told about as one having a specific spatial structure.
>
> (2002, p. 264, emphasis in original)

A fictional space, however, need not be entirely coherent. Storytellers can use a form of 'fuzzy geography' if it suits their purposes. Or they can carve a fictional geography out of a real setting, as is done in *Run Lola*

Run: 'Almost all of the film's exterior shooting was done in the streets of Berlin, but there was no effort to be geographically correct. Lola ran where it looked best for the film, not in any accurate relation to Berlin reality' ('Lola's Running', n.d.). However they go about it, authors do create a story space and readers use their understanding both of the real world and of the conventions of story in order to find ways of moving into it.

Legible environments

Talking about what makes a city memorable and possible to imagine in strong terms, Lynch describes five important elements: paths, edges, districts, nodes, and landmarks (1960, pp. 47–8). People tend to remember a well-known city in terms of paths through it, he says (1960, p. 49), especially the paths they know well and use often. Interpreting a story is a temporal act for which the idea of following a path is a helpful metaphor and we will return to this idea below. In a city, a path is a route by which citizens move from one place to another, and a node is a point where two or more paths intersect. A district may be discretely designed by architects and city planners, or it may be a more happenstance area delineated by certain kinds of usage. A landmark is often used for orientation along a path, and cities are more coherent when landmarks mark important nodes, for example. Finally an edge (such as a waterfront, or a major highway) enables city-dwellers and visitors to delimit their image of the city.

These different elements may be visible only from certain locations, or one may block or interrupt the view of another. What they have in common, however, is the fact that they all co-exist in the determinate world.

In a story world, there are no such restrictions. As we have seen with the example of *Run Lola Run*, creators are at liberty to shape their fictional world as they choose, and they may decide to invoke some or all of Lynch's markers. His terms give us ways to look at the specific spatial invitation to interpreters offered by each of the three stories here.

Run Lola Run is an obviously geographical story. Lola's path through the city is altered chronologically on each iteration but she follows the same route, and we are able to make use of specific landmarks to keep track of her progress. The nodes where her path crosses those of other characters (for example, the point where she meets Herr Meyer's car) mark specific plot pivots that vary in each incarnation. The square where Manni waits for her can be labelled a district or a node; one landmark in that square is the Spiral Bar, which provides one schematic and thematic cue to the story's organization.

Landscape is equally important in *Shadow of the Colossus*. The path is not laid out for the hero but must be discerned through use of the sword to point in a particular direction, and also through careful reading of the landscape. Players must constantly address questions to the scenery: is that a gap in the rocky wall, maybe a pass through the mountains that offers a possible path? does that river mark a definitive edge or can it be crossed by swimming? have we passed this landmark before and are we going in circles? The question of establishing the location and limits of a district is very simply answered, since a cut scene proclaims successful arrival in the district of a colossus; more general districts (the ravine, the forest) can be discerned in the landscape or on the map.

Monster, being largely set in a courtroom, would seem at first glance to offer a much less complex geography, one delineated by ceremonies and conventions as much as by physical elements. The flashbacks, however, move us into a more variegated world. The short scenes set in Steve's district in Harlem are crucial to our understanding of what brought him to the trial; the brief glimpses of Mr Sawicki's film class show us some alternative possibilities for him. And there is at least one node that is left empty for the duration of the story: the point at which Steve's path crossed or did not cross the path of the men who subsequently murdered Alguinaldo Nesbitt remains enigmatic to the end of the book.

Reading paths

Characters follow paths, but so, on a different plane, do readers.

Kress and van Leeuwen's very helpful label of 'reading paths' (1996, p. 218) is defined by Andrew Burn as 'the route the reader will take through the text, a route partly determined by the textual organization specific to the communicative modes in play' (2004, p. 11). Burn himself applies the idea of the reading path to book, film and game. Kress and van Leeuwen, specifically talking about the page, distinguish between the rectangle of print, which affords only one route in, and a more variably designed page that offers multiple pathways:

> We deliberately make a modest claim here and speak of the 'most plausible' reading path, for this type of reading path is not strictly coded, not as mandatory, as that of the densely printed page or the conventional comic strip. Different readers may follow different paths. Given that what is made salient is culturally determined, members of

different cultural groupings are likely to have different hierarchies of salience, and perhaps texts of this kind are the way they are precisely to allow for the possibility of more than one reading path, and hence for the heterogeneity and diversity of their large readership.

(1996, p. 219)

The notion of the reading path allows a way to explore the invitation offered by the text in comparative ways. The idea of multiple reading paths also gives us a convenient term for describing what readers actually do with particular texts.

It is worth noting that a reading path can also involve some fuzzy footwork with the 'geography' of the fiction. Bower and Morrow, discussing how readers create mental models of a story, suggest a metaphor of a moving and intermittent spotlight, which may not always entail a continuous line of attention: 'The protagonist's movement through space may be thought of as a shifting 'spot of light' that moves over corresponding parts of the reader's mental model' (1990, p. 45).

In *Monster*, the implied reading path entails moving between three different formats: journal entry, screenplay, and image. While the movement from journal to screenplay and back again is relatively linear in terms of the bound sequence of printed pages, readers may actually choose to skip from one journal entry to another, for example, and a codex always allows that kind of flexibility. The linear path of the story is interrupted to a modest degree in any case by the pictures (which by design invite lingering rather than forward progression); and to an even smaller extent by the over-writing on a couple of pages. Readers may choose (as did most in this study) to ignore the pictures and stick to the direct path of the words.

In *Run Lola Run*, the reading path is in some ways even more linear and in some ways something of a loop or a spiral (the latter metaphor reinforced by some of the images from the film itself, such as the Spiral Bar in the square where Manni waits for Lola). Viewers in a cinema will watch this film straight through, but they are certainly encouraged by the structure of the movie to make mental connections between different run-throughs. The participants in this study were interrupted from time to time as I stopped the film to invite comments, and on a number of these occasions they made specific references to a different prior version of an event. Nevertheless, we did not on any occasion rewind the film or browse elsewhere; our progress was always directed forwards towards the ending. It is not difficult, however, to imagine a home viewer skipping through the film to make direct comparisons between different versions of the same scene. Indeed, contemporary films and television programs often seem to rely on viewers having the capacity for home re-viewing with DVD and video; the power to pause, re-wind, fast-forward and watch again enables a form of domestic hermeneutics that contributes greatly to complete appreciation of a complex text. We did not engage in any of that kind of detailed, non-sequential explo-ration of *Run Lola Run* on this occasion (a consequence of our time constraints but also a reflection of my interest in the initial elements of *understanding* rather than the later forms of *analysing*).

Shadow of the Colossus also invites a relatively strict linear progression through the text. None of a player's actions alters the order in which the colossi are slaughtered. At a micro-level, the more skilled players in this study went down far fewer dead ends and so experienced the story in less circular and repetitive ways. At the macro-level, however, they all proceeded from beginning to end of the story in a recognizable lock step (with the single exception of the arbitrary decision for Group AB to skip two colossi and rejoin the linear progression at number 16). The colossi are significantly different from each other but the overall pattern is the same for each episode, and a successful interpretive strategy involved far less need to make *narrative* connections between episodes than was called for by *Run Lola Run*. On the other hand, most participants did make stra-tegic links between different battles, recollecting tactics that had worked on prior occasions. They also reflected on the overall patterns of destruc-tion as they considered the morality of killing these monsters at all.

Readers vary in their readiness to create their own reading paths thro-ugh a text. Some are much more obedient to the starting structure than others. Nevertheless, a convincing case may be made that many contem-porary interpreters are more open to re-casting a text since the advent of the domestic video and DVD, especially the latter with its many extra tracks pointing out the constructed nature of the movie. These partici-pants, all closing in on 20 years of viewing experience, have had many years of exposure to re-reading and re-viewing and re-playing. The DVD particularly aids the development of multiple perspectives on a story, and it seems plausible that it may contribute to the development of narrative schemas that make more room for plurality. Fifty years ago, only the book and the gramophone record came equipped with a 'replay' button, and browsing was possible but discouraged with both vehicles. The DVD mixes semiotic channels so that, for example, you can watch the story with the diegetic soundtrack or with the director's commentary – all as a matter of routine, as part of your domestic entertainment ecology. Narrative defaults are culturally constructed and it seems very likely that these members of the DVD generation would be particularly open to narrative re-working.

Reading paths through the legible environment

Games, perhaps more than the other two media being explored here, allow for a relatively blind trial and error approach. Jacob described a fairly primitive form of interpretive strategy for his computer game playing: 'Most of the time I just try stuff until something breaks through. I try to orient myself in that respect.' Most of the transcripts, however, provide examples of more sophisticated interpretive questioning that involves content as well as strategic experiment. In the conversations of the four different groups of interpreters, I found at least four different forms of consciously organized orientation:

- some interpreters stayed inside the story world, drawing on internal elements of place and time to locate themselves (Bakhtin's [1981] concept of the chronotope sheds light on this behaviour).
- some interpreters moved back and forth between assessing the characters, events and setting of the story within the narrated world and referring to the ways in which the story was presented.
- some interpreters assembled an assessment of the story in light of a more general thematic approach; themes emerged *from* the story but were also brought *to* the story by interpreters.
- some interpreters drew on genre knowledge and intertextual connections to establish preliminary expectations.

All of these approaches served to develop an initial sense of orientation. In addition, the soundtracks of film and game led to examples of what seemed to be involuntary orientation. Michael Wedel makes use of Henri Lefebvre's idea of 'rhythmanalysis' to explore aspects of *Run Lola Run*, for example, talking about how we become 'attentive to those dimensions of space, time, and subjective experience opened up by rhythms, repetitions, and intervals' (2009, p. 139). The driving pace of the soundtrack sets up rhythms of expectation from the very first moment of the movie, and was commented on by many participants.

The chronotope

A story in any medium is a temporal as well as spatial event, and some readers excelled in finding ways to use space and time together as axes of orientation. Bakhtin's concept of the chronotope (a word created out of the Greek words for time and place) describes exactly such an alignment of axes:

In the literary artistic chronotope, spatial and temporal indicators are fused into one carefully thought-out whole. Time, as it were, thickens, takes on flesh, becomes artistically visible; likewise, space becomes charged and responsive to the movements of time, plot and history. This intersection of axes and fusion of indicators character-izes the artistic chronotope.

(1981, p. 84)

Some interpreters made specific and significant use of the chronotope as an orienting guide. Here is Sebastian of Group C, for example, on the three run-throughs of *Run Lola Run*:

Things vary so it was different enough that you could tell how far along the journey was, based on what was round her. It wasn't the same thing over and over again, so even if it cuts from her to the running background you could tell how close she was to getting the money, so that helps put the time frame in perspective.

He explicitly uses space to talk about time and time to talk about space, and establishes a 'perspective' from within the story world.

Here is Sebastian again, talking about *Monster*, in terms of both time and location: 'I like how the Judge asks him how the Fourth of July was, and they talk about playing softball right in court, and the kid's up for the death penalty and they're talking about how their week-end was.'

Jarret, also of Group C, can be seen here making strategic use of the chronotope, holding the space of the film class in abeyance while he works out the correlated timeframe: 'Somebody just flashed to film classes and I haven't quite made up my mind if that is a flashback or some weird alternate storyline.'

Players were also happy to make what might loosely be classed as 'chronotope jokes'; here, for example, are Group C invoking a delib-erate clash of space and time markers in order to make fun of Jarret's 'driving' across the screen landscape:

[Jarret gallops the horse and rider across the viaduct, holding his sword aloft to look for directions]
Sebastian: Maybe you should use two hands to drive. It's like cell-phone use. 20 per cent of car accidents occur when the drivers are holding giant glowing swords in their hands.

Jacob: But 100 per cent of looking cool occurs when drivers are holding gigantic glowing swords in their hands!

In these lines, the space is the space of *Shadow of the Colossus*, the time is the time of the players, and the discrepancy is articulated in the joke – which is only funny if you register the disjuncture.

The dual focus

When I began this analysis I had a relatively simplistic sense of the import of the question, 'Where might we be going?' I imagined that having moved into the story, interpreters would be focused on the 'inside' of the story world: placing the setting, figuring out potential plot elements, assessing characters, and so forth. In fact, when I began to explore the transcripts in detail, I found many instances of dual focus, on both the story and the telling, sustained throughout all three texts; and indeed all the texts invite such an approach by the nature of their composition. A number of interpreters oscillated between the story world and the surface world of the telling, but in very purposeful ways, with the apparent intent of keeping themselves moving through the text.

As I worked through the transcripts, I was reminded of a remarkable overnight airline flight I took a few years ago from Edmonton, Alberta, to London, England, in early June. The solstice was approaching, with its 24-hour Arctic day. As we flew north to follow the great circle route to London, our flight path followed the demarcation line of constant daylight. For hour after hour as we flew east through the night, if we looked out the port windows to the North, we saw sunlight; if we looked out the starboard windows to the South, we saw twilight. Like all people who live any distance from the equator, I am used to that brief period at dusk where it is bright in the west and dark in the east, but to 'ride' the dividing line for hours was memorable.

Our plane, of course, set its path by instrumentation, but for metaphorical purposes I find it interesting and useful to imagine my pilot setting a manual course. Intrigued by the beauties on either hand, this pilot is nevertheless most significantly focused on moving forward through space.

I do not want to belabour this metaphor, but I like the idea of moving forward, navigating by means of information from two related sources, on either side so to speak. The interpreters of these three texts oscillate between the story world itself and the discourse that presents that story world, but their default priority is to move *forward* with the purpose of making sense of the text in hand. In most of the readings that are manifested in my transcripts, alternating from daylight to shadow and back again is subservient to the process of making 'straightforward' meaning (so to speak); it appears to be a tactical process much more than it seems to be a pleasure in its own right. (The plane drives ahead rather than circling between the two worlds for the sheer pleasure of the view – but that option is always open.) It is impossible to answer from this dataset the question of whether a re-reading (at least a voluntary re-reading) might be more leisurely and open to sight-seeing detours; I suspect the answer might well be affirmative. Similarly a critical perusal might well involve more side trips in one direction or another.

'Forward' progress was clearly important to all these interpreters, but other questions are also interesting. Do different interpreters navigate differently? Are individual differences distinct or do we see more of a group identity in these social interpretative exercises? What can we learn about the idiosyncrasies of the interpreters' role in setting directions? Manguel speaks of readers' ability to transform textual meaning and provides a rather daunting list of elements that may replace the automatic pilot as a reader navigates the border between the events of the story and discourse that creates these events:

> This transmigration of meaning can enlarge or impoverish the text itself; invariably it imbues the text with the circumstances of the reader. Through ignorance, through faith, through intelligence, through trickery and cunning, through illumination, the reader rewrites the text with the same words of the original but under another heading, re-creating it, as it were, in the very act of bringing it into being.
>
> (1996, p. 211)

In short, reader predilections and reader lapses are potent influences on the direction in which the story is steered.

And yet, despite the diverse potential for interpreters to go adrift, there is much agreement among them about many aspects of story development in particular cases. Group A, when asked at a very early stage of the game, could articulate links between orienting and making the step into the subjunctive world, although they naturally did not use these terms. Their conversation was interrupted from time to time by subtitled directions from the game, which apparently objected to their slow progress as they considered an external question.

Margaret: Can I just ask you. While this is going on, how much are you inside the story? How much are you talking inside the strategy of the play?

Dan: At this point in the game, I think you're still just trying
                to learn how to play it and it's more, how do I figure out
                how to do this? I think that once you get into the game
                by a couple of hours, by then you'll be more involved in
                the story, but at this point in time, it's purely problem
                solving.

Keith: You're trying what to do with this guy.

Margaret: Can I just ask you. If you compare it to the first few pages
                of *Monster* where you were reading the different kinds of
                print, is that a similar sort of thing or do you get into the
                story first?

Dan: I think it's similar, and then you're acclimating, but with
                games, I think it's different because it's combining a sort
                of manual dexterity and our problem solving at the same
                time is something else.

*(Hold up thy sword to reflect the light onto the colossus. Its
vitals shall be revealed)*

Margaret: So it's more strategic?

Dan: Yeah.

Neil: It's easier to acclimate to a book usually.

(Hero climbing up the leg)

Neil: [The game] usually involves kind of complicated move-
                ment and strategy.

(Hanging onto back of leg)

Group A also spoke retrospectively about how they oriented themselves to what is significant in *Run Lola Run*, in relation to the repeating
time-scale. Rabinowitz's rules of reading allow them to move back and
forth between the story world and the world of the telling, as we see
below:

Margaret: And yet you all seem to know how to watch this. You
                didn't have any difficulty establishing when time moved
                backwards or forwards.

Keith: Mm, no.

Dan: I thought they made that very clear.

Margaret: So what kinds of things told you?

Dan: The high use of red colouring, like when the death
                event occurred. The little conversation when they
                talked about differences in how they related to each
                other and to their relationship. I thought that actually

signified that there was something happening and then of course, you always saw the stop or the go which was the most obvious.

Keith: And the first bit of the scene is pretty much the same.

Neil: It's identical.

Keith: It's identical, so it shows.

Dan: Up to the horoscope they were talking about – Sagittarius.

In this passage, the three men are talking about notice and signification – what caught their attention and how they ascribed importance to this information. Soon Dan made use of this assessment to consider configuration – how the elements of the story might be put together:

I think the cartoon is a foreshadowing of the actual outcome because based on what she did with the guy and the dog, it affected the outcome. It was almost parallel to what happened. In the last one she was decisive so her outcome [*inaudible*] whereas the middle one she just shied away and she tripped, so of course that affected the outcome as it was a sort of foreshadowing.

The idea of foreshadowing (with its faint allusive reference to my elaborate metaphor of daylight and shade) precisely moves between the world of the story and the world of the telling. It combines the idea of '*this* is what the author is doing' with '*this* is where we might be going inside the story world'. Unlike the coarser notion of prediction, which can be developed through sheer guesswork, the idea of foreshadowing evokes what is laid down in the text itself. '*This*' is a deictic word, and its role in such thinking allows the thinker to move fluidly between the text world and the story world without stopping to specify which is being invoked.

These interpreters also moved between micro- and macro-observations. Asked to comment on the general shape of the story in *Run Lola Run*, Keith and Neil were quick with observations about how each reiteration moved towards the finale:

Keith: It seemed to get better as it went on, even though in the second one the guy dies. It seems like they get closer and closer to succeeding. Like I noticed, when that guy who got in the collision – the first time he hit him at the front, the second time he just barely and then the third time he finally didn't hit him at all until they drove off.

Neil: It depends on the character I guess. It wound up more positive for them, but the crash between the white and black cars got worse progressively.

Monster provides a singular rather than a plural account of the main action, but it is not told in straight chronological order. There are flashbacks of Steve's earlier life, which Dan and Neil found illuminating. (There were technical problems with the audio recording of this session but the drift of their comments is clear.)

Dan: I thought the flashback to his friend and that experience is interesting because it just kind of gives you an image of how he grew up. We get an idea of the dynamics behind his life and current events so we get a bit of the back story [*inaudible*].

Neil: Actually it puts it all together.

In Rabinowitz's terms, what we see here is rules of configuration leading to an initial stab at coherence.

Even with the gaps caused by the recording problems, the next extract clearly shows Keith and Dan moving between considerations of the story elements and considerations of the way it is being presented to readers in *Monster*.

Dan: You get the impression that witnesses that they're bringing up are almost to kind of discredit – I think the prosecution is bringing up credible witnesses' ... testimony. And I think that's almost a way to kind of make everyone else seem less reliable when you come back to the story later. Just so the jury [*inaudible*], so it's a pretty good method of raising doubts and what not. And then at the end, he's talking to his brother, the last part, you see the dark side, the light side [*inaudible*].

Keith: The movie part's [*inaudible*] today. Because it's in the third person. You really don't get ... exactly what these characters are actually are feeling [*inaudible*] and stuff like that. Only when he goes to a diary entry rather than some kind of [*inaudible*].

'You' is another deictic word, and Dan seems to be using it to slip between the reactions of the jurors and the reactions of the reader. Keith talks about the third person nature of the filmscript, the first person perspective of the diary entries, and the second person role of the interpreter, the 'you' who is trying to establish what characters are feeling. The deictic shifters help them slide effortlessly from inside the story world to an external perspective.

The thematic approach

Group A, as we have seen above, made use of their general understanding of how their different stories were being presented to them in order to gain some sense of orientation. They also took consistent account of what might be called the moral shaping of the stories to track movements of different characters, both literally and psychologically. The whole group regularly pondered the morality of the stories they were contemplating; it is one example of what might be called a collective signature response.

Here are some of Dan's comments, for example, on *Run Lola Run*:

- Every side-story has its own consequence within short-term and long-term.
- I think the whole movie seems to be about what effect – what are the consequences of every action and I think it's kind of like saying 'well, what if she'd done this differently? What would have happened?'
- Sort of a branch in time. All of your actions have a consequence.

The three members of Group A tackled such questions on a regular basis. This discussion is also concerned with *Run Lola Run*:

Dan: But then again, the question was about the morality [of the] original source of the hundred thousand Deutschmarks. Her outcome became progressively better, the more morality she put into her own decision regarding how to achieve that and get a hold of that money.

Keith: I don't think it was a question of morality though, I think it was just a question of the circumstance.

Dan: It was, but I think there was still a correlation between how *she* reacted and how it turned out for her.

Neil: Kind of, but I would argue that – I'm not sure, but at least for the first two, how she cut the hundred thousand was pretty much morally ambiguous.

Dan: Yeah.

Neil:　One way she held up the bank, the other way she went in the grocery store.

Dan, in particular, appreciated relatively complex morality as his account of *Monster* affirms:

> You enter into every novel with an expectation and because it was a young adult novel in this genre I thought 'happy ending' and you know, that's what you expect that he reunites with his family, they're so proud of him and happy that he didn't get caught and the lawyer's going to be happy for herself and for him and she'll wish him luck. But I think in a way, that's where this kind of diverged from being strictly a young adult novel to more of an adult novel where the realism – . And the fact is, I think the people around him had their image of him severely shaken by this whole thing, seeing him in prison, seeing him accused of this terrible crime and I think that that added a lot of realism to it for me. I think I would have had a much worse opinion of the book if that hadn't occurred.

The open question of motivation in *Shadow of the Colossus* also struck Group A in moral terms also; in this case, Neil takes the lead with his questions as Dan labours at the controls to climb up the body of a gigantic colossus:

Neil:　Yeah but we're not getting anywhere past his ass.

Dan:　I'm trying. We got there last time. It takes some time to read-just. Look at him, it's like a bear, kind of. Like a teddy bear with a big stone hand who wants to crush you.

Neil:　Why are we trying to kill them anyway?

Dan:　Because he's got the stuff that we need to make the princess come back to life.

Neil:　Yeah, I know, but what if this princess is a real bitch? [*Laughter*]

Keith:　What's the princess in *Zelda*'s name?

Neil:　Is she worth bringing back?

Dan:　Whoa, I can't believe I'm not getting hurt here.

Neil:　Yeah.

(Hops onto fur on shin)

Dan:　I'm trying to get up.

Neil:　That's the one thing with a game. There's never the back story. They want you to accomplish incredible feats –

Dan: For no reason.

Neil: Yeah! They never really – we know that this guy loves this girl and he wants to bring her back, but they haven't established any real desire to want to do it, other than that's what we need to do to get further in the story. Go around! Oh nice, ohhh!

(Falls to the ground)

This exchange mingles conversation about game play, a brief reference to a different game, and observations on the lack of back story and motivation and the consequent impact on the ethics of the game's challenge. Neil is attempting to clarify his moral stance towards the actions he is being asked to take, and using this concern to develop his understanding of the shape of the story overall.

Group A, and later Group AB, often confound Rabinowitz's idea that the rules of coherence are applied for the most part after the reading has finished. With their emphasis on the larger themes, they seem often to be looking to potential coherence as a way of establishing even the very early signposts. It seems clear that the larger questions keep them interested in the story. On the other hand, it is possible that some of Group AB's problems arise because this is actually a relatively risky strategy in some ways. If you are always backing off to look for the long shot, you may miss some of the significant details of the landscape. If your priority is always the big picture, you may become careless with some of the smaller items. If you care mainly about the themes, you may miss out on the actual story.

We will return to these questions in Chapter 7 and again in Chapter 9, as we explore some of the ways in which Group AB made less than satisfactory progress.

A moral geography

Another way to look at the responses of Group A is to consider how moral themes are built into the different stories.

Susan Brooker-Gross, discussing the *Nancy Drew* books, says, 'The use of landscape [in these books] constitutes a sort of tutelage in moral geography' (1981, p. 63). Nancy favours the suburban:

In order to receive a complimentary description, landscapes must show evidence of the actions both of human beings and of nature ... The pastoral setting – natural but managed – is Nancy's haven, her respite from the dangers of cities. Even more it is a sanctuary from the uncertain treacheries of the wilderness. Wilderness implies an absence of human management and an uncertainty of events.

(1981, p. 61)

In the *Nancy Drew* stories, a neglected front lawn is an infallible pointer to the home of a miscreant because it fails to meet the standard of 'natural but managed'.

The idea of a moral geography is very helpful in considering the responses of Group A to the moral ambiguities of the three texts under consideration. The 'hood in *Monster* is readily associated with ethical dubiousness, and the social geography of his district engages Steve in nefarious encounters with bad people. Similarly, the city in *Run Lola Run* offers both potential havens and real threats for gangsters such as Ronnie and would-be criminals like Manni (Manni loses Ronnie's money when he inadvertently leaves it behind on a train, vulnerable to theft as it crosses the city on a path that excludes him). The geography of *Shadow of the Colossus* manifests a different ethos: vast and silent, it presents both a barrier to be challenged and an atmosphere of beauty allied with a sinister emptiness. It is difficult to avoid the conclusion that something is very wrong in this land; paths, edges, landmarks all point to a haunting vacancy, an atmosphere of loss and sterility.

A moral geography offers a very particular example of Rabinowitz's idea of signification. When we see that unkempt garden in a *Nancy Drew* book, we are able to ascribe the appropriate sinister significance. But understanding this detail of signification in the *Nancy Drew* stories involves an alertness to the moral schema that is built up over the course of a series. With the free-standing texts of this project, interpreters had to build a locally derived sensitivity to forms of moral signification from first principles.

Signposts, maps and compasses: Drawing on experience

No story involving orientation would be complete without mention of maps and compasses, something that can be brought into the unknown of the story world from the outside. In many of the comments above, we may trace an implicit reference to expectations of genre (as with the moral virtues of suburbia in a children's mystery series), and generic expectations may provide some directional guidance. As Rabinowitz reminds us, expectations do not lose their power when they are confounded; so we see Dan expecting the smooth conventions of the young adult novel's happy ending and pleased to find that *Monster* offers a more jagged conclusion. We see all of Group A less than impressed with what they perceive as the convention of many videogames: a vacancy where the back story should be. We see Sebastian knowledge-able about the ways of the courtroom drama. All of these, and many more such comments, indicate that the interpreters of these stories come into the story world prepared to explore the most plausible direc-tions indicated by particular genre expectations. Yet most of the quotes above show them paying careful attention, apparently at least in part so that genre conventions do not blind them to the actual experience on offer – one hallmark of an experienced interpreter.

One of the jobs of genre is to reduce the possibilities from infinite to manageable. Umberto Eco speaks of this component of reading experi-ence using the term of orientation: '[E]very text, however "open" it is, is constituted, not as the place of all possibilities, but rather as the field of oriented possibilities' (1979, p. 76). Readers must find ways to align themselves with that field of plausible potentialities.

Specific references to other texts also offer guidance to interpreters trying to orient themselves to a new story. The transcripts supply many examples of intertextuality, not all of them strategic, and we will return to this topic later on. Some intertextual examples, however, are drawn in precisely for the purposes of orientation. Group C provide an example of an intertextual connection providing a link that led to successful orienta-tion, and, in this case, to profitable action. Jacob is at the controls.

Jarret:	See if you can jump onto that ledge and then – can you move while you're on the ledge?
Jacob:	Oh, I know what you can do.
Jarret:	Yeah, there you go.
Sebastian:	Shimmy. It's like *Zelda* except different.
Jacob:	I forgot how you do that.
Jarret:	You've got to figure out how to wall jump.
Jacob:	Yeah.
Jarret:	There you go. While still holding, press [*inaudible*]
Sebastian:	Left hand.
Jarret:	Ta da!
Sebastian:	He's good.
Jacob:	All right.
Sebastian:	This 'R1' button –
Jarret:	Here we go!

(Our hero finds the first colossus)

This gaming chatter involves two kinds of orientation, to the story and to the controls. Sebastian's cryptic and contradictory reference to *Zelda* is designed to illuminate a particular tactic, but it also draws in associations from a different story world.

Jerome Bruner's observation about the role of maps in interpretation provides an insight into how this subtle relationship ('like *Zelda* except different') helps with orientation:

> As our readers read, as they begin to construct a virtual text of their own, it is as if they were embarking on a journey without maps – and yet, they possess a stock of maps that *might* give hints, and besides, they know a lot about journeys and about mapmaking. First impressions of the new terrain are, of course, based on older journeys already taken. In time, the new journey becomes a thing in itself, however much its initial shape was borrowed from the past.
>
> (1986, pp. 36–7)

Rabinowitz's rules of signification and configuration are helpful in clarifying how interpreters draw on past experiences to help make sense of new ones.

Many elements of configuration are specific to genre, and assessment of genre contributes to how we notice signposts, thus making a strong contribution to orientation. We will consider the significance of the pretty girl in Chapter 1 quite differently in a murder mystery, a western, or a romance. But we do know, in most story scenarios, that a shaping hand is laying out events in order to make changes in the initial situation, an awareness we develop through experience of fictions.

> [E]vents have a predictive value in fiction that they do not have in life. We can experience the ebb and flow of a text – its resolutions and surprises, its climaxes and anticlimaxes – only if we assume while reading that the author has control over its shape, and that the future is *in some recognizable way* prefigured in the present.
>
> (Rabinowitz, 1987, p. 118)

An important component of configuration operates on a basis of balance and focus, especially with regard to the central consciousness of the novel (1987, p. 126). Shifts in point of view are often flagged; when they occur without warning it is usually because the author has designed 'an aesthetically significant jolt' (1987, p. 129). 'Balance works with regard to subject matter as well. Just as we usually have ways of knowing, fairly soon, who will be the main characters, so we have ways to tell what a novel is likely to be about' (1987, pp. 130–1). Our assessment of balance, Rabinowitz argues, is manifested in expectations about conventional fictions: that repetitions will continue until they are in some way blocked, that diverse strands of action will eventually be linked, that most events that are significant enough to be mentioned will produce some form of results – although cause and effect, he argues, are 'radically genre bound' (1987, p. 139).

Orientation involves deciding what kinds of expectations about balance are reasonable, and, to some extent, determines what is going to be perceived as surprising as the story proceeds.

Aligning the group response

Group C, long accustomed to playing together, were able to coordinate their comments in productive ways. Group D, all strangers to each other, consistently offered a collective signature response of diversity. Lewis was an enthusiastically immersive interpreter; Adam paid particular attention to surfaces; and Sandra was very inclined to be resistant. They brought these different tendencies to bear on their collective orientation to the stories in interesting ways. Here they are, for example, speaking about the very early stages of *Run Lola Run*, trying to assess their stance in relation to the story:

Lewis: It's good, it captivates you.
Adam: There's definitely something at stake (*inaudible*).
Sandra: It's all right.
Lewis: The crime, Manni and obviously someone's life is on the line, you want to find out what happens.
Adam: There's also a touch of the surreal every now and then with the turtle and the screaming.

Even as they take an initial turn at sorting out their initial reactions, they demonstrate different and very distinctive priorities, a collective characteristic that was repeated throughout their sessions. Thus this social interpretive occasion caused them to look for ways to orient themselves towards the text and also towards the others' responses to the text. In this ongoing dialogue they all manifested great skill in dealing with multiple deictic centres.

It could be argued that the need for this group to register each other's priorities is an artefact of the artificial construction of the project.

In fact, however, many people learn much or even most of what they understand about interpretation in social settings: when brought together in the classroom, when talking over the movie in the playground or at the bar, when clustered around a single computer screen to collaborate on a game. In collective environments, other people's interpretations may conflict or even interfere with your own, sometimes to the great detriment of your capacity to return to the immersive bubble ever again. Such interference is all the stronger when it is difficult for you to break away from interpretations hostile or damaging to your own. I will never forget the dismay of an undergraduate fan of Beverly Cleary's *Ramona* series who found herself trapped in a children's literature class discussion about Ramona's apparent attention deficit disorder. A classmate proved to be a vociferous proponent of the idea that Ramona's mother was abusive for not putting Ramona on Ritalin. The level of social interference with other readers' relationships to the characters of the series caused by this hypothesis was palpable, and very distressing to many students in the room as well as the instructor. It is difficult to 'un-think' that connection between Ramona and Ritalin; this example demonstrates how group interpretations may linger long after we might wish them to evaporate.

In the case of this project, one group provided interesting evidence of how social cross-fire can hamper collective interpretation. Group AB was the amalgamated group created when student timetables changed after the Christmas break. Dan and Neil, longtime friends, came from Group A; Keith left university at Christmas and was unavailable in the new year. Martin was the sole member of Group B able to fit in two-hour sessions at a time when other players were available. Dan and Neil are scientists and Keith is an engineer; for this and/or other reasons, they had meshed well together and we have already seen signs of the strong collective dynamic of Group A. Martin is an English major with a prior history in drama. In Group B, he was the only man, and while a study of the gender dynamics of that group is beyond the limits of this project, he seemed to have enjoyed that role.

Group AB was never really successful. At the time the three men met, each had spent approximately two hours playing *Shadow of the Colossus* within the configuration of the original groupings. Their subsequent activity was entirely game-related; we did not return to film or novel. I will discuss their lack of success at different stages of this account, but here I want to address some questions of their orientation *to each other*. Each group member came to the first meeting of the new trio with expectations established in a previous group. It is possible in the following segment of conversation from early in their first encounter to see their orientation to each other take priority over their attention to the game. They are experiencing great difficulty with colossus number 3. Dan is at the controls, and the hero has just fallen off the colossus' body and is picking himself off the ground. It is worth remembering that Martin has never met Keith, and that the other two knew him only from their three prior sessions together.

Dan:	That's within stabbing range I think.
Neil:	Yeah, oh he's going to start now; you've got to get out of there.
Martin:	[drinking water] We tried killing the colossus and I drank water out of a Styrofoam cup.
Neil:	So Keith left university?
Martin:	Here it comes.
Dan:	Keith?
Neil:	Nice guy. His name was Keith.
Dan:	Oh, Keith, right. Keith.
Neil:	Hah, you did the exact same thing I did!
Martin:	Oh, ouch.
Dan:	Yeah.
Neil:	I think you've had enough tries.
Dan:	Oh, come on, you were playing for, like, minutes.
Neil:	[*Laughs*] Just rubbing it in.
Dan:	Go ahead. [*to Martin*] What program are you in?
Martin:	No he's not swinging this time. I'm in English and writing.
Neil:	Oh okay. What year?
Martin:	Fourth but not final. I switched programs years back out of acting.
Neil:	Ohhh-kay. Fine arts. Ooh.
Martin:	I never got into fine arts. I didn't audition.
Neil:	Wouldn't acting be fine arts or no?
Martin:	Yeah, acting would have been finc arts, so I guess I was a drama major the first time.
Neil:	Ohhh – go go go – there we go – move – ugh!
Dan:	I'm attempting to.
Martin:	[*laughs*]

It would be easy to over-analyse the quotient of establishing status in this conversation; at this particular university the fine arts drama program is elite and exclusive; a very small number of students is admitted by audition every year. Drama is the more inclusive alternative, and Neil may or may not have been picking at a status question (it is very possible he had no idea of the distinction); Martin may or may not have been reacting to it. Neil returned to the subject a bit later on, and again it is difficult to assess whether he is genuinely trying to make a connection or establishing a status order:

Neil: So what are you hoping to do with your degree?
Martin: [*Laughs*] I don't know. Write a letter on the back of it, maybe.
Neil: Ah, sweet.
Martin: I'm not going to use this one.
Neil: Are you getting another one too?
Martin: Uh – no.
Neil: Oh.

It is perfectly possible that Neil thinks he is being friendly and Martin thinks he is being attacked. The need for these strangers to assess each other as they assess the project being asked of them means that many complicated assumptions were being tried out.

It may or may not be coincidence, but it is certainly noticeable that after this conversation Martin's language became stronger; although many participants talked about swearing while playing, Martin was the only one to do so regularly within the project game play, and Dan and Neil more than once mentioned to the research assistants at set-up time that they disliked this habit and increasingly disliked Martin himself.

Even before this conversation, however, before Martin and the two friends, Dan and Neil, had any real sense of each other, their lack of focus in orienting themselves towards the game's objectives began to make itself plain.

Failure to orient: Group AB

Group AB's initial discussion was about how much to use the strategy book.

Martin: You guys don't usually use the book at all?
Neil: Occasionally.
Martin: I found that for the first colossus we had to do that climbing – and in order to learn how to jump and roll and stuff like that, it was important.

Neil: Okay – we just couldn't figure out how to kill the first colos-
           sus. We had to use the book.
Martin: Yeah, we had to use the book as well, but after that it seems
           to be sort of self-explanatory.

This conversation does not seem to entail a decision to rely heavily
on the strategy guide, but from the very beginning Group AB defaulted
to the book at any point of trouble. The irony is that it really did not
help them. Here is an early sample of conversation.

Martin: [*Reading*] 'Second bridge to the left of the stone arches.'
Dan: Second bridge?
Neil: Whoa! Do not go off that!
(Hero almost gallops over the edge of the cliff)
Martin: It doesn't look like he can.
Dan: I don't know. The camera just annoys me still. There's one
           bridge there. You said the stone arches? Where the hell are
           they – I don't see them. I think this is the way to the second
           one, I don't know.
(Hero gallops across natural rock bridge)
Neil: I don't know.
Martin: You can check again [*by holding the sword to the sun*].
Neil: Yeah, check it.
Dan: I'm trying.
Neil: You can do it on the horse.
Dan: For some reason I can't.

Even with explicit instructions, none of the three can locate the stone
arches with confidence. Dan dismounts to hold the sword up and they
return to the directions of the strategy guide. Their attention is easily
diverted however. Here is the next stretch of conversation.

(Hero dismounts Agro and holds up sword to the sunlight)
Martin: [*Reading*] 'Ride along the grassy plains following the cliff
           side.'
Dan: Yeah.
Martin: And 'enter the shadowy canyon.'
(Hero back on Agro at a gallop trying to find the way)
Neil: Do the Japanese have horses?
Martin: Umh, yeah.

Dan: Didn't they get them from somewhere else though? I think they're not native to the area.

Neil: That's what I was wondering.

Dan: No they're not native to Asia there. They're European.

Martin: I think it's to the right.

Neil: Yeah, go on there.

(Enters the canyon)

Martin: The shadowy canyon.

Neil: Well this looks pleasant!

Dan: Yeah, customary scare-you-away tactic. Any tips for this one?

Martin: Yeah, 'Arrive at the misty lakeside. Swim across to a ramp.'

Even in this short extract, it is clear that these men are only half-paying attention to their surroundings, relying on the crutch of the strategy guide to substitute for their own assessment of the environment. The distraction concerning the native home of horses dissipates their focus until Martin redirects them to the right.

Other groups indulged in this kind of small talk as they galloped across the vast wastes of the game, but usually only *after* orienting themselves and establishing what they needed to do. The game features extensive periods of travelling, with plenty of scope for passing the time with chitchat. The members of Group AB, however, were much more likely than any of the others to wander from the topic even as they attempted to orient themselves. They engaged in rambling conversation and then turned to the guidebook to regroup. It was not a successful strategy, and we will return to their interpretive challenges in the next chapter.

Like other groups, at least in the early stages of their work together, Group AB develop what might be called orientation jokes, exploring the limits of the world they find themselves in.

(Swimming across the lake)

Martin: Amazing perspective.

Neil: Yeah, this lake isn't exactly clear. I never liked swimming in things that I don't know what's living in them.

Dan: Well we don't have any sea monsters here, so –

Neil: Yeah, but there could be pinworms and – a whole manner of other stuff.

Martin: I don't know if there's a dysentery function on this game.

Dan: I don't know – you are afflicted with thirty minutes of dysentery? Your strength is reduced by ten and your ability to fight is reduced by 12 or something. That would be funny.

Martin: You also require Halls Cough Drops.

Neil: [*Laughs*] Go find them.

(Reaches ramp and runs to the top)

Dan: They had something like that in Japan. They recently started selling the potions from [*inaudible*], they're selling from *Final Fantasy* and now you can buy potions in the store. They're like a beverage.

Here, the banter has a bit more purpose, allowing them to investigate, even in jest, what limits are likely to be set on the story, an essential component of orientation. It is also noticeable that this stretch of conversation happens at a *post-orientation* moment, as they are making progress in a direction already decided, rather than being distracted from making a choice.

Group AB's problems with orientation highlight the importance of this stage of interpretation. Some texts call for regular re-orientation; some interpreters find that they need to re-orient because they have lost their way. The ability to be purposeful and yet provisional, especially in initial orientation efforts, is one of those tacit skills of interpretation that is rarely taught, yet is essential to success.

We use a great deal of orientation vocabulary to talk about making sense of a text; we suggest, for example, that the text offers 'pointers' to the interpreter. Wolfgang Iser, in his famous analysis of the reading process, talks about the gaps in the text as a different kind of connector. Part of how readers orient themselves towards a text is through filling such gaps or blanks. 'Balance can only be attained if the gaps are filled, and so the constitutive blank is continually bombarded with projections', he says (1978, p. 167). In the next chapter we will look at this idea of filling the gaps in more detail.

7
Filling Gaps: Inferences, Closure, and Affect Linking

Orienting involves relatively high-level decisions about where to direct attention, and often draws on intertextual awareness. At the level of page or pixel, however, it is necessary for interpreters to flesh out the information on offer with their own supply of experience. As in so many aspects of interpretation, the top-down and bottom-up perspectives must interact and inform each other. In this chapter we look at how interpreters activate the data they are given and bring it to life in their minds.

No text provides every single possible detail about the scenes it presents. The part stands for a greater whole, and interpreters are expected to infill. 'Whenever the reader bridges the gaps, communication begins', says Iser. 'The gaps function as a kind of pivot on which the whole text–reader relationship revolves' (1978, p. 169). Elsewhere he extends this idea:

> Blanks and negations ... make it possible for the fundamental asymmetry between text and reader to be balanced out, for they initiate an interaction whereby the hollow form of the text is filled by the mental images of the reader. In this way, text and reader begin to converge, and the reader can experience an unfamiliar reality under conditions that are not determined by his own disposition.
>
> (1978, p. 225)

The reader is stimulated by gaps, according to Iser, 'into filling the blanks with projections' (1978, p. 168). Another label for this process is the making of inferences, 'the glue of narrative structure' (Lynch and van den Broek, 2007, p. 323).

Gaps, and the projections and inferences that help to fill them in, serve several purposes. The most elementary kind of gap arises when a description is simply partial and the interpreter is expected to supplement the details provided with more of the same. Iser refers to the *good continuation* principle of coherence (1978, p. 124), the closure of a *gestalt* when an image is completed in the mind.

Since no fiction can supply every single detail, a gap may be more or less *innocent*. Some are innocuous, some are playful, some are designed to be misleading, some are created to jolt the reader into heightened attention, and some are negotiated to create a situation of unclosable ambiguity. Whatever their origin, they provide readers with a way to enter their own experience into the text as part of the interpretive encounter.

Reading, as Iser reminds us (1978, p. 126), is designed for us to take another person's thinking into our own mind, yet our own mind does not evaporate under the weight of another's words. We infuse the words with life but it is partially *our own* life: we contribute the cadence of our own unspoken voicing of the words, the background details of our own world, the emotional force of our own experiences and understanding. A fusion of text and reader evolves, and we generate inferences from both our awareness of the text and our understanding of the world and of ourselves.

David Gelernter provides an interesting concept that may help us to understand the subjective and subjunctive qualities of making inferences. He speaks of affect linking – the connection of one experience to another through a mental association of a similar emotional charge. His definition of emotion includes its own subjunctive component: 'An emotion is a mental state with physical correlates; it is a *felt* state of mind, where "felt" means that signals reach the brain that are interpreted as bodily sensations, however fleeting and subtle' (1994, p. 27, emphasis in original). There are primary emotions, such as happiness or sadness. But Gelernter says we also develop compound emotions that are much more individual, that are associated with particular experiences, and that may offer a connection to a very different experience that somehow *feels* the same way.

> But these emotions are a far cry from 'happy' or 'sad.' They have two distinguishing characteristics. They are subtle. No grand passions need apply. They are *idiosyncratic*, blended to order for a particular occasion. They may contain recognizable traces of 'primary emotion' (a touch of sadness, a trace of anxiety), but these are nuanced, complicated mixtures. *They have no names.*
>
> (1994, p. 28, emphasis in original)

Our minds may make an associative leap between two apparently unrelated experiences because of the link evoked by a similar, subtle and idiosyncratic emotional flavour. Gelernter speaks of such affect linking in terms of real-life experiences recalled within a single mind that makes the association for itself. I contend further that interpreters of fiction are open to similar leaps of emotional recognition, that one mind supplies the affective link to the words of another, responding to the evocation of particular emotional charges. I may *vivify* a fictional scene with a subtle blend of emotions experienced once long ago in a different context in my own life. I may not even pause to reflect, 'I know what that feels like because' but the intuitive attribution of a complex mix of feelings brings the scene to life. In an earlier study (Mackey, 1995), I found a number of examples of readers producing such links.

Gelernter does not mention the subjunctive, but it is impossible not to make the connection when he says, '[F]or affect linking to happen, remembered feeling must be *felt*, not just dispassionately examined ... For the affect link to work, the thinker must "re-experience," *feel* his memories' (1994, p. 28, emphasis in original).

Iser's work has been available for three decades and those who are interested in reading processes have long become used to the idea of readers filling in the blanks and indeterminacies. Kendeou, Bohn-Gettler, White and van den Broek (2008) strongly suggest that the capacity to make textual inferences is common to the interpretation of a variety of media, but different media are composed by means of diverse forms of gaps and blanks that serve different ends. It seems plausible that we fill gaps and blanks with our own blend of emotional understanding as well as making other connections, and that this capacity should also be platform-neutral. What are the ramifications of this hypothesis for each of the three media being considered here?

Print

Words are perhaps the most abstract of all semiotic channels, arbitrary and referentially neutral in their physical manifestation. One set of sounds or black marks evokes one reference; a second set means something else entirely, even though in terms of their own physical attributes the two different sets of marks or sounds may strongly resemble each other.

Christopher Collins provides an interesting assessment of the implication of these abstract qualities for readers.

To put it bluntly, when we enter the imaginary space of a text, we don't know where we are. We orient ourselves only in reference to the few landmarks we are given – nouns situated in a void. These nouns are fashioned into an assumed visuospatial network by prepositions, verbs, and adverbs, but are displayed to us only in the linear, unidirectional sequence of word order. Not having actually perceived this scene ourselves, we have no peripheral field in which to detect and target an object as our next image. The fact that the speaker may be narrating events from experiential memory does not help one bit to orient us, because this is his, not our, experience: we can imitate the procedural format of retrospection, but we can never supplement another's retrospection by drawing on the contents of that person's memory. As the implied addresser several [sic] enters or reenters *his* world and names its objects, our peripheral field is as blank as the white space that surrounds each printed character and, as for our next image, that comes when and only when the text determines.

(1991, p. 151)

The author may set up these words in the white space with a view to generating individual and idiosyncratic inferences, or, alternatively, with a view to generating the kind of good continuation that actually tamps down the desire to infer anything that might cause the story to change tack from the highly predictable. Occasionally an author will be explicit about the manipulative power of these words and white spaces. Here is a very famous explication scene from the narrator of *The Murder of Roger Ackroyd* by Agatha Christie:

I am rather pleased with myself as a writer. What could be neater, for instance, than the following:
'*The letters were brought in at twenty minutes to nine. It was just on ten minutes to nine when I left him, the letter still unread. I hesitated with my hand on the door handle, looking back and wondering if there was anything I had left undone.*'
All true, you see. But suppose I had put a row of stars after the first sentence! Would somebody then have wondered what exactly happened in that blank ten minutes?
(2004, pp. 356–7, emphasis in original)?

Christie's use of the word 'blank' in this sentence is a reminder that gaps play a variety of roles, and that sometimes our facility in filling them is used against us by the author.

In the kind of novel that is told as continuous prose, the arrangement of the 'nouns in a void' provides pointers to how we should fill the gaps between them. The words alone invite us to supply our own details of setting, character appearance or nuance, and emotional quickening. In other kinds of print story, however (and, to a limited extent, *Monster* falls into this category), the design of the page also offers information of value to readers.

Scott McCloud, writing about graphic novels, points to the gutter, the space between panels as crucial: 'the gutter plays host to much of the magic and mystery that are at the very heart of comics ... [I]n the limbo of the gutter, human imagination takes two separate images and transforms them into a single idea' (1993, p. 66). We use closure, he says, to make continuous action out of separated images. In his example, a man brandishes an axe in one panel; in the next a scream echoes through city streets.

> I may have drawn an axe being raised in this example, but I'm not the one who let it drop or decided how hard the blow, or who screamed, or why. That, dear reader, was your special crime, each of you committing it in your own style.
>
> (1993, p. 68)

McCloud here is talking about a form of good continuation that attributes actions to the still image – a contribution from the reader that can only be made by inference.

Moving between image to image across the gutter invokes one kind of inference-generating closure; Lawrence Sipe and Anne Brightman draw our attention to a different kind of gap, the page turn. In a print novel, the page turn is arbitrarily established; except at chapter breaks, the main reason to create a new page is that the previous page is full. In a picture book, however, the page break is deliberately designed and, according to Sipe and Brightman, 'There is a break or gap between turning the page from one spread to the next, and this gap often requires a high degree of critical and inferential thinking' (2009, p. 74). Every page turn involves 'at least a slight rift, fissure or "aporia" (blind spot of uncertainty; Derrida, 1993) in the verbal and visual narrative when a page is turned' (2009, p. 75).

That this rift is, at least partially, filled by personal commitment to the story is understood not only by Sipe and Brightman but also (at least implicitly) by the second graders who responded to the stories that were read aloud to them in this study. Here is one charming example. The children are listening to *Don't Let the Pigeon Drive the Bus!*

by Mo Willems. The bus driver is taking a break and has asked readers to ensure that the pigeon doesn't take over.

On the fourth opening, the pigeon states, 'My cousin Herb drives a bus almost every day!' in an attempt to persuade the reader/viewer to let it drive the bus. The fifth opening shows the pigeon with its wing over its heart and the words, 'True story.' Ellen, beginning the TU [Topic Unit], commented, 'I think between those two pages there's like an invisible page *and we're on it* and we're saying, "Nuh-uh, I don't believe it"'.

(2009, p. 87, emphasis added)

Monster is neither a graphic novel nor a picture book, but it does have a graphic component, and the page breaks are rather more deliberately designed than they would be in a novel created out of continuous prose: the gaps between the journal entries and the screenplay are purposeful, the page defaced with the scrawled 'Monster,' and the image-bearing pages all call out for inference-making that does more than fill in behind the words. The readers in this project varied in the degree to which they explicitly attended to all these semiotic channels, but the spaces were there for them to inhabit if they chose.

Film

Agatha Christie's print narrator supplies a deliberately misleading example of how words can be used to create 'an interaction whereby the hollow form of the text is filled by the mental images of the reader' (Iser, 1978, p. 225). But in a movie, the images are already externally supplied. How is room created for viewer inference?

In electronic media, says McCloud, closure is 'continuous, largely involuntary and virtually imperceptible' (1993, p. 68). A film cannot present 100 per cent of the detail of a story, any more than a print narrative can. Where do we look for gaps in the world created by a movie? What kinds of inference-making are needed?

'[T]he great thing about literature is that you can imagine; the great thing about film is that you can't', says James Monaco (2000, p. 158). But Monaco qualifies that binary distinction:

The reader of a page invents the image, the reader of a film does not, yet both readers must work to interpret the signs they perceive in order to complete the process of intellection. The more work they do, the better the balance between observer and creator in the process; the better the balance, the more vital and resonant the work of art.

(2000, p. 159)

Perceptually, the viewer sees the image 'as is' on the screen. It need not be called up by the mind; it is there for the eyes to take in, with perhaps extra information being supplied by the soundtrack. Yet there are many elements to take note of; film, says Monaco,

> has its own unique connotative ability. We know (even if we don't often remind ourselves of it consciously) that a filmmaker has made specific choices: the rose is filmed from a certain angle, the camera moves or does not move, the color is bright or dull, the rose is fresh or fading, the thorns apparent or hidden, the background clear (so that the rose is seen in context) or vague (so that it is isolated), the shot held for a long time or briefly, and so on. These are specific aids to cinematic connotation.
>
> (2000, p. 162)

Viewers must infer what meanings may lie in each of these filmmaking decisions. Beyond the information of the single shot, moreover, lies the meaning of the editor's cut. A film does not have a gutter, exactly, but it does have two frames placed side by side, and the decision about what lies between the frames is supplied by the viewer.

Stephen Prince describes viewers' participation in a slightly different way, but again draws attention to the need for completion or closure:

> The viewer's participation in a narrative activates a basic operational principle of the human mind – the search for pattern. Perception and interpretation are not mechanical responses to information, but are active, goal-directed processes that organize information into meaningful patterns. Narrative activates these processes by inviting the audience to search for the overall pattern within a given narrative structure.
>
> (2001, p. 29)

Although a single shot, complete with soundtrack, holds more concrete sensory information than any abstract black mark on a page could ever do, the shots must be combined and the gaps between edited moments must be infilled by inference. But even the best inference-making must leave room for surprise; witness Jarret and Jacob very taken aback by an unexpected turn in *Run Lola Run*:

Jarret: I can't believe she got shot!
Jacob: Yeah, I didn't see that one coming.

Even this tiny snatch of dialogue indicates that they expect to make inferences and predictions but are pleased rather than dismayed that the movie is not completely predictable.

What is predictable in a story, of course, is culturally determined. The canonical expectation, described by Bordwell as 'introduction of setting and characters – explanation of a state of affairs – complicating action – ensuing events – outcome – ending' (1985, p. 35), offers a fairly singular and linear model. But many cultural factors weigh in favour of interpreters being open to more plural possibilities. Group A, for example, having watched Lola's first run through Berlin end in the red scene of death, do not hesitate to draw on a schema of plurality to help them assess what might happen next in the movie. Their schema of how a feature film tells a story clearly does not include the concept of it all being over in 20 minutes flat, so they are considering ways that the story might be extended.

Keith: I almost get the impression that she knows she's dying and she's wondering what could have happened if she'd done things differently.
Neil: Yeah. I was thinking we're going to have to watch this entire thing all over again.
Keith: She fell there so it's going to be her slower [*inaudible*] and all sorts of stuff can happen, I guess.
Dan: I think the whole movie seems to be about what effect – what are the consequences of every action, and I think it's kind of like saying 'Well, what if she'd done this differently? What would have happened?'

Their predictions of reiterated plot events are very close to the mark. My sense at the time was that they were quite happy to expect a form of story that does not adhere to Aristotle's norms; they did not speak of this possible development as revolutionary.

Different viewers will find different aspects of the film surprising or intriguing. But what viewers take for granted also plays an important role in the kinds of inferences they generate.

Game

Films 'flesh out' the story with image and sound. Games add a further physical component. Torben Grodal, in a very interesting chapter about the embodied experience of computer games, points out the significance of being able to move within and in response to the given images and sounds: '[I]n video games such activities [e.g., travelling from one site to another, shooting an opponent] often demand rather detailed cognitive maps and motor skills, and playing therefore often requires extensive training of necessary skills' (2003, p. 139). Inferences in a game, in other words, have to be acted out specifically, precisely, in detail, and in 'perceptual and muscular realization' (2003, p. 147).

Group C's approach to the first colossus includes many of these embodied inferences. They were swift to express their expectations about the game with their fingers. In this very early extract, we can see them coming to terms with how to play and how to predict based largely on what they can physically manage. Jacob is at the controls.

Jarret: You're supposed to climb him like the way you climb other objects, get on top, stab the point at his face.

Sebastian: Jump on the club. Uh-oh – you're in trouble now!

Jacob: Uh-oh! [*Laughter*]

(Colossus takes a huge swipe at the Hero with its club)

Jacob: I'm not going to lie to you – that's not good.

Jarret: Try to go up the back of his –

Jacob: Hold up thy sword.

Sebastian: See that little red flashing bar at the bottom?

Jarret: That's your health. You're about to die.

Jacob: Clearly!

Jarret: Okay, notice how he's got platforms on his back? [*Inaudible*] back in his face, back in his face, quick!

Jacob: Ahh, I got a better idea.

Jarret: Ugh!

Jacob: Uh-oh! It's time to run away – 'L1' – okay. [*to the colossus*] You're going to get climbed on.

Jarret: What are you doing?

Sebastian: Wait, I don't think he can quite step on you. Why don't you stand a little closer to his foot?

Jacob: Sarcasm aside, I am going to climb him.

Sebastian: Wow!
(Climbing onto his foot and up his body)
Jarret: Like you know, I said.
Sebastian: That's just going to piss him off.
Jacob: Okay. How do I hold up thine sword and point out thine vitals?
Jarret: It's a little late now, because you have to do it while you're in front of him, so hold down your attack button and you can do a stronger attack.
Jacob: I think that might have been a vital.
Sebastian: I think you found his Achilles heel.
Jacob: Oh that was bad. [*to the colossus*] You should be ashamed of yourself. [*Laughter*] Man, that chick better be grateful for this!
Sebastian: I think it's fur.
Jacob: I'm hoping it's fur. Climb.
Sebastian: Maybe try stabbing him again.
Jarret: No, you're almost there – at the platform.
Sebastian: You should get a jacket like that. You could like, keep your lunch in the backpack.
(Now standing on lower platform)

Group C were experienced players and moved swiftly along the learning curve of combining understanding with appropriate action. In this extract they discuss what buttons to push in what order, consider the nature of short and medium term objectives in this fraction of the game (all new to them at this point), reflect briefly on the larger plot ('that chick better be grateful'), and joke about the fantasy elements of the game (as in Sebastian's final comment about the value of a colossus jacket). This compound of layers was typical for Group C's play, though the explicit references to the buttons did abate as they moved further into the game. But Grodal reminds us that different players actually make different stories, at least to a certain extent: 'Video games are based on learning processes and rehearsals and are therefore stories *in the making*, sketches of different stories, different coping strategies' (2003, p. 147, emphasis in original). Other groups developed different compounds and although they followed the same storyline their experiences were not the same as Group C's – in part because of the physical skills they could muster, in part because of differently-based inferences.

Experiential gaps

A comparison with a different kind of literacy may clarify some of these distinctions. As a child learning to play the piano, I worked for an entire year on two books: one of easy music by J. S. Bach and one of Béla Bartók's 'Little Pieces for Children'. The overall shape of a Bach piece was familiar to me from home recordings and from church music. For Bartók, I had no such schema, and the music I produced sounded discordant and jarring, both to me and to my long-suffering family. The point of comparison is that I had to work out inferences with my fingers, had to practise *embodied* theories of what it might adequately sound like, had to assemble a 'perceptual and muscular realization' of what I was reading on the page. My piano teacher certainly played the little pieces better than I did, but Bartók was new to him too, and I do not remember it occurring to either of us to articulate a hypothesis that the short pieces should combine to create a single suite, to explore how differently each would sound if played in a sequence of the whole set.

One day, 30 years after my piano lessons had come to an end, I heard the little set of songs played properly on the radio – faster and more crisply than I had ever managed, one falling lightly after the other. It was a completely different sound from anything I had ever managed to perform (though intimately familiar to me – to my ears and to my finger muscles – from the very first note). Both my inferences about how I should play that music *and* my actual fingering skills had been inadequate to produce the delicate sounds I heard on the radio that day, and, since I had very laboriously improved (if not mastered) my rendition of the songs only one at a time (joyfully discarding each one the minute my teacher said I could move on), I had never even thought of them as a collective. Essentially, I could only imagine what I could perform, and in this case that limitation was reductive in its impact.

I am reminded of my Bartók days when I consider the physicality of working out inferences with a set of game controls. My piano playing needed to be fast, light and precise to do justice to the notes on the page (which I could 'read' perfectly well in the abstract). I needed to *practise* my inferences, not just simply take them for granted as part of the pattern, and as I practised, my powers of inference would expand along with my powers of performance.

As with playing the piano, this embodied working-out of hypotheses complicates the development of fluency in understanding the game. Not only do players have to figure out how to perform what they infer, it is sometimes the case that they can only infer what they can perform.

The surface difficulties that some of the players faced in this project as they battled to control the game serve as a reminder of how deeply we have internalized *how to perform* the reading of print and the viewing of moving images. Yet it is not very difficult to imagine a reader whose capacity to make hypotheses is hampered by the physical difficulties of decoding: just take any number of 15-year-old first-time readers of Shakespeare as an example and the point becomes clear. Such limitations shine through even more clearly when people are asked to develop a story in performative ways: invite a set of ordinary adults to produce a narrative through illustration and they will swiftly restrict the kind of story they can *tell* to the much tighter limits of the kind of story they can *draw*.

The achievement of Group AB, who struggled mightily with performing *Shadow of the Colossus*, in part because of their lack of experience in console play, provides many examples where the players' generation of inferences was curtailed by their physical limitations in handling the controls. Unlike the novice readers of Shakespeare, however, they could turn to other ways to generate inference: expectations arising from genre knowledge, cultural awareness of Japanese game design practice, intertextual hints and cues. Like the other groups, they did make it to the end of the game, however arduously. Yet without a doubt, their physical discomfort with the PlayStation2 controls restricted the kinds of inferential choices they were prepared to explore.

It is not fair to single out Group AB for all the attention in this regard. Sumana was another player who was markedly uncomfortable about handling the controls and happy to pass them over to another player at the first difficulty. Probably as a result of her modest assessment of her own capacities, she did not press her predictions except at a very general level. All the players had moments when their fingers stumbled, and, on many of these occasions, their willingness to make daring inferences correspondingly withered.

Performance may inhibit prediction; we know this restriction is also true for little children learning to read, who 'bark at print' and have no energy or attention available for broader interpretive efforts, such as understanding a complete sentence or paragraph. There was certainly evidence of such constraints in Group AB's efforts, as well as Sumana's. I suggest that their lack of automaticity in performance also distracted their imaginations for large stretches of time and limited the ways in which they were able to think about the text. We will return to the implications of such struggles in Chapter 8.

For many interpreters, their reading and viewing skills function at a much higher level of automaticity than their playing skills. Attention paid to the physical complications of managing the controller is attention not available for making observations and inferences, yet inference-making is crucial to the creation of a satisfying story. But this scenario, though perhaps commonplace, does not represent the only possibility for skewed expertise. I once taught a young woman who watched a phenomenally large number of British soap operas (I specify the national origin because British and American soap operas work on quite different conventions). She presented an interesting example of the power of experience to lead to the kind of automaticity that frees up attention. Given a literary work to assess, she laboured to produce even a sketchily plausible assessment of motivation, but, discussing her soaps before and after class, she revealed striking powers of social observation and a deep understanding of the nuances of relationships and behaviours. Her inferences about soap opera characters were subtle and grounded in a profound familiarity with the settings in which these characters operated and the particular conventions of that genre of story-telling. Nevertheless, she was not able, or it did not occur to her, or she thought it inappropriate to transfer these skills to a school setting and a print work of literature. Interpretive capacities may readily cross media boundaries but that transfer does not invariably occur. Sometimes interpreters may judge that their interpretive experience does not provide the correct kind of cultural capital that is worth importing, a case where educational assumptions may actually be damaging.

Gaps between story and discourse

This chapter has focused on the small gaps, the shortfalls where no amount of telling or showing can provide a complete picture and interpreters must supply their own closure of images, schemas, *gestalten*. Some gaps are larger and more deliberate; they represent ways in which the plot is shaped out of the available information about characters and events: the distinction between story (the events themselves) and discourse (the telling of them).

The discourse of a story need not simply be expressed in words. Where multiple semiotic channels are at work, gaps may arise between different elements of the same story: between what the music tells us and what the images tell us, between the content of the subtitles and the information conveyed by the actors' voices and demeanour, between the appeal of the beautiful landscape and the forward compulsion of the quest challenge.

The time of the story and the time of the telling are not the same. As Teresa Bridgeman says,

Whatever the temporal patterns set out within fictional worlds – whether they are those of a nineteenth-century novel that moves toward a defined and anticipated ending, or whether they are those of a postmodern narrative operating by disjunctions, loops, and effacements – it is inescapable that these patterns will be set against the reader's *temporal experience of the text*, founded on memory and anticipation. And the reader's attempt to relate these two kinds of temporality will be an important part of the effect of the text.

(2007, p. 54, emphasis added)

Meir Sternberg expresses the challenge in these terms:

In or out of language, narrative uniquely entails the concurrence of two temporal sequences: that in which events happened and that in which they unfold, the dynamics of action and of its narration, represented and communicative time, in short ... [T]he action or event line hinges for its telling and reading and very narrativizing on communicative time ... Narrative therefore uniquely lives, I argue, not just in or over time but *between* times, and so do we readers, hearers, viewers, throughout our processing of it as such.

(2003, pp. 326–7, emphasis in original)

Sternberg speaks of the larger gaps created by the duality of the two time sequences and labels the three main categories as suspense, curiosity, and surprise. These larger, structural gaps help to sustain our interest in the story over the long term, and it is to this territory of the long haul that I now turn.

8
Making Progress or Making Do: The Unconsidered Middle

The middle parts of a story don't always get as much respect as the beginning and the end. Even Rabinowitz's rules of notice privilege openings and closings; if we pay special attention to these marked elements of a text, is there a kind of 'unspecial' attention that we devote to the middle? Crago (1982) noticed that his annotations fell away as he became engrossed in the mid-stages of *A Chance Child*. I noticed the same phenomenon as I flagged my own personal reading of *Dangerous Spaces* (Mackey, 1993). Victor Nell, hoping to explore deeply engaged reading, asked his participants to read at least the first 50 pages of a book to establish that they truly liked it before bringing it along for the research project (1988, p. 103). As we move deeper into a story, it may well be that the need to be continuously on the alert and to be actively making connections devolves into a more unconsidered kind of absorption and obliviousness, and a focus on the gathering momentum towards an ending.

Although this mid-to-later stage of engaging with a story is not as interesting to observe from the outside as the earlier stages of establishing the story world, it is often the part a person remembers in a large sense as the *experience* of the book or film or game. At least some readers find, paradoxically, that it is also the part of the story about which they remember the smallest number of particular details, which may indicate that they have engaged most aesthetically (in Rosenblatt's sense of in-dwelling) and least efferently (in terms of taking information away) with this section of the narrative. This phase of the experience of the story is where interpreters establish or fail to establish some payback for the effort of 'being out and stepping in'. It is helpful to the feeling of successful connection if there are positive ingredients in the experience: curiosity aroused and satisfied; surprise as an antidote to the repeated and the predictable; suspense and its associated emotions about the possible outcomes; and pleasure in the whole achievement of being absorbed in another world.

Meir Sternberg addresses the first three ingredients in that list, curiosity, surprise, and suspense, as the 'three master interests that constitute the universals of narrative' (2003, p. 327), and says they arise from the gap between the events and the telling.

> *Suspense* arises from rival scenarios about the future: from the discrepancy between what the telling lets us readers know about the happening (e.g., a conflict) at any moment and what still lies ahead, ambiguous because yet unresolved in the world. Its fellow universals rather involve manipulations of the past, which the tale communicates in a sequence discontinuous with the happening. Perceptibly so, for *curiosity*: knowing that we do not know, we go forward with our mind on the gapped antecedents, trying to infer (bridge, compose) them in retrospect. For *surprise*, however, the narrative first unobtrusively gaps or twists its chronology, then unexpectedly discloses to us our misreading and enforces a corrective rereading in late re-cognition. The three accordingly cover among them the workings that distinguish narrative from everything else, because they exhaust the possibilities of communicating action: of aligning its natural early-to-late development with its openness to untimely, crooked disclosure.
>
> (2001, p. 117, emphasis in original)

Whether or not Sternberg's three categories do exhaust the full possibilities of story and discourse, his large-picture account of readers' attention to gaps between the time of the events and the time of the telling does help to account for what fuels the interest of interpreters through the length of the story. Other theorists may help to fill in the smaller scale of actions that interpreters pursue.

Being in and moving through

Judith Langer's description of the state of 'being in and moving through an envisionment' sums up some of the sense of pivoting between understanding *enough* to move forward relatively effortlessly and not understanding *everything* so that there are still points to be curious about. 'In this stance', she says,

> readers are immersed in their own understandings, using their previously constructed envisionment, prior knowledge, and the text itself to

further their creation of meaning. As they read, meaning-making moves along with the text; readers are caught up in the narrative of a story.

(1991, pp. 8–9)

How do readers 'move' their meaning-making along with the text? Rabinowitz's rules of configuration supply some answers to this question. 'Rules of configuration', he says, 'govern the activities by which readers determine probability' (1987, p. 112).

Rabinowitz speaks of the two meta-rules of configuration: 'First, it is appropriate to expect that *some*thing will happen. Second it is appropriate to expect that not *any*thing can happen' (1987, p. 117). Sandra, of Group D, sums up the abstract version of these meta-rules at the beginning of *Run Lola Run*: 'It's going to go wrong. It has to, or else there wouldn't be a movie.'

By the middle stages of a story, readers have probably established some information about that *some*thing, and have eliminated large numbers of possibilities so that the overwhelming need to understand the '*not-any*thing' limits of the story is somewhat under control (though in a successful story, the delightful prospect of still being surprised remains open).

Observing progress

Progress through the middle stage of a story – that most intense, absorbed and 'quiet' stage of interpretation – is difficult to capture. In this project, I used tactics from the simple to the semi-sophisticated to probe some of the underlying actions that enabled these interpreters to make headway through their stories. The challenge was to find ways of gaining access to responses that are simultaneously absorbed and very fleeting. I tried a variety of methods, all of which, in their different ways, offer oblique insights through the kinds of minimalist observations that offer as little interference with the ongoing interpretation as possible.

With the film, I could find no way of gaining insight into the interpretive efforts without pausing the movie to talk about it. In this chapter, I investigate Group D's explicit comments at some of these stopping-points for insight into their very varied responses. I explore the utility of more subliminal measures for the game and the novel, one using sophisticated technology and one making very old-fashioned use of paper slips and manual counts. Although one approach looks more scientific than the other, in fact they are probably both equally quick and dirty. Using the analytical software Transana to assess and code the technical talk relating to *Shadow of the Colossus* enabled me to explore Group C's gameplay and provide a visual account. With *Monster*, I turned to the other end of the technological spectrum of data collection, and asked readers to attach a sticky note to any page that attracted their attention; then I counted and collated their responses. Finally, I undertook a preliminary exploration of Group AB's ineffectual gameplay to see if it cast any oblique illumination on the face of successful progress.

The methodologies are diverse but the results show some common ingredients, and I believe they do shed some light on some interpretive behaviours at the heart of the story, the territory least well explored by most standard forms of analysis. I make no claim for the detailed reliability of my observations; the value is approximate at best, and all the evidence represents one group of people meeting one particular text in the context of one specific and artificial set of circumstances. Nevertheless, these findings do suggest that the individuality of interpreters persists through this most unconsidered part of the process and give rise to some useful questions about what we miss when we take this activity for granted.

Run Lola Run

Group D present a reiterating image of diversity as they progress through the story. Overall, as they move through *Run Lola Run*, for example, Lewis spends more time than the other two inside that story world. Sandra remains resistant and Adam continues to look at the techniques by which the story was told. These patterns repeat throughout the project. Their final reactions as the film comes to an end represent one iteration of the pattern.

Lewis: I really liked it. I thought it was awesome. I like the – I don't know, it fascinates me – everything I didn't get. The little changes the director does.

Adam: It's almost worthy of the cult status it has, but it was – it wasn't bad.

Sandra: I don't know. I wasn't totally impressed, I won't lie. [*giggles*] I think anyone can write a script like that and make it work out pretty good, you know.

Adam: It actually seemed kind of clichéd.

Sandra: I know.

Adam: Like, I saw *Sliding Doors* a little while ago and they had the same kind of thing except they called them parallel, at the same time.

> Lewis: I still think – I don't know – it doesn't matter what the story is. I still like seeing everything come together like that.

These different stances as they progressed through the story led them to some acute calculations of configuration. At the end of the first round of Lola's dash through the city, I asked them what they thought would happen next, and their answers were astute. Like Group A in the last chapter, they were swift to grasp the potential for plurality.

> Adam: Almost a rewind like this was *one* outcome.
> Sandra: Yeah.
> Adam: Like if she was late there, if the guy stole a moped there, [it] made that happen.
> Lewis: Yeah it changed something about [*inaudible*].
> Adam: Yeah, like even if it's just anything.
> Sandra: The song that they're playing is like 'what 24 hours can do' or something.

Accumulating evidence from various sources in the movie, tracking the events and anticipating new ones, and pooling their insights at the moments when I asked them to articulate their responses, they continued to react in very diverse ways. Here is another excerpt from their conversation at the end of the second section of *Run Lola Run*; Manni has just been hit by the ambulance, precisely at the moment when it seemed as if he and Lola would succeed.

> Lewis: It sucks.
> Margaret: What's the matter with it?
> Lewis: Well I don't know, she had everything going, had the money – a couple of the steps – good – it's done.
> Sandra: I thought it was kind of funny. [*laughter*]
> Lewis: What, that he got hit?
> Sandra: Yeah because you know, of course something had to happen. It's funny though.
> Adam: You were sort of expecting something. As soon as he started crossing the street –
> Lewis: Yeah.
> Adam: I started tensing up.
> Sandra: Yeah and it made it even funnier that it's the ambulance that hit him.

Adam: The same poor bastard.

Sandra: Yeah. Not a very good driver. [*laughter*] So then next time, because I think they're going to do it again – maybe – who knows, time that is here. I wonder who's going to die next. [*laughs*]

Lewis is emotionally involved; Sandra is detached; and Adam is on the lookout for patterns. Adam, who consistently remained vigilant to surface indicators, nevertheless reminds us how much of progressing is anticipating and how much of anticipating has an emotional quotient even for a relatively detached viewer: 'You were sort of expecting something. As soon as he started crossing the street I started tensing up.'

Shadow of the Colossus

Shadow of the Colossus is not a game where your toolkit is necessarily increased, improved, or refined as a reward for progress through the game. To the end, the hero is equipped only with sword, bow and arrow, and horse. Many players devoted much effort to making the approaches to these tools automatic. What divided successful players from those who struggled was a two-fold capacity. The first was the ability to get rapidly to the point where they thought of the tools in terms of their *fictional* use (for example, holding up the sword) more than the real-world physical requirements of which buttons to push in what order (for example, pressing the circle button while aiming and focusing with the left analog stick). The second was the power to look at the pixellated screen landscape and see meaningful alternatives that they could align with the coded guidance of the Delphic voice and with their developing understanding of the game patterns. In a way, these were two sides of the same challenge: to see 'through' the controller buttons and the array of screen images to a meaningful fictional world where meaningful actions were the focus of attention and progress could be assumed rather than fought for.

Polanyi has provided a memorable analogy for the whole idea of 'looking through', referring to the idea of using a probe to explore the back of a cavern.

Anyone using a probe for the first time will feel its impact against his fingers and palm. But as we learn to use a probe, or to use a stick for feeling our way, our awareness of its impact on our hand is transformed into a sense of its point touching the objects we are exploring ... We

are attending to the meaning of its impact on our hands in terms of
its effect on the things to which we are applying it.

(1983, pp. 12–13)

Polanyi's metaphor applies directly to the manual function of the game
controller, but it applies also in more analogical ways to the movement
'into' a book or a movie. The game, however, never fosters a complete
yielding to the story. Paying attention to the controls remains important (though none of these players ever needed to look directly at the
controller they held in their hands), even as players move 'through'
into conversation bounded entirely by the story world. The twin challenges of first locating and then slaying each colossus require some
explicit attention to the controller.

Transana offers the capacity to represent coding in graphical terms,
and the line graph of Group C's 'button talk' gives some indication of
the ebb and flow of how they approach complete immersion in the
story. 'Button talk' is a sub-category that refers to any reference to the
controls, whether serious or joking. Although, as one might expect,
it predominates most significantly at the start of the game, it never
entirely disappears. But some of the references that shape this graph are
clearly part of Group C's aesthetic experience of the game, rather than
just a switch of their attention to process. They take pleasure in teasing each other over finesse or the lack of it in managing the controls;
'hold R1' starts as a real instruction to the player, but gradually becomes
a joking catch-phrase of their play. Jarret says that telling people to hold
R1 would be 'something that we incorporate into the future games we
play ... We'll just be playing and someone is going to say, "Remember,
hold R1."' Jacob contributes a line of mock dialogue: 'But I'm playing
an X-Box – *Hold R1*!' In the battle with the first colossus, we can see the
first mentions of R1 as a serious instruction: 'To mount him faster, jump
towards him and press the R1.' And later, 'R1. Oh, that's R1, maybe
that's R1.' By the third and fourth colossi, the tone has turned sardonic:
'He's probably like, "Maybe I should press 'R2' and surprise them!"' 'To
quote a good friend of mine, R1!' The eighth colossus brings forward the
command, 'Find thine foe and stab. R1!' By the eleventh colossus, Jarret
is being regularly teased: 'Now Jarret you want to hold R1.' Fighting the
final colossus leads to sarcasm: 'Now remember Jarret, hold R1. Actually,
I think let go. Let go of R1.'

Other forms of button talk also turn frivolous. 'Press thine X button', says Jacob during the fight with the eleventh colossus. And by
the end, 'Okay, so X is demon breath, square is smashy-smashy.' As late

as the eleventh colossus, however, there is still straightforward talk to help manage the controls: 'No, no, you press the triangle to get off the horse.' 'So when you jump, do you press crouch and jump?'

The following graph sorts these references colossus by colossus. It should be read with caution as it presents an misleadingly 'scientific' picture of the gameplay experience, but it does give an indication that the need to pay attention to the nuts and bolts of keeping the game moving never entirely vanishes into the domain of the automatic pilot, even at the points where players are deep into the gameworld.

Figure 8.1 presents some significant information about how readily the skilled players of Group C adapted to the specific commands of this game. The steep drop in the graph between the third and fourth colossi represents their breakthrough from initial attending and orienting into the kind of progressing that continues relatively steadily to the end of the game from the fourth colossus onwards. References to R1, both serious and joking, mirror the rise and fall of the general button talk (and it is worth noting that they are already making R1 jokes as early as the battle with the third colossus) and comprise a large proportion of the technical conversation for the major part of the game. The need to establish and remember what the controls accomplish is turned into part of the social experience of the game, as the bottom line of the joke references indicates.

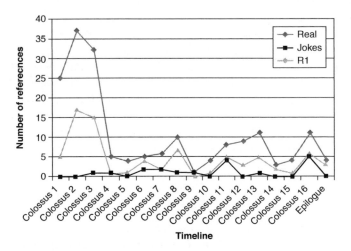

Figure 8.1 'Button talk' in Group C's game of *Shadow of the Colossus*

(A numerical table of the exact tallies that created this graph can be found in Appendix 2.)

This figure presents some significant information about how readily the skilled players of Group C adapted to the specific commands of this game. The members of Group C were also adept at combining their jokes with strategic observation. As they spotted the giant ramp that they needed to climb to find the third colossus, Jacob said, 'This colossus is wheelchair-accessible for your convenience!' It was a passing remark, apparently made for its entertainment value, but when they did locate the third colossus, they discovered they needed to climb his club as it crashed at an angle into the ground. 'Wheelchair-accessible', remarked Sebastian, and a minute or two later, Jacob was able to observe a pattern: 'This monster's all about platforming. Getting off here was a practice run to get to him.' Recognizing that the approach to a colossus might involve a dry run of the skill set that would later be helpful in bringing it down allowed the players to attend more carefully to the initial stages of making contact with colossi, with obvious improvements to their efficiency. The joke helped them focus their play.

Momentum and accountability

As we saw in Chapter 1, Chittenden and Salinger with Bussis define reading in terms of a process that involves both momentum and accountability (2001, p. 44). Cycling offers an apt parallel: a bicycle rider needs to pay attention both to the need to move forward and to the need to stay upright. An interpreter, similarly, must move forward through the text sufficiently smoothly and rapidly to make macro-sense of where the text is going, while at the same time paying at least a certain amount of attention to decoding and making accurate sense of the story at the micro-level of letters and words, or controller buttons. Achieving a balance between momentum and accountability in interpreting can involve a certain amount of personal preference, but both components need to be managed.

In the timeline of Group C's button talk, we can see a surprisingly vivid graphic representation of momentum and accountability also at work in the interpretation of the game. The left-to-right achievement of the top line marks the progress from one colossus to another. The up-and-down variation of that line reminds us of the players' need to attend to the micro-details of the controls. The R1 line starts off as a monument to accountability but the players' 'R1' references gradually become a feature of the forward momentum, and the jokes show them creating and enjoying the space between the need to move forward and the need to pay heed. The jokes also enabled them, from time to time, to look at the game from a surface rather than story-world perspective, and it seems arguable that this stance helped them to observe patterns that they then used to organize their play.

Group C's facility for noticing patterns that improved the efficiency of their play seems to me furthermore to involve a slightly different kind of interaction of accountability and momentum. They develop accountability on a larger scale, trying to make sense of and be true to the overall shape of the story and to the conditions of its platform. There are many examples of them applying ideas that Rabinowitz would describe as the rules of coherence, trying to make the best story possible. Rabinowitz describes the processes of coherence as 'retroactive' (1987, p. 140), but in this case and some others we see Group C looking to ideas of coherence to bootstrap them forward through a starkly story-reduced zone.

In some cases the three men combined their larger observations with joking. This conversation occurred during the pursuit of the seventh colossus:

Jacob:	Get on thine horse.
Sebastian:	There we go.
Jarret:	You don't have to summon him, he's right there.
Sebastian:	I just wanted to be sure of the button.
Jacob:	Maybe it's someone else's black stallion.
Sebastian:	Yeah, you've got to be careful.
Jarret:	Because there's *so* many other people around.
Sebastian:	Well –
Jacob:	Do you see another hero on a different channel? 'What are *you* doing here?'
Jarret:	You have some other heroes slaying colossi. 'Don't worry, you don't have to kill all 16. I already got four.'
Jacob:	'I'm with the Colossi Preservation Society – someone's been killing my colossi. Ahhh –'
Jarret:	Where's the horse?
Sebastian:	'Colossi are an endangered species. There's only 16 known in existence.'
Jacob:	'And someone killed six of them! What heartless person would do that?'

Sebastian:	'We've been trying to reinforce the population through captive breeding, but we've been meeting with limited success.'
Jarret:	Captive breeding! (*Laughter*)
Jacob:	That's another issue altogether, man. (*Laughter*)
Sebastian:	Save the colossi.
Jacob:	Yeah, for all we know, you're causing irreparable environmental damage.
Jarret:	Ooh – which way are you going?
Sebastian:	I don't know! The horse is taking me this way.
Jarret:	Yeah, but it is a dead end.
Jacob:	I'm telling you, you've got to show that horse who's boss, otherwise he'll just push you around.

It is worth noting the way they combine specific, local accountability to the management of the horse with larger references to the game's presiding amorality in the slaughter of the colossi to achieve one individual's personal goal – and how they coach these concerns in the joke of their mock dialogue. They returned to this question more specifically after they killed the ninth colossus.

Jacob:	Maybe the story will develop a little more this time.
Sebastian:	Yeah, so far it's pretty much been, just go forth and slay.
Jarret:	Do you need any more story?
Jacob:	I do. I don't think it took too long [*looking at the time record for the slaughter of the ninth colossus*]. 3:44 – 4:10. Yeah, that was a twenty-minute monster. Twenty-six-minute monster.

Jacob's rapid turn from the absence of story to the more competitive territory of how long it takes to kill a particular colossus is striking. It was clear throughout the game that ideas of 'progress' were multifaceted for this group of players. Yet the idea of the wantonness of the slaughter kept recurring, most often camouflaged in the form of humour. The twelfth colossus had to be mounted and then driven by means of striking his horns to steer him (the ultimate aim was to force him off a cliff). This activity gave rise to the following dialogue as they rode the monster:

(Driving the colossus once more)
Jarret: We should keep him as a pet. I don't want to kill him.

Jacob: Yeah, neither do I! How fun would it be to go running
             around the countryside in this thing?
Jarret: What are you up to, Jacob?
Sebastian: I'd put in seatbelts.
Jacob: As would I.
Sebastian: Maybe a roll cage.
Jacob: One heck of a roll cage.

Their capacity to joke with both the details and the larger pattern fuelled their momentum through the story and offered an oblique form of
accountability.

Monster

With the novel, I collected a different kind of data. As the participants
read the book, at first with me and then later at home, I asked them to
flag with sticky notes any page of *Monster* that caught their attention.
I collected their flagged books at the end of their reading and labelled
them with their pseudonyms.

This activity of flagging is worth some attention in its own right.
It represents a very rough and ready form of research, but as Martin
Heidegger reminds us, 'all the sciences concerned with life ... must necessarily be inexact just in order to remain rigorous' (1977, p. 120). In
exploring the 'unconsidered middle', I wanted to find a way to tap into
automatized forms of behaviour. Too much stopping to reflect interferes
badly with unconsidered behaviour; I was hopeful that adding a sticky
marker on the fly would represent the smallest possible interruption of
readers' usual behaviour.

Appendix 3, on page 241 presents the information provided by the
flags, in all its bald minimalism. I expected that the stickies would pre-
ponderate at the beginning of the story, with a few to mark some closer
attention towards the end. The placement of multiple flags does indeed
follow this pattern, but the single flags, marking a pointer chosen by
only one reader, persist relatively evenly throughout the whole book. Of
the 274 content-bearing pages of the book (281 minus 7 blank pages),
129 were flagged by *at least* one reader. All page numbers refer to the
paperback edition.

The dispersal of the flags merits attention. Eleven readers made at least
some use of the sticky notes (Keith did not). Only one page attracted as
many as six flags: page 24, the page defaced by the scribbled repetition
of the word 'MONSTER', three crossed out and three still unmarked.
Five pages were marked by five readers, and four of these were right

at the beginning of the book, as might be expected. 65 different pages were flagged by *only* one reader, with these stickies distributed more or less evenly throughout the book. The pattern of distribution for the 30 pages marked by two people is similarly spread out.

There was not time for a detailed debriefing from each participant, and there is a very good chance, given the time frame of the home reading section of the project, that they would not necessarily have remembered what impulse triggered the placing of any given flag. It is impossible, therefore, to glean much more information from this distribution, but it is worth noting that readers are idiosyncratic rather than simply obedient to the author's directions. It is hard to imagine how Myers, with his crossed-out 'Monster's, could have made page 24 a more vivid invitation to pause at least for a second and consider the implications of the page's design. It is of course perfectly possible that the six readers who did not put a flag on the page were so busy noticing that they forgot to place their tag, and I do not want to belabour the implications more than they will bear. The extensive distribution of single markers, however, does provide a bit more positive evidence that readers are bringing their own priorities to bear on the interpretation of the novel.

It is important not to read this table as more scientific in origin than it really is. A few observations are nevertheless in order. It is worth remembering that the participants read as far as page 58 in the 'experimental' conditions of the collective session. With two exceptions, all the pages flagged by four or more readers fall within these first 58. Page 281, marked by four readers, is the final page of the story, and displays, in the journal format, the core question of the story: why did Steve's lawyer turn away from him after he was acquitted? As the last line of the book queries, in very large font, 'What did she see?' (Myers, 1999, p. 281)

Page 214, marked by five participants, provides a different window onto these readers. It is a screenplay sequence, and starts off in the court; but partway down the page it cuts to a single paragraph of flashback to the film class in school. The end of the page moves back to the courtroom, showing instruction for a split-screen image of Steve and his lawyer.

It is very tempting indeed to think of these five flags on page 214 as marking a different kind of 'button talk'. Readers had to disrupt the flow of their mental imaging of the court sequences in order to take account of this brief change of venue and the implications of Mr Sawicki's instructions to 'keep it simple' (Myers, 1999, p. 214). 'When you see

Table 8.1 How individual readers marked the three stages of *Monster*

	beginning (pp. 1–58)	middle (pp. 59–200)	end (pp. 201–81)	total # of flags
Dan	7	8	3	18
Keith	0	0	0	0
Neil	9	3	3	15
Martin	25	17	11	53
Sumana	15	15	9	39
Tess	27	16	9	52
Jacob	0	0	2	2
Jarret	10	3	0	13
Sebastian	2	0	0	2
Adam	15	19	15	49
Lewis	6	3	2	11
Sandra	7	9	11	27

a filmmaker getting too fancy', Steve's teacher tells him, 'you can bet he's worried either about his story or about his ability to tell it' (Myers, 1999, p. 214). Is the subsequent split-screen a hint to readers to be wary of Steve's trustworthiness? Did any of these readers placing their sticky marker on the page pause to consider such a question? It was not possible to debrief in such exhaustive detail that this second question can be answered, but it is clear that a number of readers did in some, perhaps very fleeting way accept the need to take note of the shift in focus. It is not an exact parallel to 'hold on to R1', but it is a recognition of the fact that their control of the story is being shared with the author, and that to some extent they are obliged to follow where he takes them.

The long list of pages flagged by a single reader calls to mind Bower and Morrow's metaphor of the moving spotlight rather than a continuous line of attention (1990, p. 45). As with the button talk, there is a little trace of interpreters 'checking in' with the text. In some ways, the imprecision of the information provided – some reader marked this page because it struck him or her in some way – actually accords with the vague and fleeting way we take account of the individual words on the page as our 'meaning-making moves along with the text' (Langer, 1991, p. 9).

A different way of exploring this information set is to look at the behaviour of individual readers (see Table 8.1). Rather than laboriously display every page marked by each reader, I have roughly divided the book into three sections. 'Beginning' includes pages 1–58, the pages actually read in the group setting. 'Middle' is the biggest section, from page 59 to page 200; it is an arbitrary divide but page 201 does mark the point at which Steve's lawyer becomes more pessimistic about his case so it is perhaps reasonable to consider it as the stage at which the endgame of the story begins. 'End' includes from page 201 to page 281.

The variety of reader behaviours is demonstrated sharply in this chart. From Martin, Sumana and Adam, who respectively added 53, 52 and 49 flags, down to Jacob, Sebastian and Keith, who inserted 2, 2 and 0, we are looking at very differentiated use of the sticky notes. It is, of course, such an artificial way to respond to a book that I do not want to dwell on the significance of these listings too heavily. The number of times that readers might legitimately have added a sticky but simply forgot to do so is the invisible variable in this chart. However, I will take the risk of a brief look at patterns: Neil, Martin, Tess, Jarret, Sebastian and Lewis all started more attentively and added fewer stickies each time they progressed from one section to the next. Dan, Sumana, Adam and Sandra marked their attention in a more continuous line throughout the book, although Dan and Sumana tapered off towards the end, and Sandra increased steadily as she progressed towards the last page. Jacob added his two stickies right at the end of the book, and it may well be that he simply remembered at the very last moment that he was supposed to have been doing this all along.

Deficient as it is in rigour, the chart does demonstrate the important finding that readers do not behave either predictably or neatly as they make headway through the story. It was apparent from the post-reading discussions of *Monster* that, whatever method of attending they favoured, all the readers had made enough meaning out of the book to hold an intelligent conversation with me and also with each other – which is in itself remarkable, given the diversity of forms of attention displayed in this table.

Surface and flow

These tables, with all their deficiencies, shed some small light on issues of accountability. Momentum is harder to track; by definition you interrupt its flow to talk about it. Not surprisingly, therefore, some of the most interesting talk about how the interpreters moved from surface inspection to the development of an ongoing story in their heads came retrospectively. Group A and Group D provide some interesting contrasts in their discussion of reading *Monster*; all these comments came in the third session, and followed conversation about the content of the story, the enigma of Steve's guilt or innocence, and the role of the court officials. I deliberately switched the discussion to the activity of reading a book that alternated between first person narration and screenplay. Here is Group A, discussing their reading processes. I asked them to describe how they responded to the book at home.

Neil: At first the format was a little bit aggravating, just because it wasn't quite what I was used to. By the end that had really gone away. I didn't actually mind it. Once I got used to it I could pretty much visualize what was happening, similar to the way that another novel is laid out. It worked okay....

Dan: Yeah, definitely, it was almost as if you were able to read it as a stream of consciousness. At least for me, initially it was disjointed and you could see – now he's thinking, now he's writing. Eventually – obviously you visualize what you read, and I think for me it became much more tangible because you could kind of see it playing out.

Group D, as usual, took varying approaches to the complexities of reading *Monster*. In discussing the layout, the readers made it plain that while they might notice the distinctive page layout of this book, their reading processes absorbed the content in differential ways. Adam processed it more or less as written: 'I kept on reading it as a screenplay. I couldn't reconfigure it in my head as a book.' Lewis continued with his strongly visual approach: 'I definitely just turned it into a picture in my head of what was going on. And the camera angles and everything just became a part of what was going on in my head.' Sandra, however, seems to have converted the words into the equivalent of continuous prose, eliminating all stage directions.

Sandra: Oh see now, I adapted to it. Maybe it's because I don't really read screenplays ever, so.

Margaret: So you just turned it into a story?

Sandra: Yeah. Because that's what it is ... I never really read the camera angling anyways. I just kind of skipped over it [*giggles*] because I didn't really understand exactly what it meant, so.

Descriptions of momentum

Similarly, Group B found ways to make the story flow smoothly before their eyes, being converted into a mental world that they could readily access.

While the tables give an artificially precise snapshot of accountability at work, Group B provided an interesting gloss on the concept of momentum.

Martin: There was a period where for about 45 pages I didn't make a note. I was absorbed in part of the trial with his testimony and stuff like that.

Tess: I think I definitely sped up as well. I'm looking at it, you can see the cross-section of my book [*referring to the attached stickies*], but I finished the book. It was evil paper week [*referring to class assignments*] so I'm going to read it, I'm going to sit down in an armchair and finish the rest of the book, so I did with a cup of tea and read the book, but I definitely found myself slowing down a lot less, possibly because I had a goal in sight and the goal was the end of the book as opposed to ten pages later. I find when I've got shorter pieces to read I tend to look at them with closer attention, whereas I've got a longer excerpt I'll skim read and I'm pretty sure I did. Or I'll just look for the larger themes and the bigger picture as opposed to the individual details, which, again, from what I picked up was definitely smaller quantity I think.

Sumana: Yeah I find that when I'm reading large stretches and kind of reading it just like picking. Like, I want to see what happens basically, so I'm reading kind of fast because I want to see and then at the end of that I guess the difference I notice between when we were reading together is that I pick up fewer details of this character said that and so on and it's just more like images or like the mood that the book evokes and that's what I remember more. I read this pretty fast and it was interesting. It was enjoyable to read, but not as much satisfaction as I would have liked. It was just kind of back and forth and going like, from the jail cell to the trial to the jail cell to the trial.

In varied ways, all these readers took the words on the page and converted them to some form of smooth-flowing story, and it seems clear from their comments that they found this outcome to be satisfactory. They enjoyed this stage of their reading where they found ways to process the story that smoothed out disruptions and allowed the story to proceed uninterrupted by second thoughts.

Yet, while all three of these readers manifest a tapering off in the attachment of stickies to their pages, none of them actually stopped noticing particular points and recording them in this rough-and-ready way. Although they are describing an interest in moving ahead quickly with the events of the book, their actions (however coarsely recorded) continue to indicate attention to particular details (in the final section they added 11, 9, and 9 markers). It is impossible to say for sure what they were doing with their stickies, but the pattern of their attachment at least makes space for them to be recording attempts to develop some resolution between story and discourse, a challenge with intellectual as well as affective reward.

Of course, what is being described here is a form of reading that is largely unresistant. Such submission to the story is one of the pleasures of reading, and it often comes into fullest play in the mid-to-later stages of the story. In the subtitle of this chapter, 'the unconsidered middle', the word *unconsidered* has two meanings: one is that it is a stage of reading often overlooked by reading experts of various kinds, and the other is that it is the stage in the story when the interpreter is most completely swallowed up by the narrative – and possibly also most vulnerable to absorbing its ideological freight.

Group B, even as they finished describing how they just read faster and faster, also noted some of the ways that the format of the book disrupted their ability to feel themselves part of the story world. Unlike some of the other readers, Sumana and Tess were unable to normalize the screenplay into unmarked reading, and Martin describes a sensation of being 'half in and half out'.

Margaret: How did you find reading the movie script? Did it get to the point where you stopped noticing that it wasn't standard novel prose? Or did it always intrude into your reading awareness?

Tess: I think it always jumped in.

Margaret: Mmm. You didn't ever get to the point where you kind of normalized it?

Tess: No. Normal is the sections in sort of the script-like font.

Sumana: The diary format.

Tess: Because partially the change of fonts, partially the change of size, formatting was enough I think, to wake me and be, like, okay, okay, we're back in the game, we're back in the movie stage. So that's just me.

Sumana: The way it's described makes you look at it differently from how you would look at another novel because it talks specifically, it gives a section where it gives the actual camera angles, so you start to see it in that way, so that makes you picture it differently. Then the diary segments, there's not really as much physical description so it's more like you start to feel the mood of the protagonist. That kind of jumps back and forth a little bit.

Martin: The state of looking at it like a movie didn't really go over well for me because of those blocks in the text where there wasn't really any leads to think of it as a movie. I found that I was thinking about it a little more, but I found that I was reading it as more of a book and less of a movie and so now I wonder how does that affect my perspective? How does that affect the things that I'm seeing that I'm supposed to be seeing? Like, in the flesh.

Sumana: Actually, I think part of the detachment I felt towards the main character in the book is the fact that when you're watching a movie, the characters are very external to you; you kind of see when they're talking, it just goes back and forth between the two and you're outside just watching it. Whereas in a typical novel you're inside the head of everything that's going on and every minute detail is described to you. Like, the tastes, the smells, the touch, the sight and you get more involved with the characters I think. Whereas with this book, for the most part, you're on the outside.

Martin: Or you're half in, you're half out.

Tess: Exactly!

Making do

It was clear that the format affected the experience and these readers' sense of connection with the characters. It did not, however, stop them making successful meaning from the story. But what if the meaning-making simply doesn't 'move along'? Group AB, composed of three interesting and thoughtful men with plenty of experience of stories in many media, provide a different perspective on the composing of meaning out of narrative ingredients. The difficulties of Group AB with *Shadow of the Colossus* make instructive reading, and I believe the gaming transcripts offer some illuminating possibilities for a better understanding of narrative processing in book and film as well.

Not every encounter with a text offers success or real enjoyment. A seriously under-studied and under-theorized form of interpretation is the unsuccessful effort, the unrewarding trudge through a story, for reasons that are most often extraneous since the internal attraction of the story itself is manifestly very limited. It is useful to be able to see a 'slow-motion' form of such perfunctory progress in the game of Group AB, and in this section we will explore their meandering progress. We will also explore a smaller conundrum that arose in the viewing of *Run Lola Run* by Group D.

The large-scale problem: Failure to progress

Group AB was singular in its collective incapacity to make use of textual information in the game, even when it was explicitly highlighted in the strategy guide (which they used extensively). The following extract, with Dan at the controls, gives some clear sense of the group's collective inability to make straightforward progress. This extract is taken from the second full session of the amalgamated Group AB, who at this point are in pursuit of the seventh colossus.

Martin: Okay, where are we going?

Dan: Right and then right. Oh, it'll be left because it was on the right. Okay Agro, come on.

Neil: You were supposed to ride into the canyon opening on the left, but then you were supposed to take a right at the canyon intersection.

(Pulls down map)

Dan: Yeah the canyon intersection is back here.

Neil: What – no, no, no, not that canyon intersection. There should be one at the end –

Dan: The canyon intersection is right there.

Neil: There's two – look.

Dan: No, look where I am. Look where the arrow is – this is another path where I can turn right just ahead of me here.

Neil: Yeeeeah, okay, so ride [*reading*], 'ride through the canyon and arrive at the lake. Follow the shoreline, keeping it to your right then ride into the canyon.' So maybe –

Martin: There's one place that we could have gone.
Dan: Yeah we'll go there.
Neil: Okay. So now we're clearly lost.
Dan: If you were a child and your parents were in the car with you, they would tell you to enjoy the scenery.
Martin: Keeping the shoreline at your right.

Group AB's progress is laborious and very slow. A single extract captures some of the circular nature of their endeavours but does not really demonstrate the many ways they found to repeat previous misunderstandings. At this stage they are relatively good-humoured about the slow headway they are making, but they really are not making much serious effort to get better at the game.

The transcripts of Group AB's game provide numerous examples of such forms of disconnect between the guidebook's advice and the gamers' response. Their capacity to focus on orderly action was variable at best, and none of them was adept at the PlayStation controls, which meant that even when they had some strategic sense of what they should be doing, their capacity for manual execution was deficient. It was also clear that the artificiality of the situation was part of the problem. Dan in particular said that if he had been similarly stuck at home he would have just bored down on the problem for however many hours of relentless practice it took to gain a better sense of the controls, not a realistic option in this project. Neil said he would turn to a cheat card – though given the way this group failed to utilize the information in the strategy guide, it is not clear that such a procedure would really have helped him.

Whatever the causes, this group almost never managed an immersed stance, rarely moved *into* the game in a determined and focused way. For example, it was extremely unusual for them to hold up the sword for guidance. Their observation of the game scenery and surroundings was perfunctory and they often rode right past a landmark that they had just read about as marking a crucial turning point. Unlike the other groups, this trio's sense of visual salience never really improved over the many hours of gameplay; it seemed that they were expecting the guidebook to supply all the information they would need. Many passages of transcript read along the lines of the following short sample:

Neil: You'd probably be better off if you went to the middle one, that's what they said.

Dan: He's in the middle one.
Neil: No, I don't –
Dan: Yes he is.
Neil: No, that's not the middle one. There's one over.
Martin: There's one.
Neil: Yeah.
Martin: And there's one.
Dan: Middle one.
Neil: Oh, okay, never mind.

Mark Reid makes the point that many people will describe reading as a more active process than watching a movie or a television show,

> to which I usually ask whether anyone has ever read 5 pages of prose without taking in a word of it – and in fact isn't there such a thing then as 'passive reading'? And how is passive reading – or viewing – possible, if not because we're so able to process the language, so sophisticated at it that we can process it on auto-pilot? By the same token, observation suggests that young children, contrary to popular belief, don't process the moving image passively: sit with any 3 year old and watch a piece of film with them and see how their processing is all externalized; they ask the questions and 'think aloud' the sense-making that as adults we have long since learned to internalise.
>
> (2009, pp. 20–1)

Group AB, of course, were being asked to externalize their sense-making in exactly this way, and what was revealed often resembled those '5 pages of prose' that constitute Reid's empty reading example. Yet they were not without their strategies. What was very interesting about Group AB was that in the midst of often catastrophic breakdown of *configuration* (putting the game's pieces together), they preserved an instinct for *coherence* (making overall sense of the story, if only sardonically). Dan and Neil brought with them the thematic interest that showed so strongly in Group A's reflections, and Martin was very interested in the potential for symbols to relate to a higher understanding. Dan, in addition, was very ready to explore cultural explanations:

Dan: It's just like the gods speak to you and you listen. Any good
             Japanese citizen would to their gods, right?

Neil: Yeah, I know. Maybe it would make more sense if we were Japanese, but I like a little bit more back story – something.

Dan: It's almost like Shinto religion, the way that the gods get you to do tasks.

Neil and Martin added considerations of overall pattern.

Neil: Yeah, all I know is that right now we seem to be running around and killing these colossi who seem to be really stupid and live alone.

Martin: In the repetition the ritual is being formed between, like, which one is predator and which one is prey, and they keep on dancing. 'Okay, if you're going to fire your little burr at me, I'm going to come knock you off the platform' – like a dog, and his owner walking the dog, both of them thinking, 'Well here we go again, it seems to make him happy.'

Probing Group AB's play

There are many possible explanations for Group AB's lack of progress. The set-up was entirely artificial. They played in public with a platform they disliked and were not comfortable using, in company they had not entirely chosen, for arbitrarily determined lengths of time. Their sense of performing a task for somebody else seemed to overwhelm their subjunctive entry into the game. They made very ill-advised use of the strategy guide and took little apparent effort really to *attend* to the landscape or the potential weakness of a colossus.

Whatever the causes, they were not satisfied with their own progress.

One component of progressing involves assessment of the current interpretive situation. In the midst of a story, interpreters vary in how much they care about the precision and accuracy of their relationship to the text. The spectrum between momentum and accountability (Chittenden and Salinger with Bussis, 2001) offers a useful measure for considering this issue further. Momentum readers, when they hit a roadblock in their interpretation, will usually speed up, hoping that further information will make all clear. Readers whose bias lies in the direction of accountability will slow down and strive for a more accurate understanding of the detail that is causing the problem. It is a spectrum, rather than a binary divide, and not all readers inhabit an extreme end.

Nevertheless, the contrast between momentum reading and accountability reading provides a useful heuristic for understanding some of the realities of interpretation.

I made use of this contrast in my exploration of the concept of the 'good enough' reader (Mackey, 1997, 1995). Many readers, especially when reading exclusively for their own personal pleasure and not to account to any outsider (such as a teacher, an examining board, or even a book group) will sometimes compromise, make do with an interim interpretation that is less than totally rewarding but good enough to be getting on with. I define good enough reading as an interpretation that provides a balance between momentum and accountability that is sufficiently satisfying (a very personal decision) to enable an individual reader to keep going. An inaccurate interpretation that does not interfere with momentum sometimes simply fades away when counter-evidence arises; forgetting also plays a role in the temporal activity of interpretation, especially for those readers not wedded to strict accountability.

How the idea of the good enough interpretation applies to media other than print is an interesting question. Interpreting a movie, at least in the cinema, is strongly affected by the fact that viewers actually cannot slow down or speed up. Issues of momentum and accountability in watching the moving image change radically for ordinary viewers when they gain control of pacing decisions through the vehicles of DVD and videotape. A game like *Shadow of the Colossus* yields more readily to players' pacing decisions, so issues of what is good enough are more open to manipulation. In the case of Group AB, it is arguable that control over pacing was not an asset.

This group struggled with both momentum *and* accountability. Their inability to *see* the opening in the rock face, even when the guidebook told them how to look for it, meant that their forward momentum was severely hampered by their lack of accurate inspection of the text. By almost any definition their progress was *not* good enough. They kept playing, but the circular and repetitive nature of their game was very unsatisfying to them, and only possible at all because the game is open to endless cycling in a way that is difficult to imagine occurring in a novel or a movie.

In a perfect research universe, I would have given Dan, Neil and Martin each a copy of the game and followed them home to observe their more natural gaming processes as they wrestled with the controls and the camera angles that were causing them so much grief. I had neither the resources nor the ethics approval for such a venture, so continued to observe the artificial circumstances of their frustration with playing as a group. One element of interpretation that almost completely disappeared as a result is the ability to improve through practising. Dan's reference to the eight hours he would like to have spent in gaining a thorough mastery of the controls is a reminder that focused effort can also play a significant role in interpretive endeavours.

To describe this frustration in productive and useful ways is a complex challenge. It is difficult to distinguish between a relatively passive acquiescence in a practice that is apparently not good enough and a more active stance of motivated resistance. John Stephens raises the question of a story's significance:

> narratives invariably have thematic purposes and functions, whether deliberately because they seek to inculcate something about life, or implicitly because no encoding of a story can be free of societal and/ or ideological marking.
>
> (1992, p. 14)

It seems clear that Dan, Neil, and Martin, at least some of the time, are objecting to alien or insufficient significance in this narrative. Yet resistance, for whatever reason, was not the whole story. With the assistance of a short cut (eliminating the requirement to kill the fourteenth and fifteenth colossi), they did get to the end of the game in a total of 16 hours of gaming.

Throughout their play, it was interesting to explore the ways in which they attempted to compensate for failures in momentum and accountability. One recourse, naturally, was simply to complain – about the game, the controls, the camera, the horse, the Japanese tendency to evacuate narrative from the game, and more; the list was long. But interestingly, they also reverted to a grander perspective as a kind of compensation; even when details failed to function, they could talk about the larger narrative elements at work. Even as they failed to master the *physical* geography as presented on the screen image, they absorbed and commented on the implications of the *moral* geography. Although tactics of configuration often did not work well for them, they were able to speak meaningfully about elements of signification and coherence, and such subjunctive involvement in this game as they achieved often occurred at these more macro-levels. It was interesting to note the degree to which their conversations about the thematic components strongly resembled those of the more efficient players in

Group C. These men were not particularly competent manipulators of the controls for *Shadow of the Colossus* but they were perfectly capable and often thoughtful about understanding the shape and significance of story.

It is a very interesting question whether a game invites or even enables such forms of complex interpretive movement between configuration and coherence in ways impossible for a film or a book. Is it possible that Atkins' game question ('What happens next *if I* ... ?) can be answered in an *ad hoc* and happenstance kind of trial and error that keeps a player *just engaged enough* to stumble to the ending? Are there equivalent behaviours in other media? What about the viewer who becomes impatient with a movie and starts to fast-forward, slowing down for scenes that seem especially salient and for the last few minutes of the ending? What about the book group member who hates the book but wants to be in on the discussion, who skips through the chapters with the help of hints about salience and significance in the table of contents? What about the traveller confined to plane or train with a less than interesting story who browses and skims? It certainly would be difficult from the outside to call such encounters a form of good enough experience – but when interpreters are setting the conditions for their own satisfaction, it may be that 'just barely more than nothing' may qualify as just good enough for the minimal demands that the interpreter is bringing to bear. And before we delude ourselves that instructed interpretation in the classroom involves a much loftier, more detailed and more critical experience, we do well to remind ourselves of the quantity of classroom work that is based (in spite of the teacher's best efforts) on a mechanical once-over of *Coles Notes*.

The game, in its embodied and muscular working-through of every detail of the story, does make space for an observer to take more clear account of desultory story processing than might be possible with other forms of narrative interpretation. Group AB, patiently or impatiently persisting in an often unsatisfactory and perfunctory experience, at least in part to oblige me and my project, collectively offer a valuable window onto aspects of interpretation that are often overlooked in our assumptions about the pleasures of engaging with fiction. Left to their own devices, they might well have quit the game, and it might well be that quitting would actually have been the best option for them. Of how many set classroom novels is the same condition true for some or many reluctant, conscript readers?

Some keen and fluent processors of story in any medium (but perhaps especially some 'good' readers) excoriate people who fail to finish the book, or who walk out of the movie, or who reject the game. It is hard to make the argument that continuing the kind of desultory and spasmodic commitment that marked the play of Group AB actually represents a productive use of time. Lacking the means to improve their play, unsure of the value of the exercise overall, they might well have been right to decide that stopping was their best option.

And yet, they were still able to bring intelligent interpretive energies to bear on their assessment of the overall story. The end, in this case, was greater than the means. If I had devised a wrap-up 'test' on *Shadow of the Colossus*, I would not have been surprised if Dan, Neil and/or Martin had written the best essays – one more testimonial to the complexity of response.

The small-scale problem: failures of detail

Not every problem is as endemic and overwhelming as the struggles of Group AB with the game as a whole. During Lola's third dash through Berlin, she jumps in the ambulance and holds the hand of a person lying there, causing the pulse to steady. A small retrospective conversation among the members of Group D about the identity of this sick person shows these viewers making do with an insecure interpretation.

Adam:	I thought that was Mr. Meyer – wasn't it?
Sumana:	Yeah.
Adam:	Wasn't there?
Sumana:	I thought it was a woman.
Adam:	I thought it was the guy in the car crash. I thought it was Mr. Meyer.
Lewis:	No, the guy lying down, he was the security guard, right?
Adam:	I thought that was Mr. Meyer actually.
Lewis:	I thought that was the security guard.
Sumana:	I thought it was Mr. Meyer.
Lewis:	Because the security guard was feeling his heart in one of the earlier ones.
Adam:	That was true.
Lewis:	And I got the feeling – he had a heart attack this go round, he ends up in the ambulance and again, about the character development – there was some attachment between Lola and the security guard.

Adam:	I was confused. I was almost wondering, maybe he is a random guy, maybe she doesn't know him. Maybe she's just doing that so that she gets to stay in the ambulance.
Lewis:	Yeah.

Each of these viewers was temporarily prepared to be persuaded of two different possibilities for the person in the ambulance. Lewis has the most consistent theory about the security guard (and he is, in fact, correct), but he is prepared to agree with Adam, at least briefly and provisionally, about the random person. Adam argues with less conviction for Mr. Meyer, but substitutes the question about the random guy. Sumana temporarily wonders if the person is a woman but then is prepared to go along with the idea that it is Mr. Meyer. Lewis's theory provides the most cohesive story in that Lola has earlier established a bit of a relationship with the security guard, and it may be no coincidence that it was Lewis of this group who liked the movie the best (or, of course, he may have watched it more closely because he was enjoying it more; the direction of causality is impossible to establish here).

In any case, the three were all able to make overall sense of the film despite the provisional nature of their short-term theory of the little scene in the ambulance. In fact, any of these theories would suffice for the sake of the story overall, though I am inclined to find the little story arc of the security guard to be the most satisfying. Nobody mentions here that the security guard is the person who drops the ball at the very beginning of the movie, and it would take enormous powers of observation and recall to come up with that identity on a single viewing unless the actor was recognizable enough to be memorable in his own right.

Again, the slow-motion observation made possible by recording these interpretive efforts enables us to focus on this short period of confusion. In the context of normal viewing arrangements, it is possible that none of these interpreters would give that moment in the ambulance another thought. At the same time, however, it is not difficult, to imagine them having this retrospective conversation about the identity of the ill person as they left the movie theatre; clarifying small confusions can be part of the efforts after coherence, often long after the story is over.

People vary in the degree to which they are content to live with such confusion. It may be that Adam and Sandra disliked the movie in part because they did not feel secure enough in their ability to make sense of it. But they did not raise the question of the person in the ambulance until I asked them about it, so they were not overwhelmingly troubled by it. In fact, any of their putative identifications provide an answer sufficiently good enough to allow them to keep watching.

In short, the gradations of 'not good enough' may range from fleeting to overwhelming. Confusion and lack of commitment may affect the story at the level of one or two details or may sink the whole interpretive project.

9
Concluding: Reaching Provisional and Final Judgements

The fact that a story has an ending at all marks it as different from our daily, real-life 'human possibilities'. I know that my own personal life story will come to an end, but I do not know that I will have the opportunity to reflect on it after it is over. Even if there is some post-life reflecting room, it will have to take account of much accidental and incidental detritus. As we *begin* our exploration of the subjunctive world of the story, we can make connections to our own sense of human life; as we come to the *end* of this shaped and selective narrative, we can make fewer comparative links to the hodge-podge of daily existence. The ending is, in some ways, the most artificial element of the story; in Ryan's terms, we must consider 'a sequence of events forming a unified causal chain and leading to closure' (2006, p. 8). As we explore this most unnatural, most un-life-like element of the story, we must shift the deictic centre out of the events and back to ourselves as interpreter, looking to make sense of the whole.

The word 'concluding' has two main meanings: it can mean 'reaching a conclusion or judgement' or it can mean 'reaching the end.' In this chapter, we will consider the first definition in terms of provisional and temporary summings-up along the way, and then consider the 'end of the story' and interpreters' post-encounter reflections.

Judith Langer makes room for both of these stages, speaking of 'stepping out and rethinking what one knows' (1995, p. 17) and also of 'stepping out and objectifying the experience' (1995, p. 18). Even the earlier stage, however, 'stepping out and rethinking what one knows,' becomes a consideration *towards* the ending. 'Where is this going?' is a question with an *answer*, in ways that do not apply to me and my life, except for the incontrovertible fact that 'in the long run, we are all dead'.

Not all narrative forms insist on an ending in this way; the BBC radio soap opera *The Archers*, for example, which has run every weekday since 1950, gives every indication that intends to be a never-ending saga. Website enhancements enlarge the scope of the story world (for example, see http://www.bbc.co.uk/radio4/archers/ for maps, family trees, recaps, and other extensive additions to the radio drama). The parallel for such ongoing narrative, in many ways, is pretend play, and Meek, Warlow and Barton explore that comparison in ways that illuminate the composed story:

> This recognition of story as a form is based on certain recurrent features which we become familiar with quite early in our experience of them: anticipation of climax, expectation of judgement and, as Frank Kermode calls it, 'the sense of an ending'. These distinguish story from narrative, art from life. In life there are recurrent crises, temporary judgements, and only one final end. When we invent fictions in dreams and make-believe we meet ourselves in them and the end is delayed. When we tell stories for others, we draw to a close, a pay-off time, and part of the pleasure is the form as the box-lid snaps shut.
>
> (1977, p. 73)

The three stories represented in this project are finite, if not necessarily *conclusive*, and even if their endings are ambiguous, they do end. 'The box-lid snaps shut' even if every element in that box has not been neatly disposed of, and even if interpreters are left with questions.

Frank Kermode wrote about the role of endings in terms of fictional orders of time and significance:

> [W]ithin human time one can distinguish between the *chronos* of mere successiveness and the *kairos* of high days and holidays, times or seasons that stand out (red-letter days, as one used to say) as belonging to a different temporal order. It was my belief that in referring to the sound of a clock not as 'tick-tick' but as 'tick-tock' we substitute a fiction for the actual acoustic event, distinguishing between genesis of 'tick' and apocalypse of 'tock,' and conferring on the interval between them a significance it would otherwise lack. The fictive end purges the interval of simple chronicity. It achieves a 'temporal integration' – it conveys a blank into a *kairos*, charges it with meaning. So it can be argued that we have here a tiny model of all plots.
>
> (2000, p. 192)

In his terms, it is the ending of the story, the 'tock', that confers significance. It is only after the story is over that we can look back on the shape of the whole, but knowing that a deliberately contrived ending is on its way alters how we sum up interim stages of progress as well.

Reaching conclusions

It is not necessary to reach the end in order to reach a conclusion. In fact, there may be a kind of interim judging, a summing up, an expression of the gist so far, an assessment of how the gaps involved in suspense, curiosity, and surprise may be provisionally resolved, that enables interpreters to move forward. It is very difficult to ascertain, however, that such a summing up occurs naturally during autonomous and uninterrupted interpreting. I certainly encountered many instances of such behaviour during the course of this project, but I was, of course, deliberately inviting it. What can be minimally asserted is that interpreters were very readily able to gather together the threads of 'the show so far' whenever invited to do so.

One way to consider this kind of ongoing summing up before moving forward is to make use of the distinction between story and discourse, the resolving of those temporal gaps. Buckland, referring to film, describes discourse as relating to '*how* events are presented on screen' and describes the role of interpreters.

Spectators rearrange events, disambiguate their relations and order, and in doing so, gradually construct a story ... of *what* happens.

Because the film's story is a mental representation the spectator constructs during his or her experience of the film's plot, the story is in a constant state of change, owing to the spectator's ongoing generation of new inferences, strengthening of existing hypotheses, and abandonment of existing inferences.

(2009, p. 7, emphasis in original)

Buckland speaks of an ongoing 'process of readjustment' (2009, p. 7), which means that interim conclusions are known to be provisional – and indeed reaching the story's end does not necessarily mean that judgements are immediately firmed up. Tentativeness may very well survive the conclusion of the story as presented.

David Bordwell, also discussing film, suggests that it is possible to sum up at any point:

Needless to say, any portion of the film's trajectory may be interpreted as a 'summarizing' one, depending on how the critic has

mobilized semantic fields, selected person-based and category sche-
mata, disclosed cues on the basis of the concentric-circle schema,
and so on.

(1989, p. 192)

He is writing about more formal analysis than I am considering here,
but the suggestion is clear that a summary can be marshalled at many
different points of a story.

These interim conclusions will likely not be overly detailed. Barratt,
also addressing questions about film, tells us,

> Contrary to our intuitions ... we do not store a recording of
> the scene in the precise fashion of, say, a video or a DVD. When
> we are prompted to recall the scene at the end of the film [or at
> some inbetween moment when we sum up the gist so far for our-
> selves or someone else like a researcher], our recollection does not
> involve us replaying a 'memory video' in our mind's eye. Although it
> is probable that we are able to recall one or two distinctive details ...
> what primarily happens is that we reconstruct our memory of the
> scene using ... schemas and propositions ... Significantly, these
> schemas and propositions incline us to go beyond the information
> given by filling in the gaps with details not included in the original
> scene.
>
> (2009, p. 78)

The ongoing story we create in our minds is both broad-brush and personal, according to this version of interpretive activity. In the following
excerpts we can see participants reaching for details when they think
they will bolster their ongoing interpretation, but certainly not running
through them in a chronologically correct sequence.

Run Lola Run

Here, for example, are Group C after the first run-through of Lola's gallop through Berlin:

Margaret: So, we're only partway through the movie – what's going
to happen now?
Sebastian: Maybe we'll go back and see what's happened before, or
maybe she's not even dead.
Jacob: Yeah.
Margaret: Any other suggestions?

Jarret: I'm just trying to recall how many people we saw at the very beginning, when they were initially doing montages of various people and so far most of them have showed up as she runs past them. I don't know if she has run past them all or not.

Sebastian: I believe she has.

Jacob: Yeah.

Sebastian: You mean those people in the snapshots?

Margaret: What are those snapshots doing?

Sebastian: They're telling the future, like what happened to them, happened to them before. Didn't the ones who were nice to her and try to help her get good things and those who didn't got bad things?

In this sequence of comments, it is possible to see at least early instances of notice (has Lola run past all the people in the snapshots?), signification (do the snapshots indicate the future?), configuration (we could expect some flashbacks or perhaps a plot twist) and some preliminary stabs at coherence (it is possible that the degree to which passers-by were nice to Lola affected the remainder of their lives). These short summary comments entail a considerable quantity of assessment; in Langer's terms, Sebastian, Jarret and Jacob are briefly 'stepping out and rethinking what [they] know' (1995, p. 17). Langer labels this stage the third stance, and it is worth remarking that, here at least, it is a reiterative stance, and that it sets interpreters up to move forward as well as necessarily involving retrospection.

As Group B reached the end of Lola's first run-through, there was only one macro-level comment, from Martin: 'She's consistently clashing with all these authority systems – like time.' After the second iteration, however, Tess and Sumana engaged in much the same kind of summary, assessment, and deduction as we saw from Group C above.

Tess: You would think they wouldn't let anyone out of the bank though. I watch too many cop shows.

Sumana: Yeah, there's just too many strange coincidences. There's a bit of unrealistic behaviour that happens in the movie that wouldn't actually happen in real life, but I guess you need those things for a movie to go.

Tess: It's just about crazy enough to work that small little circumstances – her getting tripped on the stairs, getting that guard's gun. If he had any backup within the bank that would have gone differently, but he didn't. He just had that one gun. So I think it's a story of circumstances more than anything. If any one thing is different it ends up completely changed, like even looking at the destinies that get flipped around. It's interesting – the people who had goodish destinies before are now bums and the ones who are better – finding people to fall in love with, and so on and so forth.

I don't know – am I babbling?

Far from babbling, Tess was moving between the singular details of this instantiation of the run-through (the guard's lack of backup) to a shrewd summing-up of the movie's running motif of 'circumstances'. It is interesting in this little stretch of conversation to see Sumana reiterating her comfort with the idea that fictions work on different principles from reality – 'you need those things for a movie to go.'

Monster

In the early stages of *Monster*, Group C, both separately and collaboratively, attempt to cluster information for maximum utility in moving forward in ways that are very similar to their responses to *Run Lola Run*. After reading pages 13–19, they turned readily to summary, even on the basis of very little information.

Jacob:	Somebody just flashed to film classes and I haven't quite made up my mind if that is a flashback or some weird, like, alternate storyline.
Margaret:	Right.
Sebastian:	I think it was a flashback.
Margaret:	Anything else catch your attention?
Jarret:	I like how the stenographer wants it to last long so she can make more money.
Sebastian:	I like how the Judge asks him how the Fourth of July was and they talk about playing softball right in court and the kid's up for the death penalty and they're talking about how their weekend was.
Jarret:	I like how Briggs says that he can't run anymore.

Sebastian: I like how he's writing it down too. How he makes – he mentions that he's actually writing all this down as it happens – that's funny.

Jarret: Yeah, I marked that too – page 16.

Margaret: Are you getting any more sense of Steve?

Jacob: He used to be a good guy and he just somehow got himself into this situation.

Sebastian: He's scared. He's afraid of King too [*pause*]. That's the other – the 23-year-old. Yeah, when they were in the room together, Steve didn't seem so comfortable.

As with Group C's comments above, regarding *Run Lola Run*, we may discern all of Rabinowitz's rules at work here: notice (the clash of priorities in the courtroom), signification (the issue of the potential flashback, the importance of the fact that Steve is recording events as they occur), configuration (the implications of Steve's fear of King), and some preliminary coherence ('he used to be a good guy and he just somehow got himself into this situation'). They not only 'step out and rethink what [they] know' (Langer, 1995, p. 17), they also compare notes on their assessment up to this very early stage. This summing-up includes Langer's elements of 'what the individual does and does not understand, as well as any momentary suppositions about how the whole will unfold, and any reactions to it' (1995, p. 9).

The goodness of fit between the comments of the participants and Rabinowitz's and Langer's descriptions of interpretive processes at work is considerable, yet the artificiality of the context must also be emphasized. Perhaps this kind of assessment occurs only when the interpreter pauses for breath – puts down the book at the end of a chapter; pauses the video to get something to eat, stops the digital game for a bathroom break. It is certainly not difficult, however, to imagine an extended period of immersion without such a pause, when the pursuit of 'what happens next' continues relentlessly: the reader turns the pages as quickly as possible without looking up; the movie-goer is wrapped up in the story for two hours without so much as a glance at a watch; the gamer hunches over the console for hours at a stretch. My own personal experience of being 'lost' in a story in this way suggests to me that there is far less 'concluding' occurring under such conditions, but I am wary of generalizing too far through my own singular lens. These responses indicate at a minimum that summary information can be very readily marshalled at such moments.

Another approach is to develop tentative conclusions that cluster items of information in ways that can lead to further questions. Here is Group D, having read from page 20 to page 32, discussing the ambiguous attitude of the lawyer:

Adam: I don't know, maybe I've watched too many law shows or something, but the attorney has a lot to prove if they want to get the main character on anything except robbery, because the circumstances don't –

Lewis: They don't add up –

Adam: They don't add up so far, because they say, well he was in there but then he left. It's like, okay – and you want to put him in jail for life and maybe on death row? That doesn't make any sense at all.

Lewis: Yeah.

Adam: So I'm getting the sense that there's either something we don't know or the attorney is out to get him for some other reason.

Lewis: If the attorney is out to get him for some reason – on page 21, the automatic judgement call that Petrocelli says, *Most people in our community are decent.* Then she goes on to, *But there are also monsters in our communities – people are willing to steal and kill,* so she's already making a judgement call on him. So yeah that might pertain to something like that. That lawyer trying to get him for something other than just robbery, because if he's on for felony murder and he left – yeah I want to find out what's going to go on.

Sandra: I agree with them. [*giggles*]

Adam: I also like the little background they had in the book – the *MONSTER MONSTER crossed out MONSTER crossed out MONSTER.*

Lewis: Mmm – that was cool!

Sandra: Interesting. The lawyer's just kind of cocky. I guess that's what lawyers do.

Adam: Well I thought it was actually kind of interesting how his lawyer hasn't brought up any of that yet either. His lawyer's like, yeah I don't have any questions for this witness.

Lewis: Nothing about yes, 'Have you seen this guy beforehand – ?' or anything like that

Adam: Yeah.

Lewis: And that's weird, because she says like, when he's writing the monster in his notepad she says that he has to believe in himself but she's not going to help him out that much.

Adam: Yeah, I'm actually wondering if this is just a court-appointed kind of thing.

Sandra: Maybe she thinks though, she says he'll be more of a detriment than of a help.

Adam: Good.

Sandra: That's probably why she didn't say anything.

Lewis: Yeah.

Group D are engaged in more than summing up in this conversation. They are oscillating between two kinds of evaluation.

Their first priority is to judge the evidence against Steve inside the story world and the commitment of his lawyer to developing a robust case. To aid this cause, they bring in outside information both from other legal stories they have encountered and from their general knowledge that court-appointed lawyers may sometimes be less than devoted to the cause. This external knowledge is dedicated to creating a more coherent assessment of the shape of the story so far. They also consider evidence from the story itself: the prosecuting lawyer's comment about monsters in society and the defence lawyer's observation that Steve may not serve his own cause well. Lewis adds a value judgement on the defence lawyer's behaviour – 'weird' – that also seems to be located inside the story; in this group, it is almost always Lewis who cares most keenly about the story situation and the internal story schemas.

To these forms of intelligence applied to the interior of the story world, they add a gloss about the surface. Not surprisingly, it is Adam, always interested in the manner of telling, who mentions the word 'MONSTER', written and crossed out on the page, but Lewis is also ready to admire the effect.

Yet Adam is prepared to invest in the story world as well. At the beginning of their next set of comments, after they have read from page 33 to page 43, Adam speaks from an interior perspective.

Adam: O'Brien just went up a lot in my opinion.

Margaret: Why is that?

Adam: Because of the line of questioning she used. The whole:
             Are you sure? how can we be sure you're telling the
             truth now? isn't this just an out for you? And it's great
             because he can say yes, but he could still be telling the
             truth.

When Lewis (for once) initiates a discussion of the story-telling surface, it leads to another conversation that demonstrates the pleasures
of an engaged stance that moves in and out of the world of the story
and allows interpreters to devote internal and external evidence to
the project of making the best story possible. This little fragment of
conversation includes an assessment of how Steve is recording the
events we are reading (a reflection on the metafictional aspects of this
story, although they do not use this vocabulary). It leads to a general
conclusion about the book as a whole, even though the readers are only
a small fraction of the way through it.

Lewis: His flashbacks, I think, each of them are just going to build
             part of his character. I think that will relate to part of his
             trial –
Sandra: Right.
Lewis: So maybe in the next part we'll see *that* part of his char-
             acter, some of his morality come in, maybe a conversation
             with O'Brien or something like that. That's what I antici-
             pate just by these flashbacks.
Adam: Actually just thinking about that now, I'm kind of won-
             dering what'll happen when he eventually goes up on the
             stand. Will it be kind of disjointed then, when he has to
             put down his pen? ... I get the sense that he's writing this
             as it happens.
Lewis: I think so too, by putting these scripts in – not the typed
             parts – and throwing in those monsters.
Adam: Yeah, when she's talking to him and she's like, What
             are you doing? And he's like, I'm writing this down in
             a script.
Lewis: And she's like, Okay.
Sandra: But she told him to look interested and maybe by him sit-
             ting there writing away he doesn't really look – maybe it'll
             make him look *more* interested or *less* interested.
Lewis: Yeah, he's not paying attention or is paying attention.
Sandra: He's taking notes.

Lewis: Yeah.
Adam: So far I actually kind of like it.
Lewis: Yeah, it's good.
Adam: Because it is quick. It's actually a lot different from what I usually read, so I think that might just be why I like it.

The preliminary assessment of the story so far, not surprisingly, also involves a value judgement: am I enjoying this story? Is it worth reading in terms of my own pleasure and responses? Adam goes a step further and essays an initial assessment of *why* he likes it, which places this story in the context of others he has encountered. But it is an assessment of the value of the experience to the reader rather than assessment of the text itself that informs his preliminary summing up.

Shadow of the Colossus

With both *Run Lola Run* and *Monster*, the formative and summative comments were to a considerable extent shaped by where I, as an outsider, chose to insert a boundary and stop for discussion. As far as I could, I chose breaks at points where the text itself took a turn – at the end of each dash across Berlin in *Run Lola Run*, between a journal entry and a screenplay segment in *Monster*. Nevertheless, the pauses were imposed from outside both the text itself and the experience of the interpreters. If Rabinowitz is correct that we apply rules of notice to endings as well as beginnings, I was creating and then imposing new 'endings' as I segmented.

The game, however, did not need to stop in order for discussion to occur, so I could leave more choices to the players. The commentary on *Shadow of the Colossus* provides the most unfiltered access to ongoing summary thinking. Here are some examples from late in Group C's game; as with most other elements of their approach, their provisional and ongoing conclusions include and are sometimes expressed through jokes.

After the slaughter of the twelfth colossus, for the first time new characters enter the game: the mysterious horsemen, galloping towards the temple.

End of colossus XII

Jacob: Hey, the cut scene is right here.
Jarret: Ooh, more people!
Sebastian: Well, more horses.
Jarret: Now, you found more horses, see?

Jacob: This looks ominous.
Jarret: Oooooh.
Sebastian: They look strangely – gray?
Jarret: Because they're wearing armour.
(Masked Men on horseback – 'Only a little more to go')
Jacob: It's a Colossi Preservation Society; we are in deep trouble
             now.
[*Laughter*]
Jarret: I bet you they're coming to stop us.
Sebastian: 'We're here to apprehend you for performing crimes
             against colossi – '
Jacob: 'You are [*inaudible*].'
Jarret: 'These colossi weren't supposed to die.'
Jacob: 'The guy up there [*Dormin*] is just some bum on the roof,
             talking down.' [*He says something else in a strange accent
             – indistinguishable*]
Jarret: 'Will result in a suspension – [*Laughter*] About the re-
             moval of your colossi-killing license.'
Sebastian: 'And you! You on the roof, you are under arrest!'
Jacob: 'Thine cannot catch me – '
Sebastian: 'For impersonating a deity – '
Jacob: 'I will hide thineself underground.'
Sebastian: I will join you. [*Laughter*]
Jarret: I'm glad the story element was finally added.

The introduction of new characters alters the game briefly, but almost at
once Dormin's voice introduces the need to tackle the next colossus.

Colossus XIII
*Thy next foe is ... The vast desert lands ... A giant trail drafts
through the sky ... Thou art not alone ...*

Jacob: I thought the storyline thus far was pretty good; you just
             kind of had to fill in the blanks yourself.
Jarret: Actually more twists than just, kill the colossi and save
             your girlfriend.
Jacob: Now we're fighting a flying snake. We've fought a snake
             of every kind.
Sebastian: That we're not alone.
Jarret: We're not playing *Donkey Kong*.
Jacob: Thou art not alone.

As with their responses to both *Run Lola Run* and *Monster*, their comments are both summative and formative. The running joke about the Colossi Preservation Society both sums up the continuing questions about the relatively unmotivated amorality of the game's premise and raises the possibility that the game story may yet take a turn that invalidates all their epic efforts to date. (In fact, the masked riders do indeed serve as a kind of colossi protection unit, though the game would certainly never stoop to such a flippant and anachronistic label for this significant group of elders.) In the final stretch of conversation above, Jarret and Jacob express an evaluation of the narrative overall, even though at this point they are only three-quarters of the way through it, and Sebastian and Jacob comment on the significance of the arrival of the riders as a challenge to the solitude of the hero. Jacob mentions the repeating pattern of the different snakes.

The elision of player and character in these comments is worth attention, and a useful tool for unpicking this relationship lies in the use of pronouns throughout this passage. At the beginning of the excerpt, the perspective could be described as third person, except for the comment to Sebastian about finding more horses. The mock dialogue about the Colossi Preservation Society shifts to the pronouns (and the spoof deictic centre) of direct speech. In the final six comments, after Dormin's instructions about the new challenge, the pronouns become more intricate and interesting.

Jacob's line, 'I thought the storyline thus far was pretty good, you just kind of had to fill in the blanks yourself,' is clearly located in the zone of the player. Jarret's reply, 'Actually more twists than just, kill the colossi and save your girlfriend', shifts the ground; 'your girlfriend' is a character line. Jacob replies with an ambiguous 'we' that could entail the perspective of players or of character: 'Now we're fighting a flying snake. We've fought a snake of every kind.' But Sebastian's interjection, 'That we're not alone', is more likely to represent a character point of view. 'We're not playing *Donkey Kong*', steps right out of the story world for an intertextual comparison that helps to define the limits of the story world. Finally Jacob's rephrasing of Sebastian's remark into a mock-epic form of discourse, 'Thou art not alone', achieves several ends at once; he is quoting Dormin to respond to Sebastian's thematic insight, but he is simultaneously engaging in a ritualistic player gesture (all the way through the game, Jacob persisted in speaking in second person singular and it was easy to imagine that he has behaved this way in other games since the other two consistently ignored his translation efforts).

In other words, as they responded to almost the only example in the whole game of startling new plot events, they slid in and out of deictic perspectives, and in and out of subjunctive connection with the story world, making thematic judgements, assessing the success of the narrative so far, and addressing one of the poignant questions of the game overall: 'Am I/are we alone?'

Group AB, at the same point in the story, also responded to the sudden introduction of a new plot element.

(The masked men appear on horseback)

Martin: With riders.

Dan: Oh, they're people? Well, this is getting interesting.

Martin: Six of them with our hero as the seventh.

Dan: No, he's not the hero.

Martin: It's Dormin.

Neil: That's not Dormin.

Martin: Bet you it is.

Neil: No, because Dormin's in the castle still.

Dan: Maybe we get companions for the final fight, I don't know. Or they're here to kick our ass and take us home because we escaped prison with the king's wife or something. I don't know.

(Hero is back lying on the floor of the temple)

Neil: I think it locked up – oh, no. Never mind.

Martin: As this happens each time **(a statue crumbles)** it feels like the accomplishment is lessened each time.

Dan: Oh, I just killed another piece of stone and I get to watch Dormin say, Thy next foe is – . Fun fun. Here it goes: Thy next foe is –

Colossus XIII

Thy next foe is ... The vast desert lands ... A giant trail drifts through the sky ... Thou art not alone.

Unlike Group C, Group AB did not comment on Dormin's remark about not being alone, but they certainly registered the significance of the arrival of the masked men. Once again we see Rabinowitz's rules in coordinated action: notice (how many men?), signification (who is the hero? where is Dormin?), configuration (why might these men be coming after the hero?), and coherence (the diminishing achievement of killing each subsequent colossus – a point on which Martin and Dan agree).

With the game, I did not stop play to invite comments, either summary or formative, and it is perhaps no accident that I have selected these sample quotes from one of the few moments in the game when overall expectations of continuation and repetition, established in the very early stages of play, are thoroughly disrupted. Choosing this moment in the game increases the likelihood that players should pause for a moment of 'What just happened? What might happen?' But such reflection could be very fleeting. When Group D met the masked riders, it was right at the end of a session and Adam had just been obliged to leave early. Lewis and Sandra, clearly very close to taking the colossus, had opted to play on without him, and this was their response to the arrival of the masked men.

Lewis:	Cinematic scene.
Margaret:	You need to remember this to tell Adam about it.
Lewis:	Okay.
Sandra:	We need to remember this for next week or something?
Lewis:	Oh, just let Adam know what happened.
Sandra:	He has a funny face.
Lewis:	I think it's a mask.
Sandra:	[*whispers – inaudible*].
Lewis:	Mm – uh-oh – antagonists.
Sandra:	Who do you think all those guys were?

Colossus XIII

Thy next foe is ... The vast desert lands ... A giant trail drifts through the sky ... Thou art not alone.

Lewis:	Just his followers. I think he's going to try and unleash some power or something like that. That's my guess.
Lewis/Sandra:	Oops.
Lewis:	Opposite way. I wonder if that other guy's going to come into the picture next fight.
Sandra:	Which guy?
Lewis:	The guy we just saw.
Sandra:	Oh.
Lewis:	The masked man –
Sandra:	There's more doves. Do you think they add doves like every time we kill one?
Lewis:	Mm hmm.

This relatively perfunctory response also invites some unpicking. The cut scene arrived at the end of the session; with Adam already departed, there was a distinct feeling of winding down. Lewis and Sandra were undoubtedly weary after two hours of heavy focus. They noticed but their process of signification was relatively slight: 'Just his followers.' Lewis offers an effort of configuration in his prediction of unleashed powers to come, but Sandra has already moved on to more noticing and signifying with her comment on the doves. My necessary request that they remember to tell Adam about this scene probably reinforced their potential recall of it, but they were not really gripped by the novelty of this development.

One often neglected element of the temporal nature of interpretation lies in this issue of fatigue. Creators of stories shape their narratives according to assumptions about interpretive behaviours; they set up the possibilities of notice, signification, configuration, coherence, envisionments, stances, stories, and discourses. But interpreters, while they respond to the author's markers, also operate according to their own rhythms of engagement. As well as story time and discourse time, there is also interpretation time.

Interpreters may be wayward in other respects, and it is very likely, with *Monster* and *Run Lola Run*, that I was interfering with the unconsidered processing of these stories by asking for intermediate conclusions. Such pausing to sum up may sharpen or otherwise affect later memories of the text. A single prolonged immersion in a story certainly does not serve me well when I later try to recall details of that story. Rosenblatt's distinction between the indwelling reading of the aesthetic stance and the reading to 'take away' (that is, remember) of the efferent stance may supply a pointer to the nature of interpretive experiences that we often overlook. Remembering is not necessarily the point of an immersed, aesthetic, absorbed reading. If this is true, it is important to note the potential for distortion of the aesthetic experience posed by many psychological studies of reading that focus on memory and retelling. In this project, I was not asking for retelling or recollection, but my interruptions, exploring the interpreters' ideas of the gist so far, may well have increased their sense of coherence at an earlier stage of the story. It is hard to know how this kind of interference can be avoided in a project such as this one, but it is important to notice it as one more effect of the simulation.

Conclusion of absence or absence of conclusion

Sometimes a large conclusion about a game overrides local assessments. Dan invoked his previous experience with Japanese games on a number of occasions when Martin or Neil was reaching a judgement about *Shadow of the Colossus*. To play with the terms of this chapter in a facetious way, his conclusion was essentially that there is no conclusion. One example stands in for many.

(Hero is now swimming across the lake)

Martin: We saw him as so young at the start; I don't see him as so young now.

Dan: Well that's the animation too, right? I don't think he's –

Neil: Yeah, he's –

Dan: He's Japanese animation so it's hard to tell what age he is.

Margaret: Do you think he's being battered?

Neil: Yeah, I think he's being battered.

Martin: I think he's seen a lot. I think he's been hurt for love. [*laughter*] I just remember thinking that he looked like a young boy at the beginning and now after I've been through all of this, it's like I can't really see it as youth anymore.

Dan: I guess I have kind of a jaded view of Japanese stories because they're all the same.

Martin: You could say the same for Hollywood.

Dan: Meet prototypical animated figure, some epic fight to finish and somebody to save and some love involved and over the story he defeats epic monsters and then it's over and then they repeat it with another game.

Dan was serious in this theory about the non-arcing nature of Japanese game narratives, but his suggestions, which were interspersed through the pursuit of the twelfth colossus, may have helped to augment the sense of futility that dogged Group AB. In their efforts with the thirteenth colossus (which they actually destroyed in a reasonably efficacious time span), they expressed more and more frustration. The group of masked riders has arrived after the death of the twelfth colossus but has then simply disappeared again, which also seems to have had an impact on their attitude.

Martin: Yeah, so where are these other people?

Dan: So then I re-pop his – sacs and climb up on his wing AGAIN and then I jump down his back in the middle of the air, all the

way again, and then I kill him? Okay – just all in a day's work
for this little hero I suppose. I don't suppose you're concerned
that we have no suspension of disbelief whatsoever. Even in
the context of fantasy this is stretching things.

Yet their frustration and disillusionment did not prevent them from
reaching a relatively accurate prediction of the game story's actual outcome. Here they are after the slaughter of the thirteenth colossus, and
it is notable that they initially express their engagement with this successful stage of the game in terms of physical sensation.

(The colossus is down)

Dan: Second colossus I've killed [*chuckling*] – sweaty hands.

Neil: Yeah mine were too.

Dan: That was a crazy hard fight! So many elements.

Martin: That was a full body workout.

Neil: Same with the last one. That was pretty annoying too.

Dan: Oh well, I'm just glad I got that guy. I didn't think I had
         a hope in hell of getting that one because he was so hard
         to get onto.

Neil: I wonder if they're going to show those other guys now.
         That's the weird guys that showed last time.

Dan: Yeah.

(The black tendrils arrive)

Neil: So who keeps bringing you back [*to the temple*]?

Dan: Dormin, I'm sure.

Neil: Yeah but if Dormin can just go up there anyway –

Dan: Dormin's probably somehow prevented somehow from
         killing the colossi.

Martin: But then we wouldn't get to play video games.

Dan: I think Dormin's like an evil god and the colossi are sealing –
         they're like the keys to his prison or something. I don't
         know.

Martin: Yeah, how Dormin is abstracted?

Dan: Because it's not like he's done much for me so far. Do this
         for me and I'll raise her – well, he hasn't done it yet. So I
         don't know.

Neil: Yeah.

Dan: Oh well, at least it's somewhat progress.

Neil: Hey, yeah 13 is – you know – well, actually it's pretty
         crappy, but still.

(Hero is lying on the ground in the temple surrounded by shadows)

Martin: The circle's almost complete around us.

Dan: There's only three left.

(A statue crumbles)

Neil: Yeah, there's not a whole lot left here.

Shadow of the Colossus shares with the book (only a few pages remaining in the right hand now) and the film (we've sat here for two hours now) a clear sense of the approaching ending because of the announcement at the beginning that 16 battles will be necessary, and the repeating visual of ever-fewer statues left in the temple hall and ever-more shadows gathered around the hero's prone body on each iteration of the return scene. Not every game would be so clear, and it is possible to imagine different cultural frameworks in which the endings of book and film might not be clearly announced either (an e-book, for example, offers fewer tangible indicators of length). The sense that the end is imminent, however, currently marks most of our story encounters, and is built into the story itself as well as being externally marked in the ways I have described above. The court case in *Monster* moves towards an ending just as inexorably as the majority of turned pages shifts over to the left hand. The likelihood that Lola's third run will be the last one is culturally engrained in most of us. Dan's constant reminders that Japanese models of story shaping are different from Western conventions serve as a flag that the players of *Shadow of the Colossus* should be wary of applying more familiar story conventions to their expectations of how the ending will develop, but the number 16 winds down to one in ineluctably linear ways. In all these cases, the approach of that ending clearly looms over the participants' engagement with each story and shapes some of their sense of the interim conclusions they can reach.

Reaching these provisional conclusions is part of how the interpreters retain some control over their material – render the story elements manageable enough that they can function in working memory. 'Where have we got to?' is answered by 'This is how I understand the show so far', a pausing for breath before moving onwards.

Reaching the end

The summary conclusions of all the groups after they had completed each of the three narratives continued to reach back into the story, drawing details of notice, signification, and configuration to bear on the final effort after coherence that is recorded in this project. (Whether the interpreters continued to reflect on any of these stories after they walked away cannot be determined.)

It was not a particular consideration as I chose the texts for this project, but one consequence of my particular choices is that none of the three stories offers a clear-cut and determinate ending. Interpreters who want some kind of satisfactory closure have their own work to do. 'As readers', says Stephens, 'we learn to look for *some* sense of completeness, both aesthetic and thematic, over and above the bringing of a series of events to a close' (1992, p. 42, emphasis in original). To this challenge we normally bring Rabinowitz's founding assumption about coherence: 'We assume, to begin with, that the work *is* coherent and that apparent flaws in its construction are intentional and meaning bearing' (1987, p. 147). Endings carry a special weight in creating this coherence, he suggests.

[R]eaders *assume* that authors put their best thoughts last, and thus *assign* a special value to the final pages of a text. It is particularly easy for the reader to do so, of course, when the ending is apparently congruent with the text that precedes ... Endings, however, are not always so neat, and when they are not, the reader is often expected to reinterpret the work so that the ending in fact serves as an appropriate conclusion'.

(1987, pp. 160–1, emphasis in original)

Some of such reinterpretation occurs after the story has concluded, but we have already seen some examples of interpreters making a preliminary reconnaissance of how much reinterpretation is likely to be necessary. The most noticeable of such forays is Dan's recurring warnings that *Shadow of the Colossus* is probably based on a Japanese story/game schema that may culminate in an ending that does not satisfy Western notions of story propriety.

All the groups, however, were clearly at home with the idea of a post-story retrospective to sum up and to assess the story's overall shape and outcome. In their final discussions, they continued to think about the implications of each story; in some of their comments it is possible to see them almost in the act of perceiving new details as they reflected on an experience that is, in one sense, 'over'.

Monster

Here is a sample of different groups' retrospective comments on *Monster*. Group C combined assessment of thematic issues with overall judgement on the enjoyability of the experience.

Jacob: It was quite a good read, as far as – I was quite entertained, it was probably a book I'd actually read on my own given the chance. A pretty startling insight into the justice system – the people involved.

Margaret: Do you want to expand on that a little bit?

Jacob: All the lawyers seemed to be jaded and two-faced. And not much better than the criminals they represent in most cases. It's all based on fear.

Sebastian: I think it was interesting just what people remembered and what could be used as evidence and whether they actually knew what they were doing or whether it had been suggested to them by the police. I think that was misconceived in the different testimonies.

Jarret: Yeah. I agree especially with the lawyer statements, like at the end when his own lawyer won't even hug him. I thought that was an incredible turning point in terms of the emotional backdrop of the book.

There is a strong thematic component to this discussion as the three men establish what makes the book important and interesting.

Group D were also positive, and more in agreement at the end of the book than they had often been during the reading, though their personal predilections still manifested themselves. The ambiguity of the ending struck them in different ways.

Adam: I honestly wasn't a huge fan of the ending. I thought it fit and I thought it worked for the book. As an ending to a book I think I really liked it. But as an ending to this particular story I didn't. I wanted there to be some closure, I wanted there to be some validation, but I didn't get that.

Margaret: So you wound up not knowing? Is that what you're saying?

Adam:	Well no, I mean – to me I think he was innocent, but innocent in my eyes and innocent in the public eye is completely different.
Sandra:	Well actually after I read the book I read the little questions in the back and there's one question, like *'Why did you decide to acquit him?'* and he [Myers] pretty much said because he wanted the story to be about Steve and not the judicial system, so I liked that because obviously he made the ending a certain way because he wanted to tell a certain story. He wanted everyone to take an idea of it because if he had been guilty, then it would have really changed the way you thought about it, or I thought about it, anyways.
Lewis:	Yeah, I wanted Steve to, you know, get acquitted, but at the same time throughout the trial, it was – the author did a really good job I thought on convincing both Steve and the reader at the same time, that he was less and less guilty you know. Like going through his mind, you know, 'I went there and I was just looking around. I wasn't the lookout'. Stuff like that. So yeah I just fed into that and sympathized with Steve and wanted him to get off. So I thought the ending was good. And ah – yeah.

The readers here can be seen applying the rules of coherence quite explicitly to achieve, as Rabinowitz puts it, the best text possible (1987, p. 45). Lewis may be wondering, in his final three words, if he could improve on his sense of the book by considering questions of ambiguity, and then deciding against it – but I may be reading too much into a short phrase.

Group A relished the ambiguity.

| Neil: | Of course they're skipping a lot because normally when they put a witness on the stand they go through stuff like, what's your name, what's your occupation, relationship status, your position in the community, all kinds of stuff, and for the most part they skip past all that, so it didn't really bother me so much. Even from the very beginning you could see that he was being very selective of what he decided to shoot. |

Dan: That almost made me think, though, I guess on a side note. You know, at least from what you read in his monologue later on, that he wasn't involved, but at the same time because of the whole nature of the story being edited where often in a movie they cut out the undesirable, especially like when his defence council was training him to respond desirably in the courtroom. You do get a bit of an impression that there's kind of an aspect of tuning what he was saying there and I think that that just added a question. A minor question to me was – is he really being honest with himself about his involvement in this case?

Keith: Yeah you do wonder about the biases.

Neil: I almost couldn't determine for myself whether he was guilty or innocent. I had to wait until the jury actually came to their conclusion, whether to decide the whole back story – what actually happened. If I was a juror on this thing I would have no idea. I couldn't come to a decision because we aren't shown everything.

Dan: But that's reasonable doubt, right?

Neil: Yes exactly.

Dan: That's all part of the court of law. If there's any doubt at all you can't make him guilty. So I think that's the whole thing about this case is, I think, the amount of obscurity was almost like a literary device. Like, it wasn't so much an image of a real courtroom, but it was used to sort of enhance the story he was telling.

Margaret: Yeah, because when it comes down to the crunch, it is a novel being produced here, isn't it?

Dan: Exactly. But it did almost throw [me] for a while, so it was pleasantly enjoyable.

In such an assessment, the need to tell a story and the means chosen to do so form part of the whole that Dan, in particular, takes into account when he thinks about the book overall. He is not only considering the story's overall shape, he is consciously thinking about the book as deliberately *shaped* and the nature of the authorial shaping process is part of the book's appeal.

Group B supply a range of approaches in one relatively short discussion. Martin, as usual, is most inclined to consider the book as a construct, Tess weighs the evidence and wonders if ambivalence is the only possible response, and Sumana comments on the emotional connections that are hampered by ambiguity, and on the importance of character growth. Here is Martin:

I think they isolated the question of perspective so much that concepts like truth and guilt and right and wrong were effectively sort of scattered, so that I didn't know what to believe, and so I've read the book and I found that I've become totally separated from the things that Steve was sort of thinking about in the book such as, am I guilty or not? Who says, who's right, who to believe – it's an interesting sort of alienation from what the book was about in reading it.

Sumana thought in terms of involvement with the characters, Steve and the lawyer:

I didn't end up caring for the character as much as I thought I would by the end of it. He just didn't seem like a very sympathetic character. So I mean, typically when you read a book with just one protagonist you kind of expect to become involved with them, but that didn't really happen in this case. Maybe it's because the question still lingers about whether he's guilty or not but the fact that he was so – even if he actually didn't physically do it himself, the fact that he was so involved with the criminals who did do it makes it – he's almost guilty by association. And it's sad kind of, right at the end when he's acquitted and then he turns to hug his lawyer and she turns away from him. I think that's sad – but I can understand her herself wondering whether he was guilty or not or even thinking he's guilty and being conflicted about the fact that he was acquitted and that's a victory for her because she's the lawyer, but on the other hand, what if he is guilty and he's getting off now.

Tess agreed about the power of that ambiguity.

That was definitely a scene that hit me as well was probably one of the strongest images in the book was because she just looks at him pretty much and that's it and then the book ends with what have I done or *what did she see* and so the question of the monster really, it isn't closed. I don't think he wants to believe, but you have to wonder, is that just a denial at this point? Is he not a monster? Is he becoming one because of what he's absorbing? Steve I also found to be a difficult character to sympathize with. There were points where I was like, okay I understand where you're coming from, but then other tangents I just go – did you do it or did you not? And then there's one passage where he actually says he doesn't so, okay well that's kind of what I wanted to know, but –

Sumana is more committed than some readers to reworking the story to make it 'better'. She extrapolates a satisfactorily moral conclusion from her reading of the story and persuades at least Tess, at least for the moment, that her argument is sustainable.

Sumana: But then, in a way it ends on a positive note because as he's making his films and he's starting to think about what his life has been so far and he's kind of on this path of self-discovery, the fact that he was acquitted has given him a new lease on life, so I think in a way that's true. More self-awareness and more awareness of staying at home with his family rather than getting into a criminal lifestyle.

Tess: For sure.

Run Lola Run

Because of the triple story arc, *Run Lola Run* demands a certain kind of wrap-up assessment at all three end-points of Lola's run. All the group members were acutely aware of the emphasis on patterning in this story, but Group B articulated it very strongly, though they focused as much on its absence as its presence. As Lola started her third run, Martin, for example, observed: 'So this is the third time; they're expecting some sort of tying together of the pattern.' And as the movie concluded, Group B's comments offered a very strong focus on making a coherent story out of the three conflicting versions and they invoked *lack of pattern* as a cohesive element:

Margaret: So what do you think about that then?

Sumana: A lot of things happened.

Martin: So many different aspects of faithful agency; like, destiny, chaos interacting at once. There was no way we could have known that *that* was going to happen. If the pattern was correct then she should have bashed right into the homeless person on the third try and seen the bag and been like, 'Oh right, a homeless person taking it', but like, there was ... there *was no* pattern I guess.

Tess: That's what made it work, I guess.

Sumana: And you could pull a lot of lessons out of it if you wanted to. Like, the fact that she gets all that money in a casino and you could be like, 'Well, I guess that means you should take risks in life and then it'll pay off' ... and you notice a kind of progression in each episode.

Margaret: Well, she was later the second time wasn't she?

Sumana: Yeah. And you see the different ways that Lola deals with her relationships and what the impact is – it's interesting from that point.

Martin: The three things that stick out at me the most are the running. It's in the title: the running is the most important facet of the story. Her appearance, like how she's being portrayed to me, and then the discombobulation of time. Essentially, what she is doing with running the whole time was gambling. She was hoping for a miracle. She was hoping for something and she happened to get it the third time.

Tess: The trick is – do we all get multiple chances? What are they trying to say by running us through multiple realities, or maybe different aspects of the same reality? If you're moving as fast as she is, like she's always moving, she's always running, she never really ever stops and when she does I guess the scenery starts moving in the background. The one time, like when she's trying to figure out 'okay, who's going to help me with this – Dad', things are still spinning, things are still moving. Nothing really freezes. I also thought the two scenes between Lola and Manni –

Martin: See I disagree because I think those are two scenes where things freeze.

Tess: Well that's true. They do stop there. I thought it was interesting positioning, though. In the first scene where she dies, she's under his arm and then when he dies, he's under hers. And then, of course, in the third you never really see anything, but I think it's interesting that the movie ends when you hear sort of the sound of the flash developing on him and you never really know what's going to happen after that. Like, they could be caught, the guys could come back and be like, 'Well there's not enough money', because the bum must have taken some to buy the bike, to buy the jacket he was wearing. The money's probably not complete.

Martin: No, but I don't know if there's support for that in the movie because they show you explicitly that everything's cool with Ronnie. So, 100,000 Deutschmarks – she goes to the casino and she's short by 80 and it doesn't matter.

Tess: Yeah, that's true.

As with the discussions at the end of *Monster*, the members of Group B are here rehearsing elements of the story to place them in the most satisfying relationship with each other. To use a metaphor that is in keeping with the subject matter, it is as if the lens of their discussion is in a camera that zooms in on particular details and then retreats to a long shot to fit those details into a larger thematic picture. The interaction of destiny and chaos, the idea of risk-taking as a life lesson versus the notion of gambling on a miracle, the question of whether we do get multiple chances in life are very large questions, but as they discuss them, Tess, Sumana and Martin zoom back in on some of the corroborative details: how Lola and Manni are positioned in relation to each other in the two death scenes (a piece of visual information), the sound of the flash ending the story (an audio element), and the assessment of the importance of the missing money (an ingredient involving story logic).

It is interesting to see Group B assessing the thematic importance of Lola's relationship to the person in the ambulance because in terms of specific detail they could not establish who this man was.

Sumana: She's just such a caring person; you even see that in the ambulance. She holds that person's hand and she's just – I guess she chose Manni as the object.

Martin: She says to the patient in the back of the ambulance 'I'll stay with him.' 'I have to make a decision' is what she says in the beginning of the movie. It's like, okay, if this is fate, if this is the random sequence of events and here I am at the back of an ambulance and here's where I'm supposed to be, and goodness comes out of it.

Margaret: Was he a random guy at the back of the ambulance then?

Tess:	I wasn't quite sure
Sumana:	I thought he was Mr. Meyer or something like that because he got hit by [*inaudible*].
Martin:	I thought so too.
Tess:	I thought that it was, but it didn't really look – it looked too young to be either of them.
Sumana:	You couldn't really tell from the angle.
Martin:	So if there's no evidence to support – if these are all speculations that we're making, what I take from that is that we're not meant to know. Like, at the same time as we're trying to establish a pattern, at the same time there's a classic like, tertiary pattern going on. It's almost like nothing is supposed to be connected. Chaos – here's what happened and it happened to work out in this version. In the first one, people are dying, in the one she has the money, one she doesn't, in one they both have the money. In one she cares, in one it seems like she's having second thoughts at the very end of the movie.

Many viewers struggled with the identity of the man in the ambulance (it was actually the security guard from the bank, the man who threw the football into the air in the opening credits, but the image is clearly confusing in a context where we have seen several middle-aged white men in brief succession). What is of particular interest here is that Group B were collectively happy to surmount that missing detail and settle for a 'pattern of no pattern', to take chaos as an appropriate explanation of the ending.

Shadow of the Colossus

The video game provides a fascinating window on the ways in which interpreters, to use Rabinowitz's terms, actually configure coherence as they approach the end of the story. After the sixteenth colossus is killed, there is a long scene – mostly cut scene but players are not certain if they will be given further opportunities to take action so they maintain their game gaze. In effect they are watching a silent movie, where the only spoken words are also provided, in translation, on title cards. In the previous accounts of the endings of *Monster* and *Run Lola Run*, the comments are chronologically separate from the decoding itself; with the game they are simultaneous.

Group D's comments as the game wound down to an end offer us a window on their thought processes whose immediacy is difficult to replicate with other media. In their comments (which are mostly very brief indeed), we can see synchronous live-action interpretation as it develops. The rarity of such direct access to the thinking of interpreters seems to me to justify some extended consideration.

We pick up this conversation as the sixteenth colossus collapses. As reported earlier, this final scene reveals that the hero has all along been the tool of Dormin, and as the sixteenth colossus dies he turns into something like a colossus himself and must be killed by the masked riders. The girl and the horse both return from the dead, and there is an ambiguous conclusion in which the hero appears to return as a baby.

This whole scene takes about 25 minutes to play out, and there is plenty of time for conversation during most of the events. As this conversation begins, Lewis is at the controls and the sixteenth colossus has just been slaughtered.

(Success at last!)
Lewis: Very impressive.
Sandra: Ooh I can feel it shaking!
Adam: I'm still waiting for another boss to pop out or for him to start walking.
Lewis: Shh, you're ruining the ending!
Sandra: Ooh! Look!
Lewis: That was awesome. The tower collapses.
(The black tendrils arrive)
Adam: As we fall and die.
Lewis: Yeah where are we? Oh – sweet.
Sandra: Uh-oh!
Lewis: I like that his armour busted. His armour busted off.
Adam: Yeah that was pretty cool.
Sandra: This is big!!
Adam: I still think there's somebody else to play.
Lewis: No.
Adam: And there's only ten more minutes!
Lewis: Are you kidding? That guy took like an hour and a half to beat! Here we go; this is a masked guy I bet.
(Men on horses gallop across the bridge)

The initial comments are evaluative, with Lewis's comment at the end registering new information, as the scene shifts to the bridge to the temple.

As they continue to watch the lengthy cut scene that concludes the game, Group D start to theorize about the story's overall shape.

(Statue crumbles)
Sandra:	I don't know.
Adam:	At the very least we should never have to fight that thing again – hey, crossbow!

(One of the men raises a crossbow)
Sandra/Lewis:	Ohhh!
Adam:	No – see, he's a bad guy.
Lewis:	He doesn't want the Colossus dead.
Sandra:	I liked when – where is [*inaudible*]?
Adam:	We're evil! We're totally evil!
Lewis:	That'd be sweet if that happened.
Adam:	Because now the darkness has gone inside us, we're totally evil.

Adam is the first to forecast the plot turn that recasts the moral shape of the entire game. Lewis is swift to respond with admiration for the potential upheaval of the story that such a twist would represent. The pronouns in this little section reflect intense movement in the deictic centre: Adam begins with 'we', but then he and Lewis switch to 'he' (it seems as if Adam is referring to the hero and Lewis to the man with the crossbow, but it is not entirely clear). Adam reverts to 'we' as he makes his new prediction. Sandra is meanwhile using 'I' to refer to herself in a spectator role.

Adam relished the narrative shift but Sandra needed some explaining.

Adam:	Ooh yummy.
Sandra:	What do you mean we're evil?
Lewis:	What if it got turned around in the story that we were working for the bad guy and now –
Adam:	We killed her. We had to bring a sacrifice in order to get into the valley of the colossi –
Lewis:	And this Lord Emon guy is like, 'No you've unleashed evil on us that the colossus was supposed to protect.'
Adam:	Yeah.
Sandra:	Oh –
Lewis:	Like you know, lock away?
Sandra:	Maybe.

Lewis: Like lock away a being or something.
Sandra: This is interesting.
Lewis: That would be a good twist.

Sandra helpfully asks for further explanation so it is possible to see that both Adam and Lewis are very engaged by this possible plot turn. Adam goes one stage further and suggests that the hero has even killed the girl to have a token body to cover his quest for evil.

As the story progresses, the three continue to develop theories of plot.

(Hero is stabbed and black 'blood' starts to spew – he stands up clutching at the sword and the masked men back away)
Sandra: That was a good call in saying that we're evil, you know?
Adam: All right. Time to beat the crap out of these guys.
Lewis: Suddenly we're immortal? Like –
Adam: I don't think we're immortal, I think we're a colossus.
Lewis: Maybe.
Adam: Because that's the same kind of blood as a colossus had.
Lewis: Yeah for sure.

Adam is still expecting to fight, but he is looking at the screen with more than a game gaze at this point. His comments summarize the swiftly changing plot developments, and again, he is first to notice that the logical development of evil is that the hero turns into a colossus himself, an observation he backs up with the evidence of the black blood/shadow. As the hero pulls the sword from his body and collapses on the ground, Adam continues to develop his theory: 'Oh, and we become one of the dead shadows. Sealed up in stone maybe?'

One final snatch of dialogue comes from the last part of the story as the credits are rolling, and, though it is brief, it does give us a view of active processing continuing to the very end. As the heroine picks up the baby and leads the horse out of the temple, a deer comes into view, the first sign of life larger than a lizard or a bird that we have seen in this desolate landscape throughout the whole game.

Lewis: A deer.
Sandra: It's Bambi!
Adam: Shoot it!
Lewis: There's life, it's showing life.
Adam: Food!!! [*Laughter*]

Lewis: No, symbolism!
Adam: They got to survive somehow!
Lewis: It's symbolism.
Adam: Fine. Shoot the mother then.

Adam and Lewis disagree about how to interpret the role of the deer, and, as a compromise, Adam offers an intertextual joke created out of Sandra's mention of *Bambi*. Lewis is, at this point, still more whole-heartedly invested in the story world, but he is not 'reading' it simply for verisimilitude; he is happy to look for larger meanings in the appearance of the deer – a classic example of reading for maximum coherence.

Group AB were eloquent after the fact about the impact of putting so much of the story at the end of the game.

Margaret: I just want to start asking what the ending does to the game?
Martin: It tries to legitimize it. It tries to legitimize the repetitive violence that we just went through.
Dan: And the lack of story line. It feels like they're trying to sort of vindicate themselves for writing an all-in-all linear and boring game.

Their analogies were also very telling. Martin, for example, said, 'I feel, seeing as how they weren't integrated, the shape and the action ... If you want, this is sort of like a porno – and then doing all the character exposition afterwards.' Dan and Neil talked about the varying importance of the story in different kinds of games. Dan's view is that the story matters less if a game is designed for social playing.

Dan: [A social game is] like ping-pong or another sport. You know, you're playing the competition for the social aspect, not for the story. But when it's single player, linear, you definitely want the story to be good.
Neil: If I had a set of 16 solitaire games that I was going to go through, I'd be like, no. Like if they set up the same thing with 16 solitaire games? To do solitaire games, I wouldn't really –
Dan: You mean, you'd finish the last solitaire game on a piece of paper with a note on it to tell a story?

The late introduction of so many story elements clearly offended them on many levels, though Dan continued to assert that the game fulfils many Japanese story schemas. They would have liked some of the complexity of the ending to accompany their slaughter of the colossi. Yet parts of the ending did appeal to them.

Dan: To make you the colossus was a neat idea. I'll give them that. That was an interesting way to finish off a very –

Neil: But they didn't do anything with it.

Dan: Yeah it was too minimal.

Martin: Like what does it mean? It's a neat idea but again, relating to the story and relating to the action, it's like –

Dan: I think the whole game focused on puzzles a little more. On solving puzzles to get to the colossus and then if you kill the colossus and 'thy next foe is' times 16, with one little video and you get the story all at the end and I think that way of doing things doesn't appeal to me. It removes the significance of the story from the game play because you don't really see anything happening as you go. You don't see any of the workings behind the scenes and that's what makes the story kind of fall flat.

Martin: I think the action would have been more significant and we would have felt that it was more important if we'd had plot all along. Being like, oh crazy, this Emon guy is like – wait a minute – and then by the end you don't end up killing the sixteenth colossus.

Dan: But that's the thing I think they want you to kill the sixteenth and to feel the whole thing at the end – the letdown/betrayal.

Martin: Maybe 16 was too many repetitions?

Dan: Maybe.

Neil: Nah, they were all different.

Dan: Yeah they were all different. It was fun, killing them was fun, but – I didn't like this 'thy next foe is – ' times a million.

Neil: Well yeah that seemed – you kind of want some variation, like some more story that goes along with each one. Normally you'd have the progression of a plot but you didn't.

This conversation takes late story elements and weaves them into the effect of the whole. It is evaluative both of the game as played and of some possible alternative scenarios. It relates parts to whole and whole to parts. It takes Rabinowitz's idea of coherence and blends it with elements of assessment and considerations of engagement.

There are many pages of such transcript from all the groups, absorbed in very complex retrospective thinking about the story and the game. The game analysis is every bit as elaborated as that involved in discussions of the book and the film, even though the story component of the game is so minimal. The narrative achievement of these interpreters is impressive and intriguing.

10
Inhabiting the Story: Comparative Perspectives

Gunther Kress and Theo van Leeuwen make the strong case for a mono-modal past:

> For some time now, there has been, in Western culture, a distinct preference for monomodality. The most highly valued genres of writing (literary novels, academic treatises, official documents and reports, etc.) came entirely without illustration, and had graphically uniform, dense pages of print. Paintings nearly all used the same support (canvas) and the same medium (oils), whatever their style or subject. In concert performances all musicians dressed identically and only conductor and soloists were allowed a modicum of bodily expression. The specialized theoretical and critical disciplines which developed to speak of these arts became equally monomodal: one language to speak about language (linguistics), another to speak about art (art history), yet another to speak about music (musicology), and so on, each with its own methods, its own assumptions, its own technical vocabulary, its own strengths and its own blind spots.
>
> (2001, p. 1)

Even if Kress and van Leeuwen are correct about texts (and the history of magazines or museums suggests that they are themselves a little monocular in their perspective on past media trends), *interpreters* have never been confined to the single medium they were inspecting on any single occasion; their overall experience invariably includes multiplicity. Nor have narratives been confined to a single form of expression; from at least the time of the Greeks, stories have been represented in multimodal ways: in songs, as statues, on vases, across friezes, and so forth. For the best part of a century since the introduction of domestic

199

radio, some forms of multimodality have been close to ubiquitous in the households of the West. Disciplines may be constrained, but people cross over media boundaries all the time.

The first fact about the young people in this project is that they cannot address any explicit question about a single medium or format, no matter how monomodally phrased or intended, from any standpoint but that of a multimodal interpreter. However singular the focus, their stance is unavoidably comparative. Although I deliberately selected texts without cross-media cognates, I know that all 12 participants came to the project with an extensive background of comparing the same narrative across a variety of media projections. Their comparative instincts may indeed be almost as highly automated as their ability to process print or moving image. This is not to say that such understanding was necessarily explicit, but there is no question that at least some elements of it could be readily articulated on request. In this chapter we will consider some of the explicit discussion of interpretive processes.

Much of this book derives from analysis of how participant response manifests tacit understanding. Such information is highly productive in terms of creating the 'spokes' that enhance our understanding of the particularities of other people's narrative interpretive processes. Some information, however, can be acquired only through direct questioning that attempts to explore the inside of that 'black box' of personal understanding. In this chapter, I will present some of the explicitly articulated descriptions of how these 12 interpreters explored and experienced both the story world and the text surface.

Most of the comments in this chapter come from the third session with each group. At this point, everyone had watched *Run Lola Run* and finished reading *Monster* at home; they had all played one initial hour of *Shadow of the Colossus*. After we finished talking about *Monster* and before we moved on to the second round of game playing, I conducted a set discussion on aspects of reading, viewing and playing. I asked specific questions and explicitly invited participants to describe how they go about interpreting different forms of text. I was impressed at how fluently all 12 participants were able to articulate details about their own private interpretive processes, and, once again, it bears noting how readily they understood each other's predilections. Their understanding of the mental world of narrative was sufficiently strong that they could extrapolate into the experience of others, even when their private practices seemed to differ. It is easy to underestimate the extraordinary nature of this common achievement.

All 12 participants encountered the same initial texts. All 12 followed interpretive paths with recognizable similarities. Yet in the end, no matter how many 'spokes' round that imaginary circle we can establish in terms of attending, orienting, progressing, and so forth, the experience inside the black box of each interpreter's mind was specific to each of them and was *felt* and *thought* in different ways. Direct access to the black box is impossible but explicit questioning elicited indirect descriptions of aspects of that experience. The variations described in these discussions provide a sharp reminder that the differences also matter, that the core of the interpretive experience is personal and distinctive.

We may readily generalize that interpreters conceptualize narratives in different ways, but the default of our own 'black box' experience is seductive and persuasive, and it is easy to revert to the imperial singular of our own preferences. The particularities fleshed out by these 12 young people vivify the cognitive range of their distinctive experiences in ways that testify to the ineradicably plural nature of interpretive success.

Ways of reading

Take a relatively simple example. Here are readers talking about visualizing. Not all readers inhabit a story through the creation of a visual image as they read a scene, and not all visualizing readers do it all of the time, as the members of Group A made plain.

Dan: Everything for me when I read is very – it's kind of strange, but it's almost like, as I read, a scene is *rendered* in my head and I say that word, I guess, because I'm a computer geek, but it's very much like as a scene is described it starts to build in my mind and I can definitely visualize it very easily every time I read something, especially when it's descriptive, more so than this where it's ambiguous. I definitely do visualize the scene in my head.

Neil: I guess it's not quite like a movie for me, it's not quite as developed. It's an understanding and I actually almost prefer it to a movie at times. It's a little bit more powerful way to move through it, but I'm not really sure I can quantify that.

Keith: I can just move through it.

Neil: I can just move through a story subconsciously, experiencing it.

Keith: Yeah, it's more of a feeling you understand, but it's not like you're looking, you're reading and you see a movie going through.

Lewis is a visual reader but he also adds other elaborations to his mental imagery. 'I am a visual reader the whole time', he said. 'I played it as a movie going through my head while I read it. Different things, you know, would pop into my head. What music would go well here, stuff like that.'

Sumana added another component to her description of the experience of reading *Monster*.

It's quick dialogue going back and forth; sometimes, for me anyway, it's kind of like voices. Hearing the voices, not necessarily picturing every move that the person makes, especially if it's just two people talking. As you're reading it you can kind of hear slightly differentiated voices.

Adam of Group D was even more committed to an audio as well as a video element to his reading experience. I asked if he saw images as he read.

Adam: Yeah. Partially because I was reading it as a screenplay and again, the background is playing into that whole thing because I read plays and I need to pay attention to that because I need to know how it's going to be staged and everything like that. The entire time I was actually considering about what would this be like if it was a movie. There were times every now and then where I'd say, 'Oh I don't think a close-up would work here. I don't think a long shot would work here.' But –

Margaret: And did you have a definite image of the characters and the court scenes and that sort of thing?

Adam: Oh yeah.

Margaret: So you had faces in your mind?

Adam: Yeah.

Margaret: And is that how you always read?

Adam: Yeah.

But he was equally explicit about hearing the book as he read to himself.

Adam: I definitely give each character a different voice.

Margaret: And you hear the voices?

Adam: Well I need to, actually, or else I can't keep them straight in my head. So they need to have these separate identities, these separate voices that argue. Especially during the courtroom scenes where the lawyers are getting angry at each other and they're shouting out 'Objection!' I imagine their voices getting higher and angrier.

Margaret: So you hear in detail.

Adam: Definitely!

I asked him about the narrative voice that supplies setting, descriptions, and ongoing events, and he did not hesitate:

In a regular book, that's generally just my voice and then in this one as well it was my voice reading the stage directions. I find it really hard to separate a word, because a word on paper doesn't really mean anything until it's spoken, so I need to give it that … Even when looking at certain sentences I need to do that because I need to decide where the inflection is. And decide where the person is putting the emphasis because it will completely change the way it's taken.

Interestingly, Adam applies the same audio strategies when gaming: 'When I play a video game I even give the characters voices when they don't have them.'

The variety of ways in which a story is manifested in sensory terms in different people's heads is striking and intriguing. Visuals are clearly important to some interpreters, audio to others. Keith and Neil, the non-visual readers, both speak of 'moving through' the story and it may well be that some of the pleasure they describe could be labelled as kinaesthetic. Affective vividness, the act of creating a 'live' story in the mind, is clearly achieved in varying ways – some of them related to other media and some of them simply connected to the multimodal percepts of our daily experience.

I have never seen formal research on this topic but over the years I have asked hundreds of readers (research subjects, students, audiences) about visualizing as they read. My informal sense is that a large majority does create mental pictures – some to a high degree of specificity and stability – but a reliable minority does not. The auditory reader and the reader who 'feels' presences and moves among them both appear in this project, and they also show up every time I ask a group of readers this question.

The kind of 'virtual kinaesthetics' created by the 'moving' reader are particularly interesting to me because this cognitive approach is so under-reported and under-theorized. And yet, it makes sense that a chronotope, thickening time and space in the artistic representation, should be experienced through a feeling of moving, an activity that also involves both time and space. We know that most of children's early experience of the 'as-if' state of the subjunctive is experienced actively through pretend play. Why should the abstractions of narrative text not be enlivened dynamically through a sense of virtual movement?

I must acknowledge a small degree of special interest. I read this way myself and can report that, while inside my own black box it is possible with great effort to create a visual setting (which has no staying power, no matter how detailed I make it), my mind simply balks – refuses outright – when instructed to picture a face. I am aware of every nuance of characters' emotional states and can feel them around me, but their faces insist on remaining a fuzzy blank in my mind.

The idea that most people do create a mental picture but some do not would be interesting but not necessarily significant if the visualizers were less insistent on the importance of their own mental processes as a guide to every reader. There is a considerable educational discourse that is adamant about the necessity to visualize as part of successful reading. For example, Gunning, in his *Reading Comprehension Boosters: 100 Lessons for Building Higher-Level Literacy*, lists visualizing as a key strategy:

> *Strategies* are deliberate, planned procedures designed to help readers reach a goal … Previewing, predicting, summarizing, visualizing, connecting, and questioning are strategies. In contrast to strategies, *skills* are automatic processes that are usually performed without conscious control. When strategies are applied automatically, they become skills.
>
> (2010, p. 1, emphasis in original)

Bergeron and Bradbury-Wolff, addressing primary grade teachers, list visualizing on their book cover as an essential strategy, and define its utility as follows:

> Visualizing (word level): Creating mental visual images to keep your mind focused as you read or listen: Visualizing helps readers with comprehension by conjuring up images of a story as it is being read.
>
> (2002, p. 11)

Such exhortations are every bit as monomodal as Kress and van Leeuwen's list of high-culture exclusivities above. It does seem clear that narrative comes to life when interpreters find a way to *inhabit* the 'as-if', but that sense of experiencing the story need not necessarily be visual in nature. In popular theories of learning styles, visual, auditory, and kinaesthetic categories are familiar. I have no idea whether people's cognitive preferences in interpretation are related in any way to their possible learning styles. Nevertheless, the breakthrough of considering the plural nature of cognitive potential has a virtue that could be applied to questions of interpretive strategy as well. Acknowledging the validity of varied cognitive and affective approaches also supplies an interesting lens for looking at critical thinking about texts.

Comparative thinking: Media affordances as critical lens

Jason Mittell draws our attention to the active processing required to make sense, referring in this case to film.

> Cognitive schemata are used, often without conscious awareness, to collect bits of information presented in a film and construct it into a seemingly naturalistic narrative world; viewers strengthen comprehension and acquire new schemata through the repetitive act of viewing media and become more skilled as spectators ... A key aspect of narrative comprehension is that we tend to notice ourselves making such inferences and hypotheses *only when narration is ambiguous or mysterious*, as typical narrative connections and assumptions that we make from moment to moment ... are processed nearly automatically following learned schemata at a cognitive level that we are barely aware of.
>
> (2007, p. 168, emphasis added)

I think Mittell is partially correct. Much of our narrative interpretation occurs subliminally and swiftly, and even an exercise in slowing down such as this project cannot capture many interpretive assumptions made automatically and on the fly. However, I think he underestimates the sophistication of narrative interpretation that is *always already* a feature of contemporary life and does not just spring to life when the narrative surface is recalcitrant, as he suggests. Even as the participants in this project attended singularly to *Monster* or *Run Lola Run* or *Shadow of the Colossus*, they invariably did so as interpreters of multiple media forms. Moving from one format to another also often foregrounds interpretive strategies because it throws them to the surface, rather than burying them deep below the level of conscious attention. The surface of the text is also *experienced* in vivid and lively ways. Comparative questions make immediate sense to such users, as we can see in the following example.

When I invited Group B to compare *Run Lola Run* to a videogame as they came to the end of watching the movie, they explicitly drew on the potential for comparison as part of their assessment of the overall coherence of the story. The ability to move between different media possibilities gave them vocabulary for considering and critiquing the film.

Margaret:	One of the reasons I picked this movie is that it has actually been compared to a video game and I just wondered if you'd like to reflect on that for a second?
Tess:	I can see that – the mixing of media, the different shots and the camera angles – the treatment of violence in the underground, as well, I think is less sensationalized, maybe. Like, what Sumana was saying earlier, this money's going to either some form of black market and a drug dealer, but we get wound up in Lola's story and we don't really care where the money's going. What matters is, can she get it within the time frame of what, 20 minutes.
Sumana:	And she gets three chances just like [*inaudible*].
Martin:	It's like, you lose, play again sort of thing.
Tess:	The phone flipping, yeah. It's like, three – two – one.
Margaret:	Yeah, once you die you start all over again
Tess:	Yeah.

The comparative potential of the video game analogy continued to be productive for them for some time.

Martin:	The detachment that Lola shows at the end of the movie is striking to me because it seems like – okay, so what has she been doing? She's been showing superhuman endurance, and she's been running, as opposed to like, taking a cab or opposed to making a phone call –
Tess:	Or getting a friend to –
Martin:	Yeah, as opposed to just phoning her dad at the bank or something.
Margaret:	Well, there's a video game quality to that too, isn't there?
Tess:	Oh for sure.
Margaret:	The main characters do a lot of dashing, don't they?

Sumana: Yeah. And the thing is, when you're playing a video game you see the same situations coming up over and over again as your character walks through the environment and that just makes you feel like you should be able to win because you've seen these certain things along the way.

Martin: Her encounters with these other characters, and then those characters' features are exposed and those characters' features are different each time, just like Manni's and Lola's are. It's almost like she's interacting in this network. Obviously people on earth and interactions are totally random and chaotic and these other peoples' futures are also being chaotically determined as well. One of them would be a really good future and the next time it would be, oh random events conspired to – like, they show you progression – they show you how it happened.

Later in our discussion, the video game comparison served me as a lens for raising questions about the role of three cartoon segments that initiated each of Lola's three runs; it was clear this cross-media metaphor was productive for these interpreters.

Tess: I found it interesting that in the opening sequence where she's running, she does get caught in the spiral, but – you see the other three where she goes down the stairs again, that's kind of an interesting way of looking at it. Down the rabbit hole if you will, but she manages usually to land at least on her feet. Either she'll soar over the dog or she'll tumble down the stairs, but she'll land. She won't get sucked in by the gravity, by time, whatever the vortex is supposed to represent.

Martin: From my experience with playing video games, she handled it the exact same way that I do. When Mario was approaching the little Koopa Troopa or whatever it is, he'll avoid it one time, and it'll get him one time and he'll sort of fall off the screen and you'll start again or you learn to jump over it. It's these little tiny obstacles continuously that you have to learn how to avoid them and there's not really any pattern, it's just a random computer program.

Sumana: I don't know. I didn't pay that much attention to the cartoon. It was a good way of splitting up the different

> episodes, but it just seemed ... I don't know, it didn't
> really make that much of an impression.
>
> Margaret: You did notice they were there?
> Sumana: Yeah I did.

Sumana reminds us that different viewers see the pattern differently. Her final observation is crucial. One weakness of a study such as this one lies in the relative difficulty of observing what interpreters *don't* notice. One person's key observation leaves another person oblivious. Such initial lack of notice may be one factor in the pleasures of re-visiting a story subsequently – or it may be that an element of a story may remain forever unattended, no matter how many times it is encountered. Not all gaps are artfully composed by the creator; some are obliviously inserted by the interpreter.

Nevertheless, the comparative perspective offered these viewers many productive angles on the film. Thinking in comparative terms was clearly very comfortable for them.

Ways of living the game: Group C discuss sources of appeal

It is a truism that different people may enjoy the same text for different reasons, but given a strong popular tendency to group all gamers into one monolithic and mindless category, it is interesting to explore how Jarret, Sebastian and Jacob articulate the refinements of the pleasure they take in games. Interpreters are often very happy to compare and contrast one text with another, and in this short section, Group C make a number of such comparisons. But they also take the opportunity to compare themselves as players; they know each other well and their long history of playing together comes through very strongly in this discussion. I think it is also clear why they enjoy the experience of gaming with each other; their collective sense of humour is cumulative and many of their jokes have long pedigrees.

Unlike the discussions featured elsewhere in this chapter, this conversation took place during game play. As they hunted for the eleventh colossus, I asked them to pin down some of the appeal of the game.

> Sebastian: I like the accomplishment of defeating the big foe.
> Jacob: Yeah.
> Sebastian: That about the biggest one for me. The feeling of accomplishment that you've taken one out or it was a big

challenge and when you first got there you were kind of getting swatted around and didn't really know what to do, but then you kind of figured it out and were able to best it.

Margaret: If it were just blobs, would it be the same thing? How much is the personality of the colossus part of the pleasure of the achievement?

Sebastian: Oh, that really helps – like, having a really characteristic monster. If all the monsters are kind of the same and they all do the same sort of thing, then it gets kind of boring and mundane. But if each one has different character-istics or a different flavour to it, where it really makes them stand out and they're unique – like, the flying one, and the swimming one and the one where you have to run it into the wall. The first couple of the ones where it was the man walking around with the big stick – those, I thought, were kind of boring because they're all the same.

Jarret listened to his teammates' assessment of what makes a game engag-ing but raised a new point of appeal for himself.

Jarret: Anyway, I'm rather different. I'm all about the competi-tion.

Margaret: Mmm hmm.

(Hero back on Agro galloping towards the bridge)

Sebastian: Yeah, you probably got the biggest kick out of the one Jacob and I failed, and you beat. That's probably, like, the greatest thing to you.

Jacob: Jarret's like, 'I put it in my diary' [*chuckles*].

Sebastian: 'December 16th, 2005.'

Jarret: I'm okay fighting the same monsters. Today –

Sebastian: 'Today I played a video game with Jacob and Sebastian and they both failed, but I succeeded. I am clearly the higher calibre man [*chuckles*] and a better person.'

Jacob: 'I feel justified and no longer feel ashamed that I couldn't beat the easy one, but Sebastian did.'

(Hero off horse and descending into a quarry-like structure)

Jarret: That's right. It's all about the hard ones.

Margaret: So would *you* care if this were just a little blob? Do you have any investment at all in the character of the story, or the horse, or anything?

| Jarret: | Well, it has to have a bit of a challenge, or obviously there's no point. |
| Jacob: | You have to have really good game play if there's no story. Kind of like *Pac Man* or *Tetris*, because they can get by completely on game play. |

I raised the subject of how their conversation so frequently took an intertextual turn.

Margaret:	I notice, just when you're chatting as you play, you do a huge amount of referring to other stories.
ALL:	Yeah.
Margaret:	Is that part of the pleasure too?
Sebastian:	Partly, but a lot of themes re-occur, so sometimes it can help. Plus it's funny to see how different works draw on each other. I really like games that include that in the game, where they're actually making fun of other things I've seen.
Jarret:	We've all played a lot of games together for a lot of years.

As they continued to move through the game, they reverted to the idea of where their pleasures lay, and raised the question of their collective humour. The following discussion took place during the hunt for the twelfth colossus.

Jarret:	More than any video game itself is the witty banter that comes with playing video games.
Jacob:	I know, we had some pretty good wit during *Halo*, I thought.
Sebastian:	We played so much of *Halo*.
Margaret:	So it's a social event above everything else?
Sebastian:	Yeah, I really like games that are multi-player that I can play with my friends. If I have a game that I'm just playing by myself, it gets boring after a while.
Jacob:	I like some games that are by yourself, but they have to be pretty involving.

A major role of story in a game for Group C is to enhance the interest of the game play, and one strong element of the pleasures of the game play comes from the social connection. Story is but one ingredient in a complicated web of appeal, yet its absence leaves a serious hole in that web.

Issues of competition, accomplishment, and social connection are clearly important for these three men, and games offer the potential for all three in ways more difficult to achieve with book and movie. As the story is extended in the game by its full muscular realization, openings for social commitment are created; as players affect the outcome, accomplishment and competitiveness come 'into play'.

Comparative media pleasures: Group A and the joys of reading

The men of Group A were all explicit about the excitement and challenge of gaming; watching movies they described in more passive terms. What surprised me a little was the passion they brought to their description of reading. Here is a relatively short extract from a very long conversation on this topic. In it they discuss pleasures both at the surface level and at the level of being 'lost' in the story.

Neil: It's easier to lose yourself in something that's like a book because it's so much more real, I guess. The only other thing that I can think of that you could lose yourself in as effectively would be like complete virtual reality, which you're moving in your environment and your skills sets are changing, but when you're in a book, the character's ability to be able to understand Russian or something almost becomes your own. And a game could never give that and neither could a movie. Whereas with a book, one just kind of accepts that and moves on. So that's kind of a unique ability. But I suppose VR if it was life-like enough.

Dan: It's so hard to describe, I guess, it's really tough. But yeah, there's something about a game that just isn't present and it almost feels like it's two dimensional compared to a book and so does a movie. It's the somewhat intangible quality of a book that makes it so enjoyable because not only are you experiencing the story but you can almost live it, you can become the character or you can view the character. The option is literally unlimited because you're just in the book. In a game, while you have control, you still can't control some aspects. You're still required to view it from a third person point of view and you have to move this way to beat the game. So I think that's the one thing about a book is that, even though the story is laid out, the way you approach that story is entirely up to you.

Keith: You know, I almost think it's because it's so easy to lose yourself in a book or a movie and not a game is because if you had a game where you were perfect at it and there was never any interruptions, maybe then you could lose yourself in it, but you will never, ever finish the game perfectly and there's always obstacles and then you've got to think. As soon as you've got to think about what you're doing rather than the story it kind of separates you from it whereas a book you keep reading and it just happens automatically.

Dan: That's a good point, yeah. The one game I really enjoyed that I played again, and that I knew all the puzzles, tricks and stuff aside, it definitely was different. It wasn't like gaming for me. This game was *Half-Life 2* and my second time through it literally felt very much more like an experience rather than an interaction because it was just automatic. And I think that's what reading is, because throughout life you read so much, that's the advantage the written media has is that this is always going to be something that you can do almost automatically and there's none of this game thing where, 'how do I jump up the colossus because I have to hit these buttons' and it's very mental.

Neil/Keith: Yeah.

Dan: And when you don't have to intellectualize it, as in a book, I think that's what makes it so enjoyable.

Neil: Well, even if it wasn't for the controls in a game, [*chuckles*] what makes the game is the fact that there's some difficulty involved, there's a puzzle to solve, like a jumping puzzle at the low end or other puzzles involved like where to go or what would be the best move at this point. That's what makes a game a game and if you lost that it really wouldn't be a game anymore. It would be something you were walking through, which would be not nearly as good.

Dan: Yeah, that's it I think – like a problem. I mean a game has to be solved but a book's already been answered. That's one way I can kind of explain what I experience, but it is very much a subconscious awareness that the game definitely has to be – there's things I have to do and in a book I know they've already been done, I just have to kind of see how they turn out.

The three men are vividly unanimous in their account of the superior power of reading to absorb them, even as they occasionally struggle to articulate the source of that controlling force. Keith, talking about how the need to think about your actions in a game interferes with your ability to lose yourself in the story, offers a textbook example of the differing pleasures of engagement and immersion as defined by Douglas and Hargadon (2001). He also provides a testimonial to the significance of automaticity as an important part of immersion.

These men suggest that reading is so familiar to them that automaticity is what fuels their deep immersion in a print story. They further posit the control of the author as another component in the capacity of a book to sweep them away, without responsibility for actions that might change the story. They do not raise the issue of the abstract nature of print, but it is worth considering whether the percept-reduced affordances of print play a profoundly important role in its ability to commandeer the attention of these readers.

Not everybody agreed with the particular power of print. Sebastian would allow only that it had the potential to be as immersive as film:

I like movies generally better than books because they're more engaging. I can see it, I can hear it, it's more immersive than a book. It's reading, and I suppose once you get into it, it reaches that same level, but it takes more work, whereas a movie you're just thrown in and it kind of engulfs you right away ... Well, with a book, once I sit down and start reading it and I don't have anything to distract me, then I'll enjoy it just as much as a movie, but I find it a lot easier to get immersed in a movie.

And Jacob made a strong case for the game as offering the most profound form of immersive experience:

Jacob: But some very immersive games that I've played have been more intense than any book or movie I've ever watched.

Margaret: Any idea why that is?

Jacob: Because you're there. It feels like it's you. You're making
              your own decisions, but that's only a certain manner of
              games. Not this one [*Shadow of the Colossus*]; it's got to be
              like a first-person RPG.

Margaret: Right, so you actually have the Tommy gun in your hand.

Jacob: You can solve problems in multiple ways, you don't
              always have to use violence.

All of these comments place a high value on immersiveness and its role
in the pleasure of the text, but Group C also demonstrated that engagement is also compelling.

The spectator position

When questioned directly about an absorbing interpretive experience,
interpreters often find they can actually articulate quite a bit about the
telling of the story. Engrossed in their reading, for example, interpreters do not always stop to investigate the virtual vantage point from
which, as spectators, they observe that narrative world. When asked
to describe that position, some participants were surprised. In all
cases, I mentioned the child who described herself as a 'dark watcher',
who could perceive but not be perceived from within the story world
(Benton and Fox, 1985, p. 9). Participants' responses to this description
were intriguing, and it is worth noting the comparative vocabulary that
ensued.

Sebastian, for example, took that metaphor and augmented it with
one of his own. 'I usually think a bit more in the third person view,
where almost like in a video game, where you're just hovering behind
the character and you can see them and you can see what they see, but
you're not necessarily looking through their eyes or even among them.'

Jarret replied by turning the question of involvement back to the
game: 'Even when I think about this, like the game we've been playing,
I haven't really related to the character, just sort of watching from above
and he happens to be the avatar – my actions, what I wish to do.'

Dan, speaking about *Monster*, came up with an account that clearly
invokes the 'dark watcher' position:

Towards the end I started … it was really weird because again, reading is more experiential than visual, but it was definitely like I was
sitting – floating next to the judge, you know, the little conversation
with the bailiffs and the prosecutor, and then I see O'Brien sitting

next to Steve talking. Well it's an experience. Again it's that sort of strange in-between experience.

At this point in the project, Martin and Dan had not met, but I think each would have understood the position of the other. Here is how Martin described his virtual place as reader of the court scenes:

> I'm not a member of the jury, I won't be in the courtroom but I'll be seeing the courtroom as though I was in it. I have no role – I'm not physically in anything and there's no entity where my point of view – there's no entity centered in the action that my point of view is seeing this from. I think it's just evoking images and then my imagination – well, it's just evoking my imagination, really.

Tess and Sumana also corroborated this *unplaced* sense of place, in comments following directly from Martin's remark, but they raise other important points as well.

Tess: I think it definitely depends on the style of prose because there are some where it does seem like you're watching from behind the character, but largely I guess the best way to describe it is a consciousness of what's going on. I don't think I've ever felt that I'm present within the novel, but it just – this is terribly corny – but it almost materializes around me and the fact that the words are what I'm looking at – well, it's sort of like a daze.

Sumana: In this book I think it evokes images. Just the fact that it uses different fonts makes you more aware of your own visual sense while you're reading it. But in general when I'm reading, I think it varies a lot. Like, sometimes I'll read and I'll just get totally absorbed in it. Especially if it's a lot of description, I just read it really quickly and then I just get kind of in the mood of it. Then other times if it's like a really poignant or a really well-written or exciting moment, then sometimes I can picture it in my head for that instance. So it really depends a lot on what's going on, it's not like always visual all the time.

Presentation matters, say Tess and Sumana, both in terms of word choice and organization, and also in terms of page design. Yet they also supply descriptions of the same vagueness mentioned by other readers: 'sort of like a daze'; 'kind of in the mood of it.'

Being a spectator is different from being a participant, and both Adam and Dan, in different discussions, specifically mentioned this situation of *not* being able to make a difference to the story. Adam, describing the pleasures of a game, said, 'It's a story you have control over to some point. But you *want* to relinquish control at other points because you want to see why you're doing this. If that makes sense at all?' Dan and Adam never did meet but Adam seems here to be recognizing what Dan elsewhere described as the reader's sense of *futility* in a book where everything has 'already been answered.'

What many of these interpreters are describing is a very abstract, disembodied experience, and their accounts both complement and contrast with some of the more sensual descriptions supplied earlier. It is actually surprising how compatible their different descriptions seem to be, not only because the remarks arise in different conversations but also because they appear to be describing *the same kind* of very nebulous perspective, even as they struggle to articulate what it is like. Their comparative conversations are based on private feelings and sensations but there is enough overlap to allow different interpreters to confirm a variety of perspectives in very real and convincing ways, even as they attempt to name the ineffable. The seeing, the hearing, the moving, and the feeling interpreter all inhabit what is in many ways a common space but they inhabit it in different ways. Comparative narrative experiences help these interpreters find vocabulary to articulate this nebulous phenomenon, and provide us with a gleam of provisional and fleeting access to the interiors of their own black boxes.

The metaphors for this private experience over and over again invoke interpreters who are multimodal in ways that feel instinctive or intuitive to them, though they are of course learned from a very early age. Their internal processes are multimodally tuned.

Intertextuality and the canon

It is time to feed these tacit and explicit elements of the interpretive experience back into the metaphor of circle and spokes that I developed in Chapter 1, and to explore the implications for how we think about our definitions of young people's literature in academic and professional ways. Over the course of this book I have attempted to establish that the 'spokes' of implicit approaches to narrative, manifested in these participants' responses, create a coherent pattern that is reliable across the media boundaries that this project established and explored. The spokes describe a circle, in short. And yet the articulated descriptions of the imaginative experience in this chapter provide a salutary reminder that, however organized and tidy the set of spokes, the 'inside' of the actual 'circle' of personal experience is nowhere near so neat. These 12 young interpreters reliably draw on multimodal experience to inform, and also to describe, their imaginative incarnation of the three narrative worlds. At the same time, they outline different perceptual priorities in how they vivify each story in their own minds. Occasionally we see very particular accounts of 'signature responses' (Sipe, 1998) that apply to different media. Adam supplies internal voices wherever they are missing, for example. Sumana looks for morals and messages in all her texts. These personal 'signatures' reinforce the larger pattern represented by the assembled 'spokes' of the various responses: these twenty-first-century interpreters are able to cross media boundaries in a variety of fluid ways, both generic and personal.

What is gained and what is lost when the schooling of contemporary young people focuses almost exclusively on strengthening their approaches to singular text forms (book or film most often)? Would the study of children's and young adult literature, for example, be enriched if the canon included a broader set of materials? Such an approach might make better use of the cultural assumptions that today's young people develop in their vernacular lives. The elaborated responses of these participants to each of the texts featured in this project suggest that the loss of that kind of complexity we commonly think of as literary might be radically less than many defenders of book culture may fear.

At the same time, all classrooms and many other arenas for interpretive conversations would greatly benefit from an improved awareness of the potential for different modes of internal vivification of a story. Not only are plural interpretations viable and productive, even the initial experience of the text is not nearly as uniform as many experts have posited.

One immediate benefit of enlarging the canon of children's and young adult fiction is that the scholarly and professional repertoire of intertextual connections would expand to come closer to that of very many young people. Although I have included very many intertextual comments in my selected transcripts, I have omitted many more. The richness of this field of reference is arbitrarily limited when only print (or print and film) references are visible or comprehensible to teachers at all levels who aim to strengthen their students' ability to reach critical conclusions.

Moreover, as the world of narrative options becomes ever more elaborate, the risks that attend a closing down of critical horizons can only increase. Already too many children and young adults consider print as something reserved for stagnant and restrictive classroom applications. By treating literary value as an either/or proposition (print good, gaming and online experiences a deficit rather than a strength), and by relying on a monolithic concept of interpretive vigour, teachers risk antagonizing rather than recruiting the imaginations of their students.

Obviously, not all video games engage the player's own psychology as complexly and delicately as *Shadow of the Colossus* does. We are still, however, in the early days of game development, and the potential range of transmedia hybrids that may include games and other new text forms is almost limitless. Now is the time to start paying attention.

11
Understanding Narrative Interpretation

The battle between the narratologists (the game presents a story) and the ludologists (the gameplay itself is what matters) has abated. But as platforms merge and mutate, as ways of presenting fictional worlds become more complex and multimodal, we may find ourselves perplexed at proliferating new forms, wondering how to understand them and how even to approach them in ways that maximize their interest and value. In 2010, new forms include the vook (e-book with video inserts), the digi-novel (e-book with audio and web extras), the augmented reality version (offering 3-D capabilities for a variety of flat screens and even book pages), the social media game (such as Farmville – see Ebner, 2009, B6), and the wiki novel – among many others. How will we navigate this complex territory, bringing our astonishing repertoire of conventional understanding to bear on new ways of making stories?

For this project, I made conservative choices; games have been around for decades, film for more than a hundred years, and books for centuries. Nevertheless, even in these relatively stable formats, questions about narrative potential arise. As stories become more diffuse, established in transmedia worlds where the complete fiction is available only to those who comb a variety of media for its separate but interlocking components, our questions about what makes a narrative will become even more complicated.

At the same time, a variety of narrative interfaces offers interpreters many opportunities to attend to the surface of a story, to be more aware of what can and cannot be done in one medium or another. As interpreters become more sophisticated, creators can presume that their readers will follow them further, and can take more daring chances. This situation leads to further experiment and innovation, and raises further complex questions about interpretation.

All these developments could lead to a crisis of definition about narrative form. I am not sure about the usefulness of attenuating our understanding of narrative ingredients to cover every possible category of change. What happens if, instead, we consider the rough-and-ready idea that 'narrative is what narrative *does*' and attend to the behaviours and strategies by means of which interpreters make as much narrative sense as suits them from a text or set of texts?

It is clear from the records of this project that the participants identified some narrative potential in all the texts they were given. The texts did not display all the standard attributes of classic narrative; they did not manifest rising action, definitive climax, explicit tying up of loose ends, and so forth. Nevertheless, they provided enough indicators for at least preliminary narrative strategies to kick in.

It is possible therefore that, in a world of fluctuating structures and possibilities, we are better off identifying narrative potential as a *strategic* option, as a guide for interpretive *actions*. Where will narrative interpretive processes take me? Is it productive to attend to narrative possibilities, to move into the fictional world subjunctively, to orient, to infer, and so forth? Identifying narrative potential in the face of ever more complex presentation becomes the vital first step, prior even to the initial forms of attention I describe in Chapter 4. Will the addition of this step allow us to understand our responses to new forms of text in more subtle ways?

Identifying narrative potential

Recognizing and responding to the narrative potential of a text is undoubtedly influenced by explicit information in the paratext in situations less contrived than that of this project, which stripped away much of the paratextual framework for the selections. But the trigger to recognize narrative possibility is tacit and swift – and productive of further options. To explore the potential of this strategic stance more fully, I turn to a highly unlikely analogy.

Jeremy Mynott, in his delightful book *Birdscapes: Birds in Our Imagination and Experience* (2009), discusses how a truly skilled birder can swiftly identify even highly unlikely birds, birds that nobody is looking for or expecting to see, birds whose distinguishing features remain invisible to lesser observers who are looking with less subtle eyes. The capacity to 'spot' (to use a birding term) narrative potential and to kickstart narrative interpretive strategies until they cease to be helpful may include the following attributes that Mynott describes as essential and very powerful tools: '(1) active attention, (2) informed expectation, and (3) ambition of imagination' (2009, p.67). The links between this account and the stages of interpretation described in this study are not accidental, but it is interesting to see them described almost as a kind of highly productive *flash* that triggers subsequent forms of attention.

Active attention, says Mynott, 'is the means by which we concentrate in a selective way on specific features of the world' – or the text.

> There is an almost infinite number of potential external stimuli, which would threaten to swamp our senses if we were just passively open to all of them. So we narrow our focus on those that interest us at any one time and make a positive effort to attend to them, like turning up the power of a searchlight and directing the beam.
>
> (2009, p. 67)

Active attention has been seen at work in Chapter 4; as narrative forms become more complex, the need for that searchlight to be directed in actively attentive ways will become more and more essential.

It is *informed expectation* that hones attention. Mynott suggests that such an attribute plays an important role in science and in sport; I suggest that it also plays a part in the identification of narrative cues in the early stages of a text – not so much as a way of adding a tick or a cross to a list of possibilities but as a strategic guide for beginning to interpret.

Finally and most importantly, comes *ambition of imagination*, which, according to Mynott,

> is what distinguishes the great observers from the merely good ones. This is what marshals, integrates, and then finally transcends all the other skills. I mean by this the critical ability always to question what has seemed accepted, established, or obvious. It means doubting those same informed expectations I was celebrating above. This is going that one creative step further, or more likely in the other direction (2009, p. 68).

The variety and intricacy of the world of birds is complex and beautiful. Understanding this world, however, is a process limited to the finite (though admittedly enormous) number of options concerning species, location, and season that our experiential world supplies. Narratives, especially fictional narratives, are not only infinite in their possibilities, they are also crafted to *attract* and *enhance* attention, expectation, and imagination.

As opposed to the limits of the real world of birds, the literary work, as Wolfgang Iser explains it, offers a 'triadic relationship among the real, the fictive, and the imaginary' (1993, p.3). He distinguishes between the imaginary as spontaneous and the fictive as intentional (1993, p. xiii) and elaborates further:

> In our ordinary experience, the imaginary tends to manifest itself in a somewhat diffuse manner, in fleeting impressions that defy our attempts to pin it down in a concrete and stabilized form. The imaginary may suddenly flash before our mind's eye, almost as an arbitrary apparition, only to disappear again or to dissolve into quite another form ... The act of fictionalizing is therefore not identical to the imaginary with its protean potential. For the fictionalizing act is a guided act. It aims at something that in turn endows the imaginary with an articulate gestalt – a gestalt that differs from the fantasies, projections, daydreams, and other reveries that ordinarily give the imaginary expression in our day-to-day experience.
>
> (1993, p. 3)

Just as Mynott has analysed the instantaneous flicker of recognition of a particular bird into component elements, so we may consider whether such attributes flash into action to identify narrative potential, a productive narrative *gestalt*, when the more coherent and shaped form of a story potentially flickers into view.

Like Iser, Brian Boyd distinguishes between the inchoate glimmers of the imagination and the patterned world created by the fictive:

1. Randomness, nature's way of exploring new possibilities, seems an intrinsic part of brain function.
2. But without selective retention, randomness alone could not generate creativity that accumulates in force: as in dreams, a cascade of new ideas would take and lose shape almost without trace. Art involves not just private ideas but patterned external forms, sound, surface, shape, story, durable or at least replicable, like the patterns of melodies and rhymes that make music and verse memorable and transmissible. Pure imagination, on the other hand, alters unstably and irretrievably as brain activation spreads.
3. Because art appeals to cognitive preferences for pattern, it is self-motivating; we carry innate incentives to engage in artistic activity.

(2009, p. 121)

Boyd also says,

> Fiction, like art in general, can be explained in terms of cognitive play with pattern – in this case with patterns of social information – and in terms of the unique importance of human shared attention ... [Narrative] does not depend on language. It can be expressed through mime, dance, wordless picture books, or movies [or video games].
>
> (2009, pp. 130–1)

A story is designed to appeal to human attention, and a fictional story need not be limited by the exigencies of daily reality. But it does need to be able to communicate very early on that it may be read *as narrative*; the pragmatic mode of its initial patterns must be established swiftly. The mental flash that suggests a narrative approach may be useful, incorporates the potential for the other steps described in this book; but its first appearance is fleeting.

Tacit skills are enhanced through experience. As Margaret Meek so famously reminded us, texts teach what readers learn (1988); and like readers, viewers and gamers also learn tacit and explicit lessons about interpretation through exposure to experiences that have been pre-shaped by other hands exactly in order to develop such attributes. It is very clear that the participants in this project all came to play with relative quotients of active attention, informed expectation, and ambition of imagination. I find it very intriguing indeed that the two participants who struck me as the most fully able to articulate Mynott's three attributes were Dan and Martin, both members of the dys-functional Group AB. Unlike birdwatching, which is largely visual, game-playing calls for that full muscular realization of the story that regularly defeated Dan and Martin and Neil; yet their capacity to be open to both story and critical reflection was very well developed and articulated.

Identifying slippery strategies

However strict the boundaries of the initial text, however stand-alone it seems inside its covers or between its rolling credits at beginning and end, all texts now, in Kristie Fleckenstein's useful term, are potentially 'slippery' (2003, p. 104). Slippery texts, she says, are 'artifacts that slip and slide across the boundaries of an imageword ecology ... [They] keep us positioned on the edges that blur, the edges where literacy evolves' (2003, pp. 104–5).

Developments in the slipperiness of all media offer the potential of merging different formats of story. Do such developments make the central questions of this book more important, or do they indicate that they are becoming historically irrelevant as media distinctions become less salient? My own analysis is that this historical moment of increasing slipperiness offers a unique opportunity to explore what we take for granted and what is new in our 'imageword ecology'.

By the standards of change I have mentioned above, the three stories I offered to the participants in this project were 'old-school' traditional forms. But such an assumption ignores the boundary-nudging qualities of these particular stories. Although each is freestanding, they all manifest a certain internal slipperiness, and an awareness of such slipperiness was evident in many of the interpreters' comments.

When setting out to locate three useful texts for this study, I certainly did not aim to be transgressive; my main focus was on locating materials that would be unfamiliar to my participants (leading me to choose a subtitled European movie and a brand-new video game rather than working from selection criteria more internal to the form of the story). Yet the reality of my choices is a set of three narratives in which no story is told by means of secure chronological progress from beginning to end.

The most conventional schemas (the standard 'plot diagram' for example) are thus not reliable for this little text set. It is extremely clear, however, that all of the participants in this project are generally intrigued rather than disturbed by such anomalies. They early identified the need for, and then systematically applied, a variety of interpretive strategies that recognizably involve narrative thinking in order to engage with each of these formats (attending, entering, orienting, inferring, progressing and/or satisficing, judging, reflecting). A platform-neutral sense of narrative understanding underpins these interpretive efforts. Furthermore, these interpreters are prepared to accept ambiguity as an aesthetically appropriate ending; it is as if they will apply their narrative strategies as far as possible without necessarily holding out for narrative closure as the appropriate finish. The social setting meant that they had group support that sustained them as they considered unsettling issues of ambiguity. Whether this support increased their tolerance of an ending that they might have considered unsatisfactory if they had encountered it in privacy and solitude cannot be established, though it is a question worth asking.

Warren Buckland describes David Bordwell's cognitive account of film comprehension in ways that resonate with the descriptions established here, yet head in a direction that this study does not validate. Here is how Buckland describes this process:

> Bordwell developed a cognitive theory of comprehension using the concepts of schemata, cues and inferences ... When watching a film, which cognitivists posit as being inherently incomplete, spectators use schemata to organize it into a coherent mental representation. Schemata are activated by cues in the data. Gaps in the film are the most evident cues, for they are simply the missing data that spectators need to fill in. Films cue spectators to generate inferences to fill in the gaps. When comprehending a narrative film, one schema in particular guides our inferences – the Aristotelian-based canonical story format.
>
> (2009, p. 7)

I suggest that these interpreters followed all the cognitive steps described here, but I question whether these young readers are quite so wedded to the Aristotelian schema of narrative as their primary organizer as Bordwell would seem to suggest. At the very least, most of them seem very ready to drop such a singular model at the first hint of its poorness of fit. These viewers did not say, 'Wait a minute. I don't understand what's going on in *Run Lola Run* – she just did this already.' They were swift to articulate the advantages of the internal perspective of the diary placed alongside the external viewpoint of the screenplay in *Monster*. Dan was explicit from a very early stage that a culturally different narrative model was available to assist with the interpretation of *Shadow of the Colossus*. As denizens of the kind of plural and ever-expanding world of narrative possibilities described above, they appear quite ready to pursue relatively conventional narrative interpretive strategies without committing themselves to a conventional outcome. The interpretive tools are familiar but they are readily adaptable to new purposes. These interpreters are able to manage the orchestration of known strategies while incorporating some new elements as the text and format seem to call for them.

Indeed it is possible that some of the hitches in smooth narrative progression offer a form of friction that enhances attention and enjoyment. It may be inbuilt, as in the video game, as Tom Bissell describes:

> Stories are about time passing and narrative progression. Games are about challenge, which frustrates the passing of time and impedes narrative progression. The story force wants to go forward and the 'friction force' of challenge tries to hold stories back.
>
> (2010, p. 93)

Contemporary interpreters become familiar with this kind of friction at a very early age, and possibly long before they learn about video games. The earliest texts many children encounter include exactly this kind of conflict. Lawrence Sipe describing one form of early text suggests,

> [T]he best and most fruitful readings of picturebooks are never straightforwardly linear, but rather involve a lot of rereading, turning to previous pages, reviewing, slowing down, and reinterpreting. Doonan (1993) suggests that there is an inherent tension in picturebooks; the words impel us forward to find out what happens, whereas the pictures invite us to savor and linger.
>
> (2008, p. 27)

Friction may be part of the inherent design of the text. Alternatively, it may be accidental. In this project, the subtitles in *Run Lola Run* mean both that viewers must spare attention for reading and also, simultaneously, that they must charge their ears to attend even more carefully than usual to tone and inflection in the voices of the actors as they speak their opaque dialogue. They must pay extra attention to the cues of body language as well, in order to flesh out the extra-large gaps created by the terseness of the translation. In a subtitled movie, the forward press of words, acting, and *mise en scène* is disrupted by the need to shift attention to the different work of processing print subtitles, and also by the meaninglessness of the spoken dialogue. All the participants were able to manage this disruption, though not all liked it. Their experience is a reminder that the creator's design efforts cannot determine every element of the reception event; many other factors come into play.

Interpreters may sometimes choose to override the potential for friction. Words on the page invite forward momentum; the page turn is rendered invisible in the press to the ending. Pictures, as we have seen, invite pausing; they resist the page turn. Without exception, the readers of *Monster* in this project succumbed to the rhythm of reading the words and more or less ignored the pictures – as is their prerogative.

The role of drag in narrative processing is thus neither novel nor fatal to enjoyment and understanding. Indeed it may well enhance the pleasure of the experience.

Multimodal metaphors for mental states

This study has established many interpretive strategies that cross over all three media. Participants do seem to subscribe to an overarching sense of narrative proprieties and potential, even if they are not tied to one explicit cultural model. Their descriptions of their own experiences also supply metaphors that invoke a platform-neutral mindset, even when they are talking about reading print. Dan describes how he *renders* his visual sense of a narrative world while reading. Adam, also talking about reading, elaborates on how he needs to hear different voices in order to distinguish one character from another, with his own voice reserved for the words of the narrator. Lewis turns his read story into a movie and adds mental music. Sebastian makes a comparison to the player's position in a video game to describe where he 'is' in a story he is reading. Jacob is categorical about the visual nature of his reading experience: 'In the book you always see it the way you think it should be seen.'

Neil and Keith, on the other hand, use the example of the movie screen to point out that reading a book is not exactly the same experience. It's 'not quite as developed', more of an 'understanding' that they both say they 'move through'. Neil says he is 'subconsciously, experiencing it'; Keith describes it as 'more of a feeling ... you understand but it's not like you're looking'.

These and many other examples offer powerful indicators that what the mind experiences is its own reworking of the narrative data on offer in the text itself. The predilection to express the abstract meanings of the printed words in terms of multimodal metaphors is not universally shared, but it is very clear that the abstraction of print is transposed into something vividly experienced in the different minds of the readers, either through perceptual or affective translation into a form of 'lived' experience. But this infilling is not confined to print; we see it at work in the other media as well.

If anything, Fleckenstein's 'imageword ecology' is too restrictive a term; the experiences described here are more multimodal than her term would indicate, and at a minimum we need 'imagewordsound'. But 'slippery' is a powerful descriptor for this movement between modal possibilities. Such interpreters would seem to be well poised to take on the complexities of the new possibilities looming on our media horizons.

Torben Grodal, writing about film, describes this complex phenomenon in the following terms:

Although we receive our information by sight or sound, this activates many other mental processes, and it is not really possible to isolate perception from cognition, memory, emotion, and action, and our perception of 'space' is not independent of our concepts of active motion; our perception of objects is not independent of memories and emotional relations. A given percept, a given scene, exists as a phenomenon within a complex set of mental processes, and our understanding of 'reality' further depends on complex mental models.

(1999, p. 10)

Dan, Adam, Lewis, Sebastian, and Jacob seem to be involved in further transformative mental work, almost as if some kind of conversion from the abstraction of the word into a 'percept' or 'scene' was occurring in their minds. Neil and Keith, however, attest to an alternative mental model of reading, which is experientially alive without being so perceptually specific. Their struggles to articulate a very nebulous sensation do not appear to reflect a less vivid encounter, however – just a different one.

What these responses collectively indicate is that all these media, including even print, that most abstract medium, give rise to 'lived' sensations on the part of interpreters. How can we understand what brings these various marks to life?

The multimodal subjunctive

In 'Rethinking the Virtual' (2006), Nicholas Burbules addresses important issues of the subjunctive mode without ever using that term or addressing Bruner's concept of 'trafficking in human possibilities' (1986, p.26), though he clearly occupies the same conceptual territory, with many references to the 'as if'. Instead of the subjunctive, he talks about the importance of *immersion* as part of virtual reality:

> the key feature of the virtual is not the particular technology that produces the sense of immersion, but the sense of immersion itself (whatever might bring it about), which gives the virtual its phenomenological quality of an 'as if' experience.

(2006, p. 37, emphasis in original)

The platform neutrality of this statement, combined with its interest in the lived experience of the virtual, offers a promising starting point for revisiting the interpretive efforts captured in this project. Initially, it would seem that Burbules is speaking of *immersion* as delineated by Douglas and Hargadon (2001) and distinguished by them from engagement. He talks of 'engrossing experiences of multisensory worlds which, when we are immersed in them, fill our experiential horizons' (2006, p.37), a description that sounds very much like participating in the single schema of the imagined world, as Douglas and Hargadon define immersion, rather than dealing with the multiple schemas entailed by their concept of engagement. But it soon becomes clear that Burbules offers an account that makes room for acknowledging the pleasures of the act of interpreting itself, as an essential part of the delights of the virtual, a perspective that takes him into the territory of *engagement*:

> any reality we inhabit is to some extent actively filtered, interpreted, constructed, or *made*; it is not merely an unproblematic given while the virtual is not merely imaginary. *The virtual should not be understood as a simulated reality exposed to us, which we passively observe, but a context where our own active response and involvement are part of what gives the experience its veracity and meaningfulness.*
>
> (2006, p. 38, emphasis in original)

Confusion of vocabulary mounts when Burbules speaks of 'four processes of engagement through which immersion happens' (2006, p. 38). His four processes, however, provide a very valuable tool for investigating the vast dataset imperfectly reduced and represented in this book; and it is to these terms that I now turn.

The four processes that lead to immersion are interest, involvement, imagination and interaction, and Burbules says they apply to many forms of virtual experience: 'watching a film, reading a book, listening to music, or being caught up in a reverie or a conversation' (2006, p. 41). In this list we see a hint that the interpretive conversation itself (displayed at length in this book) may represent part of the 'as if' experience, a subject to which I shall return later.

Burbules outlines his four requirements as follows:

- 'An experience is *interesting* to us when it is complex enough to allow us to pick out new elements, even with repeated encounters.
- An experience is *involving* when we have reason to care about what we are experiencing: we pay attention to it because it concerns us in some way.
- An experience engages our *imagination* when we can interpolate or extrapolate new details and add to the experience through our own contributions.
- An experience is *interactive* when it provides us with opportunities to participate in it, not only perceptually or intellectually, but also through embodied action and responses.

(2006, p. 41, emphasis in original, bullets added)

Burbules describes this physical response as important, and reminds us that embodied response was not invented with the game scenarios now commonly described as interactive:

> This deeper engagement of our body's movement, activity, and sensations triggers unconscious responses that make us *feel* 'this is really happening,' below the level of conscious analysis ... But ... it is a mistake to think of this as a factor only in ... technological 'VR' environments. When watching a film or hearing a story, our posture, body tension, and startle responses – or, to take another example, our relaxation, rhythmic movement, and kinesthetic sensations listening to music – are a key dimension of the quality of immersion that makes the virtual seem or feel 'real' to us at the moment it is happening.
>
> (2006, p. 42)

That seeming and feeling 'real' involves a subjunctive move into the world of human possibilities and a deictic shift into a point of view other than the interpreter's own.

Interest, involvement, imagination, and interactivity are not dependent on a particular medium or technology; they are 'outgrowths of the *relation* between observer and observed: qualities of response to an experience' (2006, p. 42, emphasis in original). Such an analysis, says Burbules, 'makes it clear that immersion is a consequence of our active response and engagement with them – it is not something that happens "to" us' (2006, p. 42). It is we, as interpreters, who call up the subjunctive mode of thinking, who shift centres into the perspective of someone else. This active commitment to interpretation is itself a source of pleasure, as many lively and funny stretches of commentary from my transcripts make plain.

Interest, involvement, imagination, and interactivity are 'operationalized' in the fictions presented to my participants through an initial recognition that narrative strategies would open the doors to these texts and then through the various interpretive headings I have used in my chapter titles. Once again we have a set of nouns that are activated through the performative verbs of interpretation. Different media make different kinds of room for interpretive *performing* and it is to this topic that I turn next.

Performing the text

These transcripts present a strong element of performance. Burbules suggests that, even in private interpretation of virtual experience, it is our own involvement that brings the story to life. Active response and engagement become performances in their own right in many of the examples provided here, not just among the three friends of Group C but also among the members of the other groups (who, with the exception of Dan and Neil, were complete strangers to each other at the outset of the project).

There is a risk of interpolating too many layers of 'meta' into this project, but I find it interesting that my own interpretation of the responses also took on some of its own subjunctive tenor. On these pages, I am *performing* an analysis of the comments of my participants; I am shaping my sentences and building my thoughts towards as clear and convincing a construct as I can manage. It may already be obvious from the extended nature of the quotes I have provided that I had no difficulty in re-submerging myself into the ongoing 'trafficking' of interpretation building. The ability to re-read and re-listen to the words of the participants as recorded and transcribed afforded me the leisure to move my own deictic centre from my remembered position as observer into an effort to understand the interpretive exercise from inside the perspectives of the participants. To a lesser extent, I also shifted into the story worlds of the three narratives, but my interest was less focused on these fictional universes than on the interpretive zone in which the interpreters met the stories. This initially unacknowledged interest in 'performing what I announce' (Lather, 1991, p. 11) is what led me to reject extensive use of the cumulative data threads that the Transana software made possible and that are represented in their non-subjunctive detail in the table of Group 3's button talk in Chapter 8. Such tabulation created too much of a distortion of the integrated social events of interpretation, and I found it interfered rather than assisted with my thinking about the processes at work.

This project has taken many years to accomplish, from my first inkling of its potential interest in 2003 to the writing of this final chapter in 2010. During those years, social zones of interpretation have expanded, mutated, and become far more commonplace, in ways I was only partially aware of in 2003 (though my work on online social interpretation of the television series *Felicity* [Mackey 2003a, 2003b, 2006] had certainly enhanced my appreciation of its potential). Compared to the sheer scale and the breadth of multimodal options of online interpretive communities, my little project can be seen as conservative. The instinct for cooperation that fuelled even the dysfunctional Group AB's efforts towards interpretation, however, demonstrates a taste for collective thinking that bears further examination.

New 'ethos stuff' and the nature of social interpretation

In their account of the evolution of literacies, Colin Lankshear and Michele Knobel have made a useful distinction between new 'technical stuff' (2007, p. 7) and new 'ethos stuff' (2007, p. 9). For the most part, this project focused on (at least relatively) old 'technical stuff;' books, films, and even games have been around for (at least) many decades, and (at most) many centuries. Yet in the performance of interpretation that we see in these pages, I perceive elements of new 'ethos stuff' at work.

New 'ethos stuff' manifests itself in new literacies in ways that mark a difference from conventional literacies; according to Lankshear and Knobel, 'new literacies are more "participatory," "collaborative," and "distributed" in nature than conventional literacies' (2007, p. 9). Group C's rapid-fire improvisations around the game space mark the most participatory, collaborative and distributed performance of this project, but there are many examples of collective response that satisfy these descriptors.

If I am correct in my sense of what happened in this project, I offered specimens of relatively conventional *literacies* for inspection, but the interpreters were themselves 'new *literates*' and brought traces of new literacy attitudes and aptitudes to bear on the project. It would be surprising if such an outcome had not occurred. This project, willy-nilly, investigates the development of narrative understanding among *practitioners of new literacies*. The ways in which they attend to the three stories, and the ways in which they play with the opportunities afforded by the three stories, do provide some generalized pointers to our narrative hard-wiring, but they also rely heavily on the social, cultural and temporally grounded mental software that these young interpreters have developed over their two decades of particular forms of narrative experience.

Associative openness and the social turn in narrative interpretation

In the implausible setting of a review of a book about baseball stadiums, I came across a very helpful phrase: 'associative openness' (Kimmelman, 2009, p. 23). Kimmelman admires the leisurely pace of baseball, which, he says, 'doesn't take up all of your mental space as you watch it. It takes up a degree of it, and you're free, the rest of the time, to experiment with thoughts you might not ordinarily have' (2009, p. 23).

Associative openness both complements and contrasts with the notion of affect linking (Gelernter, 1994, p. 27). Decoding (in any format) takes some of your attention but your wits are also open to making the kinds of links with your own experience that will enable you to bring the presented events to life inside your mind. As I make use of the term here, affect linking employs a kind of closed loop between the presentation of the material and your own memories and emotions; the result is a profoundly personal and private experience that rivets our attention through connecting with our own lives. I propose to appropriate the term associative openness to question whether a less intimate form of interpretation is also viable. Associative openness, for my purposes here, involves the *collaborative* invigoration of a set of representative symbols with lived meaning. The performance of interpretation is opened up for collective associations. The Internet abounds with sites where exactly this practice is being carried out (see Anelli, 2008, for one extensive set of such activities in relation to *Harry Potter*).

If interpretation is a performance, it may be either internalized privately or externalized collectively. What matters, as Burbules says, is 'the *relation* between observer and observed: qualities of response to an experience' (2006, p. 42, emphasis in original). All these interpreters (but Group C in particular) are very happy to establish a relationship between observer (interpreter) and observed (text) that quite happily involves other observers, and to pool their associations in a collective performance that they orchestrate together.

The private experience of contemporary novel reading is part of our schema of literacy. But it is a relatively new schema. Robert Darnton discusses the role of the commonplace book as a feature of seventeenth-century reading experience in England, and speaks of

> some underlying similarities in the reading practices of early modern Englishmen. They had all sorts of opinions and read all sorts of books. But they read in the same way – segmentally, by concentrating on small chunks of text and jumping from book to book, rather than sequentially, as readers did a century later, when the rise of the novel encouraged the habit of perusing books from cover to cover.
>
> (2009, p. 169)

Jennifer Rennie and Annette Patterson remind us that another component of contemporary reading – the expectation of enjoyment – is also not a given.

> This form of reading practice ... also has a history. Pleasure was not considered a part of reading in the classrooms of scholastic teachers or in the homes of early Christians. Therefore it is possible to think

about reading for enjoyment or pleasure as a learned practice ... [In] the 20th century ... we could claim that reading for pleasure and enjoyment was not only accepted as a natural part of the activity of reading, but it was a *requirement*.

(2010, p. 209, emphasis in original)

It is not much of a leap to equate the reading of segments and the making of connections between books as a form of engaged reading as opposed to the immersed experience of much novel reading. Neither, of course, is it hard to make the connection between the linked extracts in the commonplace book and the hypertextual universe we inhabit today. The implication of Rennie and Patterson's point is also that immersion is a historically located form of reading, not an essential element in the process itself – although I suspect very few avid readers would want to abandon the pleasures of complete absorption, no matter how enticing the delights of engagement or of social follow-up.

There is no reason for engaged forms of interpretation to replace immersed experiences; the two can live happily side-by-side. We do appear, however, to be living through a cultural shift in which the personal associations of immersion are more strongly augmented by social forms of interpretive performance.

Technology facilitates more socially oriented forms of engagement with texts. Social viewing is enabled by real-time interactive options, even across North America's many time zones. *The New York Times* reports television viewers sharing responses to particular programs via Skype video chat, and lists some options for social viewing and social gaming:

The online streaming TV site Hulu.com, owned by NBC Universal, the News Corporation and the Walt Disney Company, has experimented with real-time interactive systems but has yet to make them available.

Verizon Communications offers a Facebook connection tied to its FiOS Internet service where people can post messages while they watch a program. Video-game console makers like Microsoft and Sony seem to have come closest to offering an interactive experience with their voice chat and messaging systems

(Vance, 2010)

The kind of instant online response to television that I found in 2003 when I looked at reactions to *Felicity* is today augmented by various forms of social networking. Twitter, for example, not only allows for rapid-fire collective interpretation, it also enables swift connection to expansive support material.

A slipperier academy

Social and collaborative response to and assessment of contemporary stories is assisted by technology; young people have developed strategies that make them very much at home with slippery texts. Where in this shifting territory do we find the academic field of children's and young adult literature? How do scholars and researchers locate themselves in a slippery landscape? Should they be shifting their remit from a study of literature (defined by its etymological links to letters and thus confined to print, or even print on paper) to a broader effort to explore and critique fiction in all its media guises? As interpreters gain more and more access to public vehicles of response, to what extent do scholars confine their study to the limits set by the covers of the book? For example, do online and real-life manifestations of social response merit critical attention – in their own right, in relation to the literary text, in some cases but not others, or not at all? Not every expert in children's or young adult literature will answer these questions in the same way, nor should they; but the importance of the questions themselves cannot be denied. Defining the nature of the disciplines that explore this landscape is itself going to represent a slippery project over the next few years. My own responses to my data suggest that our own 'ethos' may change whether we intend it or not, simply through the force of changes in the atmosphere around us. Scholars and professional practitioners need to reflect on and articulate our own changing responses, to ourselves and to each other.

Reframing initial assumptions

This project was set up to be social, so it is not surprising that social performance of interpretation is a central element in its conclusions. What has altered for me is my own understanding of the role and significance of 'ethos' in social performance. At the outset of this project, my intent was to design a social framework as a methodological tool. Articulating their understanding to each other, I reasoned, would enable the participants to present me with a more naturalized window onto their private interpretive processes. And indeed the sense of watching normal processes at work was noticeable, particularly in the game playing where interpretive commentary was formative rather than summative or retrospective;

and also when interpreters pursued an overall sense of coherence, in Rabinowitz's terms (which is often retrospective in any natural setting, and which occurred, in this project, with all three media).

But the social element turned out to be generative as well, providing a stage for the *performance* of interpretation. The ambiguity of the word *performance* is relevant here. One can perform a task, so it has a connotation of *work*. With a slight tweak of meaning, performance is closely associated with *assessment*; one can perform in order to be evaluated. But there is also a connotation of *play-acting*, of producing some kind of pretense. In very real ways, all three aspects of this word played a part in the collaborative production of meaning that we see on these pages.

The shift in my own thinking became clearer to me when I returned to Reid's list of six essential verbs of literacy outlined in the first chapter (choosing, accessing, understanding, analysing, creating, and expressing oneself [2009, p. 21]). At the start of this work, I was clear that my focus was on the two receptive verbs, understanding and analysing. Now I find that the social framework of my project makes it far more difficult than I had anticipated completely to exclude issues of creation and expression. All the groups, at different times, drew on forms of collective associative openness to produce a performance of interpretation that was indeed creative and expressive, if largely in modest and small-scale ways. Humour was often the main vehicle for this exchange, but humour is a form of *social* expression, *par excellence*.

I, of course, invited performance with my video cameras and my field-note-writing observers. Yet it was clear that the power of this social performance was indeed generative in ways that plainly felt comfortable and familiar to these interpreters. I had subliminally thought that I would be provided with performances in the evaluative sense; what I got in addition was performance as a form of collaborative play.

'One of the key differences between the old media and the new is what we call the balance of agency,' say Cope and Kalantzis (2010, p. 90). They imply an 'either/or' distinction, but 'both/and' leaves more forms of potential pleasure on the table, as my participants implicitly recognized. Dan, for example, says that reading a pre-printed book that allows no room for interactive changes in the story can sometimes feel 'futile', but he is very clear that the submissive delights of print reading remain very powerful, in part because of the subtlety enabled by the control of a single author. Immersion retains its appeal even as engagement on an ever-larger stage is facilitated by technological and cultural developments. The delights of socially improvised interpretation do not eliminate the pleasures of private absorption, as all of these participants testify.

The new technologies and formats that I described at the beginning of this chapter – and all the other innovations that we can expect over the next few years – will succeed or fail as they enrich our narrative pleasures, both for private enjoyment and for social connection. If my participants are in any way representative of their peers, these experiments will find an audience unintimidated by new forms and formats, able to identify the potential for narrative pleasure and to draw on active attention, informed expectation, and ambition of imagination no matter what kind of challenge they face.

None of my three texts told an entirely simple and unidirectional story. All of my 12 participants were at ease in the complex narrative worlds engendered by *Run Lola Run*, *Monster*, and *Shadow of the Colossus*, even though they had no say in their selection and no initial sense of any potential for deep personal salience in these stories. Their willingness to go with the story indicates an open-mindedness about narrative possibilities that is broader than that manifested by many of their textbooks and teachers, who cling to the virtues of the singular standard of quality.

The interpretive toolkits brought to bear on these three narratives were recognizably similar across groups and across media. A climate of cultural mutation works most successfully when creators can anticipate that their audiences will bring both a reliable toolkit and a flexible mind to bear on new materials, new forms, and new devices. Recognizing, making sense of, and appreciating the storyline in ever-changing settings is a challenge these participants (and, I suggest, many others like them) are clearly well qualified to meet. Such adept and resourceful interpreters provide the essential condition for narrative experimentation by those who create the stories. Exciting and interesting times lie ahead; these young readers, viewers, and players are well equipped to enjoy and encourage many forms of change.

Appendix 1: Details of Groups and Sessions

Work began on the project in the fall of 2005 with an advertisement calling for participants in the student newspaper at the University of Alberta. The advertisement called for participants to be aged between 18 and 21, and to have at least some minimal experience of gaming. About 20 people applied, providing details of their available times, and of these, 12 could be scheduled within a group of three for a two-hour session at a regular time each week. Each of these groups completed at least three two-hour sessions before the Christmas vacation and the new semester's timetable interfered with scheduling.

The first session was held on 16 November 2005, and the final session of Group AB was held on 24 March 2006. Each session was video- and audio-taped. Appropriate ethics consent was obtained from the Research Ethics Board of the Faculties of Education and Extension at the University of Alberta and participants all signed a consent form.

The groups were labelled A, B, C, and D simply on the basis of their order of meeting during the week. The holiday break led to some changes in these group arrangements.

Keith, of Group A, left university at Christmas. Group B ran into major scheduling problems in the new semester (which had the unfortunate effect of reducing the female participation even further). As a stopgap, I moved Martin from Group B into Group A to replace Keith. The amalgamated group never did gel, with consequences that I discuss in the book. By mid-March they were mired in the game, and, anticipating that they would still not have finished by the end of the winter semester, I skipped the slaying of two colossi (numbers 14 and 15). This team reached the end of the game in 16 hours of play, two with their original team and 14 in the amalgamated group.

Sebastian of Group C was scheduled to participate in a co-op term after Christmas. The members of Group C had all been friends since junior high and had a long history of gaming together; they were by some margin the most expeditious and efficient gamers of the whole pool, in terms of making effective use of their time. They were extremely keen to finish the game and we scheduled two longer special sessions in the short interval between exams and their departure for the holidays. They did indeed finish the game (in a total of about 11 hours) before Christmas, but Jarret had to leave about half an hour before the conclusion in order to catch his lift home. As the other two were also in danger of missing their lifts, the post-game discussion was very truncated (but I did get the feeling that reflective post-game discussion was not a regular feature of this group's gaming activities in any case; they prefer to embed discussion of previous games in the banter that accompanies the next game).

Only Group D proceeded tidily on the schedule I had originally envisaged, doing three sessions before Christmas and six afterwards, completing the game after much effort in a total of 14 hours.

I initiated a major discussion about the different experiences of reading, viewing and gaming in every group during the third session. At that time, Groups A and B were still running separately and all four trios participated in their original formation. As a result I have comments from all 12 participants.

In total, Group A and Group B each met for six hours. Group C met for a sum of 15 hours. Group D took 18 hours, and Group AB met for 14 hours altogether. There are nearly 2000 double-spaced pages of transcript from these meetings.

Appendix 2: 'Button talk' in Group C's game of *Shadow of the Colossus*

Appendix A.2   'Button talk' in Group C's game of *Shadow of the Colossus*

	Real Button References	Joke Button References	R1 References
Colossus 1	25	0	5
Colossus 2	37	0	17
Colossus 3	32	1	15
Colossus 4	5	1	1
Colossus 5	4	0	1
Colossus 6	5	2	4
Colossus 7	6	2	2
Colossus 8	10	1	7
Colossus 9	1	1	0
Colossus 10	4	0	1
Colossus 11	8	4	5
Colossus 12	9	0	3
Colossus 13	11	1	5
Colossus 14	3	0	2
Colossus 15	4	0	1
Colossus 16	11	5	6
Epilogue	4	0	3
Total	179	18	78

Appendix 3: How the collective of readers flagged *Monster* by page numbers

Appendix A.3 How the collective of readers flagged *Monster* by page numbers

	Flagged by a single reader = 65 pages	Flagged by two readers = 30 pages	Flagged by three readers = 14 pages	Flagged by four readers = 7 pages	Flagged by five readers = 5 pages	Flagged by six readers = 1 page
Page numbers	1, 4, 5, 15, 23, 25, 31, 38, 39,46, 48, 63, 66, 73, 77, 79, 80, 83, 89, 92, 93, 94, 98, 99, 106, 110, 113, 123, 129, 132, 135, 138, 147, 150, 154, 156, 158, 169, 173, 175, 177, 180, 183, 190, 195, 197, 199, 201, 212, 217, 225, 229, 234, 235, 241, 242, 246, 249, 253, 255, 260, 267, 270, 271, 277	14, 17, 20, 27, 28, 35, 42, 53, 54, 56, 68, 82, 88, 95, 109, 111, 121, 155, 189, 198, 215, 221, 222, 239, 251, 263, 265, 266, 275, 280	9, 12, 29, 41, 43, 45, 49,57, 59, 115, 136, 146, 151, 205	13, 18, 19, 50, 51, 55, 281	3, 7, 16, 21, 214	24

References

Aarseth, E. (1997) *Cybertext: Perspectives on Ergodic Literature* (Baltimore: Johns Hopkins University Press).

Afflerbach, P. (2002) 'Verbal Reports and Protocol Analysis' in M. L. Kamil, P. B. Mosenthal, P. D. Pearson and R. Barr (eds) *Methods of Literacy Research* (Mahwah: Lawrence Erlbaum).

Anelli, M. (2008) *Harry, a History: The True Story of a Boy Wizard, His Fans, and Life inside the Harry Potter Phenomenon* (New York: Pocket Books).

Atkins, B. (2006) 'What Are We Really Looking At? The Future-Orientation of Video Game Play', *Games and Culture*, 1(2), 127–40.

Bakhtin, M. M. (1981) *The Dialogic Imagination: Four Essays*, M. Holquist (ed.), C. Emerson and M. Holquist (trans.) (Austin: University of Texas Press).

Barratt, D. (2009) '"Twist Blindness": The Role of Primacy, Priming, Schemas, and Reconstructive Memory in a First-Time Viewing of *The Sixth Sense*' in W. Buckland (ed.) *Puzzle Films: Complex Storytelling in Contemporary Cinema* (Chichester: Wiley-Blackwell).

Bartleby (2009) American Heritage Book of English Usage, subjunctive. Available online at: http://www.bartleby.com/64/C001/061.html, date accessed 25 January 2009.

Barton, D. and M. Hamilton (1998) *Local Literacies: Reading and Writing in One Community* (London: Routledge).

Bazalgette, C. (2008) 'Literacy in Time and Space', *PoV*, 1(1), 12–16.

Benton, M. and G. Fox (1985) *Teaching Literature: Nine to Fourteen* (Oxford: Oxford University Press).

Bergeron, B. and M. Bradbury-Wolff (2002) *Teaching Reading Strategies in the Primary Grades* (New York: Scholastic Professional Books).

Bissell, T. (2010) *Extra Lives: Why Video Games Matter* (New York: Pantheon Books).

Bizzocchi, J. (2005) '*Run Lola Run* – Film as Narrative Database', *Media in Transition 4*, retrieved from http://web.mit.edu/comm-forum/mit4/papers/bizzocchi.pdf, date accessed 26 March 2011.

Bolter, J. D. and R. Grusin (1999) *Remediation: Understanding New Media* (Cambridge, MA: MIT Press).

Bordwell, D. (1985) *Narration in the Fiction Film* (London: Routledge).

Bordwell, D. (1989) *Making Meaning: Inference and Rhetoric in the Interpretation of Cinema* (Cambridge, MA: Harvard University Press).

Bower, G. H. and D. G. Morrow (1990) 'Mental Models in Narrative Comprehension', *Science*, 247(4938), 44–8.

Boyd, B. (2009) *On the Origin of Stories: Evolution, Cognition, and Fiction* (Cambridge, MA: Belknap Press of Harvard University Press).

Branch, J. L. (2000) 'Investigating the Information-Seeking Processes of Adolescents: The Value of Using Think Alouds and Think Afters', *Library and Information Science Research*, 22 (4), 371–92.

Bridgeman, T. (2007) 'Time and Space' in D. Herman (ed.) *The Cambridge Companion to Narrative* (Cambridge: Cambridge University Press).

Brooker-Gross, S. (1981) 'Landscape and Social Values in Popular Children's Literature: Nancy Drew Mysteries', *Journal of Geography*, 80(2), 59–64.

Bruner, J. S. (1986) *Actual Minds, Possible Worlds* (Cambridge, MA: Harvard University Press).

Buckland, W. (2009) 'Introduction: Puzzle Plots' in W. Buckland (ed.) *Puzzle Films: Complex Storytelling in Contemporary Cinema* (Chichester: Wiley-Blackwell).

Burbules, N. C. (2006) 'Rethinking the Virtual' in J. Weiss, J. Nolan, J. Hunsinger and P. Trifonas (eds) *The International Handbook of Virtual Learning Environments*, Springer International Handbooks of Education, Vol. 14, (Dordrecht: Springer).

Burn, A. (2004) 'Potterliteracy: Cross-Media Narratives, Cultures and Grammars', *Papers: Explorations into Children's Literature*, 14(2), 5–17.

Burn, A. (2006) 'Playing Roles' in D. Carr, D. Buckingham, A. Burn and G. Schott, *Computer Games: Text, Narrative and Play* (Cambridge: Polity Press).

Carrington, V. and J. Marsh (2009) *Forms of Literacy*, Beyond Current Horizons. Available online at: http://www.beyondcurrenthorizons.org.uk/forms-of-literacy/print/, date accessed 14 July 2009.

Chittenden, E. and T. Salinger with A. M. Bussis (2001) *Inquiry into Meaning: An Investigation of Learning to Read*, revised edn (New York: Teachers College Press).

Christie, A. (2004) *The Murder of Roger Ackroyd* (New York: Berkley Books).

Ciccoricco, D. (2007) '"Play, Memory": Shadow of the Colossus and Cognitive Workouts', in *Dichtung-Digital – Journal für Digitale Ästhetik*, 37. Available online at: http://www.dichtung-digital.org/2007/ciccoricco.htm, date accessed 26 March 2011.

Collins, C. (1991) *The Poetics of the Mind's Eye: Literature and the Psychology of Imagination* (Philadelphia: University of Pennsylvania Press).

Cope, B. and M. Kalantzis (2010) 'New Media, New Learning' in D. R. Cole and D. L. Pullen (eds) *Multiliteracies in Motion: Current Theory and Practice* (New York: Routledge).

Costikyan, G. (2007) 'Games, Storytelling, and Breaking the String' in P. Harrigan and N. Wardrip-Fruin (eds) *SecondPerson: Role-Playing and Story in Games and Playable Media* (Cambridge, MA: MIT Press).

Crago, H. (1982) 'The Readers in the Reader: An Experiment in Personal Response and Literary Criticism', *Signal: Approaches to Children's Literature*, 39, 172–82.

Darnton, R. (2009) *The Case for Books: Past, Present, and Future* (New York: PublicAffairs).

DeRienzo, D. (n.d.) 'ICO/Shadow of the Colossus', *Hardcore Gaming 101*, retrieved from http://hg101.classicgaming.gamespy.com/icosotc/sotc.htm, 14 January 2009.

Derrida, J. (1983) *Aporias*. (Trans. T. Dutoit). (Palo Alto, CA: Stanford University Press).

Douglas, J. Y. and A. Hargadon (2001) 'The Pleasures of Immersion and Engagement: Schemas, Scripts and the Fifth Business', *Digital Creativity*, 12 (3), 153–66.

Dresang, E. T. (1999) *Radical Change: Books for Youth in a Digital Age* (New York: H.W. Wilson).

Ebner, D. (2009) 'EA Makes Bet on Social Media Games', *Globe and Mail*, 10 Nov., B6.

Eckert, L. S. (2008) 'Bridging the Pedagogical Gap: Intersections between Literary and Reading Theories in Secondary and Postsecondary Literacy Instruction', *Journal of Adolescent & Adult Literacy*, 52(2), 110–18.

Eco, U. (1979) *The Role of the Reader: Explorations in the Semiotics of Texts* (Bloomington: Indiana University Press).

Elfenbein, A. (2006) 'Cognitive Science and the History of Reading', *Publications of the Modern Language Association of America*, 121(2), 484–502.

Eliot, T. S. (1942) 'Little Gidding', V. *Four Quartets*. Available online at: http://www.tristan.icom43.net/quartets/gidding.html, date accessed 26 March 2011.

Elsaesser, T. (2009) 'The Mind-Game Film' in W. Buckland (ed.) *Puzzle Films: Complex Storytelling in Contemporary Cinema* (Chichester: Wiley-Blackwell).

Fleckenstein, K. S. (2003) *Embodied Literacies: Imageword and a Poetics of Teaching* (Carbondale: Southern Illinois University Press).

Force (2009) Run Leia Run. Available online at: http://www.theforce.net/fanfilms/animation/runleiarun, date accessed 1 August 2009.

Frasca, G. (1999) 'Ludology Meets Narratology: Similitude and Differences between (Video)games and Narrative', Finnish version originally published in Parnasso #3, Helsinki, 1999. Available online at: http://www.ludology.org/articles/ludology.htm, date accessed 26 March 2011.

Frasca, G. (2003). *Ludologists Love Stories Too: Notes from a Debate that Never Took Place*. Available online at: http://www.digra.org/dl/db/05163.01125.pdf, date accessed 26 March 2011.

Gelernter, D. (1994) *The Muse in the Machine: Computers and Creative Thought* (London: Fourth Estate).

Gerrig, R. J. (1993) *Experiencing Narrative Worlds: On the Psychological Activities of Reading* (New Haven: Westview Press).

Grodal, T. (1999) *Moving Pictures: A New Theory of Film Genres, Feelings, and Cognition* (Oxford: Clarendon Press).

Grodal, T. (2003) 'Stories for Eye, Ear, and Muscles: Video Games, Media, and Embodied Experiences' in M. J. P. Wolf and B. Perron (eds) *The Video Game Theory Reader* (New York: Routledge).

Gunning, T. G. (2010) *Reading Comprehension Boosters: 100 Lessons for Building Higher-Level Literacy, Grades 3–5* (San Francisco: Jossey-Bass).

Harding, D. W. (1962) 'Psychological Processes in the Reading of Fiction', *The British Journal of Aesthetics*, 2(2), 133–47.

Hatt, F. (1976) *The Reading Process: A Framework for Analysis and Description* (London: Clive Bingley).

Hayles, K. (2008) *Electronic Literature: New Horizons for the Literary* (Notre Dame: University of Notre Dame Press).

Heidegger, M. (1977) *Contributions to Philosophy (from Enowning)* (Indianapolis: Indiana University Press).

Herman, D. (2002) *Story Logic: Problems and Possibilities of Narrative* (Lincoln: University of Nebraska Press).

Hogan, P. C. (2003) *Cognitive Science, Literature, and the Arts: A Guide for Humanists* (New York: Routledge).

IMDB (2009) Lola Rennt (1998) – Awards. Available online at: http://www.imdb.com/title/tt0130827/awards, date accessed 10 January 2009.

Iser, W. (1978) *The Act of Reading: A Theory of Aesthetic Response* (Baltimore: Johns Hopkins University Press).

Iser, W. (1993) *The Fictive and the Imaginary: Charting Literary Anthropology* (Baltimore: Johns Hopkins University Press).

Jenkins, H. (2008) *Convergence Culture: Where Old and New Media Collide*, revised edn (New York: New York University Press).

Juul, J. (2001) 'Games Telling Stories? A Brief Note on Games and Narratives', *Game Studies*, 1(1). Available online at: http://www.gamestudies.org/0101/juul-gts/, date accessed 26 March 2011.

Kendeou, P., C. Bohn-Gettler, M. J. White and P. van den Broek (2008) 'Children's Inference Generation across Different Media', *Journal of Research in Reading* 31(3), 259–72.

Kermode, F. (2000) *The Sense of an Ending: Studies in the Theory of Fiction with a New Epilogue* (Oxford: Oxford University Press).

Kimmelman, M. (2009) 'At the Bad New Ballparks', *New York Review of Books*, LVI(18), 22–3.

Klawans, S. (1999) 'Born Cool', *The Nation*, 12 Jul., 34–6.

Kress, G. (2003) *Literacy in the New Media Age* (London: Routledge).

Kress, G. and T. van Leeuwen (1996) *Reading Images: The Grammar of Visual Design* (London: Routledge).

Kress, G. and T. van Leeuwen (2001) *Multimodal Discourse: The Modes and Media of Contemporary Communication.* (London: Arnold).

Langer, J. A. (1989) *The Process of Understanding Literature. Report Series 2.1* (Albany: National Research Center on Literature Teaching and Learning).

Langer, J. A. (1991) *Literary Understanding and Literature Instruction.* Report Series 2.11. (Albany: National Research Center on English Learning & Achievement).

Langer, J. A. (1995) *Envisioning Literature: Literary Understanding and Literature Instruction* (New York: International Reading Association/Teachers College Press).

Langer, S. K. (1953) *Feeling and Form: A Theory of Art* (New York: Charles Scribner's Sons).

Lankshear, C. and M. Knobel (2007) 'Sampling "the New" in New Literacies' in M. Knobel and C. Lankshear (eds) *A New Literacies Sampler* (New York: Peter Lang).

Lather, P. (1991) *Getting Smart: Feminist Research and Pedagogy with/in the Postmodern* (New York: Routledge).

Lauer, A. R. (2003) '*Run Lola Run* at the Dawn of Postmodernity', *Studies in Media & Information Literacy Education*, 3(1), n.p., retrieved from http://utpjournals.metapress.com/content/v7462472k15n873l/?p=907d7e07acff4d71ab07d8f85da6cb03&pi=0, date accessed 26 March 2011.

Lee, C. D. (2007) *Culture, Literacy, and Learning: Taking Bloom in the Midst of the Whirlwind* (New York: Teachers College Press).

'Lola's Running on Video: Part 3: "Lola" Locations' (n.d.). Available online at: http://german.about.com/library/weekly/aa122099c.htm, date accessed 14 January 2009.

Lynch, J. S. and P. van den Broek (2007) 'Understanding the Glue of Narrative Structure: Children's On- and Off-Line Inferences about Characters' Goals', *Cognitive Development*, 22(3), 323–40.

Lynch, K. (1960) *The Image of the City* (Cambridge, MA: Technology Press).

Mackey, M. (1993) 'Many Spaces: Some Limitations of Single Readings', *Children's Literature in Education*, 24(3), 147–63.

Mackey, M. (1995) 'Imagining with Words: The Temporal Processes of Reading Fiction', unpublished PhD dissertation (Edmonton: University of Alberta).

Mackey, M. (1997) 'Good-Enough Reading: Momentum and Accuracy in the Reading of Complex Fiction', *Research in the Teaching of English*, 31(4), 428–58.

Mackey, M. (2003a) 'Television and the Teenage Literate: Discourses of *Felicity*', *College English*, 65(4), 389–410.

Mackey, M. (2003b) 'Did Elena Die?: Narrative Practices of an Online Community of Interpreters', *Children's Literature Association Quarterly*, 28(1), 52–62.

Mackey, M. (2006) 'Serial Monogamy: Extended Fictions and the Television Revolution', *Children's Literature in Education: An International Quarterly*, 37(2), 149–61.

Mackey, M. (2007) *Literacies across Media: Playing the Text*, revised edn (London: Routledge).

Manguel, A. (1996) *A History of Reading* (London: Viking).

McClay, J. K., M. Mackey, M. Carbonaro, D. Szafron and J. Schaeffer (2007) 'Adolescents Composing Fiction in Digital Game and Written Formats: Tacit, Explicit and Metacognitive Strategies', *E-Learning*, 4(3), 273–84.

McCloud, S. (1993) *Understanding Comics: The Invisible Art* (Northampton, MA: Kitchen Sink Press).

McLuhan, M. (1994) *Understanding Media: The Extensions of Man*, revised edn (Cambridge, MA: MIT Press).

Meadows, M. S. (2003) *Pause & Effect: The Art of Interactive Narrative* (Indianapolis: New Riders).

Meek, M. (1988) *How Texts Teach What Readers Learn* (Stroud: Thimble Press).

Meek, M., A. Warlow and G. Barton (1977) *The Cool Web: The Pattern of Children's Reading* (London: Bodley Head).

Meisel, M. (2007) *How Plays Work: Reading and Performance* (Oxford: Oxford University Press).

Mittell, J. (2007) 'Film and Television Narrative', in D. Herman (ed.) *The Cambridge Companion to Narrative* (Cambridge: Cambridge University Press).

Monaco, J. (2000) *How to Read a Film: Movies, Media, Multimedia*, 3rd edn (New York: Oxford University Press).

Murray, J. H. (1997) *Hamlet on the Holodeck: The Future of Narrative in Cyberspace* (New York: The Free Press).

Myers, W. D. (1999) *Monster* (New York: HarperTempest).

Myers, W. D. (2001) 'Escalating Offenses. (Compass Points)', *Horn Book Magazine*, 77(6), 701–2.

Mynott, J. (2009) *Birdscapes: Birds in Our Imagination and Experience* (Princeton, NJ: Princeton University Press).

Nell, V. (1988) *Lost in a Book: The Psychology of Reading for Pleasure* (New Haven: Yale University Press).

Off, G. (2005) *Shadow of the Colossus Official Strategy Guide* (Bradygames).

Oxford (2009) *Oxford English Dictionary*, subjunctive. Available online at: http://dictionary.oed.com.login.ezproxy.library.ualberta.ca/cgi/entry/50240757?single=1&query_type=word&queryword=subjunctive&first=1&max_to_show=10, date accessed 25 January 2009.

Penguin (2009) The Penguin Blog. Available online at: http://thepenguinblog.typepad.com/the_penguin_blog/2007/02/a_million_pengu.html, date accessed 3 April 2009.

Polanyi, M. (1983) *The Tacit Dimension* (Gloucester, MA: Peter Smith).

Pressley, M. and P. Afflerbach (1995) *Verbal Protocols of Reading: The Nature of Constructively Responsive Reading* (Hillsdale: Lawrence Erlbaum).

Prince, S. (2001) *Movies and Meaning: An Introduction to Film*, 2nd edn (Boston: Allyn and Bacon).

Rabinowitz, P. J. (1987) *Before Reading: Narrative Conventions and the Politics of Interpretation* (Ithaca: Cornell University Press).

Reid, M. (2009) 'Reframing Literacy: A Film Pitch for the 21st Century', *English Drama Media*, 14(June), 19–23.

Rennie, J. and A. Patterson (2010) 'Young Australians Reading in a Digital World' in D. R. Cole and D. L. Pullen (eds) *Multiliteracies in Motion: Current Theory and Practice* (New York: Routledge).

Richards, I. A. (1942) *How To Read a Page* (New York: W.W. Norton).

Rogers, T. (2005, 25 October) *Shadow of the Colossus*. *Insert Credit*, retrieved from http://www.insertcredit.com/reviews/wanda/, 26 April 2006.

Rosenblatt, L. (2005) 'The Literary Transaction: Evocation and Response', in *Making Meaning With Texts: Selected Essays* (Portsmouth: Heinemann).

Rudnev, V. (2003) 'Run, Matrix, Run: Event and Intertext in Modern Post-Mass Cinema', *Third Text*, 17(4), 389–94.

Rudolph, E. (1999) 'A Runaway Hit', *American Cinematographer*, 80(June), 20–6.

Run Lola Run, (1998) [DVD] Directed by Tom Tykwer. Germany: Bavaria Film.

Ryan, M.-L. (2006) *Avatars of Story* (Minneapolis: University of Minnesota Press).

Ryan, M.-L. (2007) 'Beyond *Ludus*: Narrative, Videogames and the Split Condition of Digital Textuality' in B. Atkins and T. Krzywinska (eds) *Videogame, Player, Text* (Manchester: Manchester University Press).

Scarry, E. (1999) *Dreaming by the Book* (New York: Farrar, Straus, Giroux).

Scholes, R., J. Phelan and R. Kellogg (2006) *The Nature of Narrative*, 40th anniv. edn (New York: Oxford University Press).

Segal, E. M. (1995) 'Narrative Comprehension and the Role of Deictic Shift Theory' in J. F. Duchan, G. A. Bruder and L. E. Hewitt (eds) *Deixis in Narrative: A Cognitive Science Perspective* (Hillsdale, NJ: Lawrence Erlbaum)

Sennett, R. (2008) *The Craftsman* (New Haven: Yale University Press).

Shadow of the Colossus (2005) [PlayStation2 digital game] (US: Sony Computer Entertainment America).

Sherman, Ben. (2006, 28 March) 'Story Mechanics as Game Mechanics in *Shadow of the Colossus*', *Gamasutra*, retrieved from http://gamasutra.com/features/20060328/sherman_01.shtml, 7 January 2009.

Sipe, L. R. (1998) 'Individual Literary Response Styles of First and Second Graders', *National Reading Conference Yearbook*, 47, 76–89.

Sipe, L. R. (2008) *Storytime: Young Children's Literary Understanding in the Classroom* (New York: Teachers College Press).

Sipe, L. R. and A. E. Brightman (2009) 'Young Children's Interpretations of Page Breaks in Contemporary Picture Storybooks', *Journal of Literacy Research*, 41(1), 68–103.

Squire, J. R. (1964) *The Responses of Adolescents While Reading Four Short Stories*, NCTE Research Report No. 2 (Champaign, IL: National Council of Teachers of English).

Staunton, J. A. (2002) *Monster* (Review), *Journal of Adolescent & Adult Literacy*, 45(8), 791–3.

Stephens, J. (1992) *Language and Ideology in Children's Fiction* (London: Longman).

Sternberg, M. (2001) 'How Narrativity Makes a Difference', *Narrative*, 9(2), 115–22.

Sternberg, M. (2003) 'Universals of Narrative and Their Cognitivist Fortunes (1)', *Poetics Today*, 24(2), 297–395.

Stibbs, A. (1993) 'The Teacherly Practice of Literary Theory', *English in Education*, 27(2), 50–8.

Tabbi, J. (2002) *Cognitive Fictions*, Electronic Mediations, Volume 8 (Minneapolis: University of Minnesota Press).

Vance, A. (2010) 'Watching TV Together, Miles Apart', *New York Times*, online 4 January. Available online at: http://www.nytimes.com/2010/01/04/technology/internet/04couch.html?hp, date accessed 4 January 2010.

Wedel, M. (2009) 'Backbeat and Overlap: Time, Place, and Character Subjectivity in *Run Lola Run*', in W. Buckland (ed.) *Puzzle Films: Complex Storytelling in Contemporary Cinema* (Chichester: Wiley-Blackwell).

Wikipedia (2009) Run Lola Run. Available online at: http://en.wikipedia.org/wiki/Run-lola_run, date accessed 10 January 2009.

Yearwood, S. (2002) 'Popular Postmodernism for Young Adult Readers: *Walk Two Moons*, *Holes*, and *Monster*', *The ALAN Review*, 29(3), 50–3.

YouTube (2009) Spoof Preview, *Shadow of the Colossus*. Available online at: http://www.youtube.com/watch?v=jqd9GiaUos, date accessed 1 August 2009.

Index

Page numbers in **bold** refer to illustrations, page numbers in *italic* refer to tables.

249